Introspection and Contemporary Poetry

INTROSPECTION AND CONTEMPORARY POETRY

Alan Williamson

Harvard University Press
Cambridge, Massachusetts, and London, England   1984

Publication of this book has been aided by a grant from the Andrew W. Mellon
Foundation

This book is printed on acid-free paper, and its binding materials have been chosen
for strength and durability.

Library of Congress Cataloging in Publication Data

Williamson, Alan, 1944–
    Introspection and contemporary poetry.

    Includes index.
        1.   American poetry—20th century—History and criticism.   2.   Self in liter-
ature.   3.   Introspection in literature.   I.   Title.
PS310.S34W54   1984   811'.54'09353   83-8583
ISBN 0-674-46276-9

Pages 201–203 constitute an extension of the copyright page.

For David Perkins

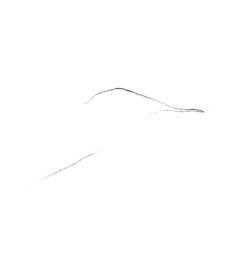

CONTENTS

ACKNOWLEDGMENTS

A number of the following chapters have appeared in different versions in periodicals and anthologies. Chapter 2 appeared in *The American Poetry Review*, March 1974. Chapter 4 incorporates an article of the same title published in *American Poetry since 1960—Some Critical Perspectives*, edited by Robert B. Shaw (Carcanet Press, 1973), and "Gary Snyder: An Appreciation" (*The New Republic*, November 1, 1975). Chapter 5 is a melding of "Silence, Surrealism, and Allegory" (*kayak* 40, November 1975) and parts of "The Energy Crisis in Poetry: News from Pittsburgh" (*Shenandoah*, Fall 1974), and "Three Poets" (*The New York Times Book Review*, October 10, 1982). I have also allowed myself to lift a sentence here, a paragraph there, from omnibus reviews written over the years.

My debts to the other critics who have written about contemporary poetry will be acknowledged as they occur. Three studies I particularly admire—Robert Pinsky's *The Situation of Poetry*, David Kalstone's *Five Temperaments*, and Helen Vendler's *Part of Nature, Part of Us*—appeared after my own project was well under way; I have tried to note coincidental overlaps with these books, as well as the second thoughts they induced in me as I revised.

But some of my largest, and least calculable, debts are not to published criticism; they are—for example—to the students who took my course in contemporary American poetry at the University of Virginia in the early 1970s, especially Paul Breslin, Francis Glosser, Mary Hayne North, and Kerney Rhoden. A letter from Richard Wertime, more than ten years back, set off the whole train of thought that produced the second chapter, by its brilliant exposition of what I have there paraphrased as the "classical and reader-centered" argument. I would like to thank David Perkins, Paul Breslin, and April Bernard for reading the manuscript at different stages of revision; their invaluable comments have made it a richer and more coherent book. I would like to thank Gary Konas for typing the final draft, and the University of California at Davis for the Faculty Research Grant that paid him to do so. My largest debt of all is to my wife, Anne Winters, for encouragement, and for our conversations about poetry, which over the years have become inextricably intertwined with my own thinking.

Introspection and Contemporary Poetry

1
INTRODUCTION

My purpose in this book is to examine the images of the self—or of
the nature and quality of subjective experience—in contemporary
American poetry, and to show how these images inform, even help
to explain, the immense variety of contemporary styles. To attribute
such a shaping role to ideas of the self is not to say that the images of
the world, found in the same poetry, are unimportant. But it is to
follow out a fairly general consensus that what is most exciting and
original about the poetry of the last twenty-five years is its individu-
alism: its willingness to set values of universality at risk, in favor of
the authenticity of specific autobiography, or of the momentary and
immediate, or of the deeper levels of the psyche. The Romantic
premise that, to quote Coleridge, "we receive but what we give, /
And in our life alone does Nature live"—that the inner self is the
source of our understanding of, as well as our blindness toward,
what lies beyond us—has enjoyed a new lease on life in the work of
writers as different, otherwise, as Lowell and Ginsberg, Ashbery,
Creeley, and Bly.

This turning inward has, of course, not been universal; good poets (Bishop and Wilbur, to name two) have ignored or resisted it. But it has been widespread; and some of the reasons for it are fairly evident, at least in hindsight. In terms of literary history, a poet starting out in the 1950s faced, at the same time, the daunting achievements of an authoritative public voice in the great Modernists, and the rather dull and predictable poetry of impersonal statement which contemporaries were producing, when they looked to Eliot's precepts rather than to his practice. There was the feeling that the New Criticism had perhaps shed too much light on the paths which a poem traditional in form and symbolism could follow; the feeling that, in Robert Lowell's words, "we've gotten into a sort of Alexandrian age."[1]

Beyond these strictly literary pressures toward a more personal poetry, there were, of course, others. The diffusion of psychoanalysis in the general culture, and the sheer amount of inner conflict and turmoil experienced by some of the most talented poets of the period, are factors that should not be underestimated. But the larger political history may have been even more important. The poets who shaped contemporary poetry all came of age sometime between the rise of Hitler and the fall of Joe McCarthy—that is to say, during a time when the relative influence of irrational hatreds, fears, and identifications, as against pragmatic interests, in political life seemed more disproportionate than it had, perhaps, for several centuries. The responses of the great Modernist writers to this history—wrongheaded, symbolic, and personally driven as they often were—I suspect helped later poets conclude that a psychology beginning at home was a necessary middle term between poetic sensibility and impersonal or ideological judgment.

But whatever the causes, if one expected this turning toward the subjective to produce a uniform new tradition, one could not have been further wrong. Never has the spectacle of American creative ferment been stranger or more variegated than in the last twenty-five years; never has it been harder to distinguish innovation from trash. The first wave—chiefly Lowell, Berryman, Ginsberg—which made autobiographical detail and the avoidance of New Critical "symbols" the touchstone of an unpoetic authenticity, was soon countered by a school for which the "deep" self was, after all, best expressed in a series of grand and haunted archetypal images. Poets who staked everything on honest statement, a "pure clear word," played off against poets who felt that Modernist tactics of montage and indefinite reference must be exalted into a veritable Uncertainty Principle before the quality of subjectivity could be discerned. Finally, in some cases preoccupation with the self has led to a sickness of the self, even a nostalgia for impersonality: witness the recent prominence of aesthetics of the "mythic self" (the phrase is Mark Strand's), or of unmediated contact with the outside world as an end in itself.

This splintering of styles, I would argue, is the consequence not merely of personal temperament or literary history, but of the difficulties which the concept of the self has presented to the modern mind generally. It is one of the paradoxes of modern thought that all of the advances that have made internal states more describable— made our individuality seem more intricately patterned, and therefore more unique—have at the same time cast doubt on the concept of an essential self, and even on its usefulness as a legal fiction. This paradox will be familiar to most readers. Yet it would take a book (or two or three) really to explore or substantiate it; so I will content myself with two particularly salient examples.

Let us take, as the most obvious and important instance, Freud. As a result of Freud's work, the very concept of subjective significance expands immeasurably, as the dreamed life and the lived life, the monumental and the trivial, reveal their hidden interfaces. It becomes possible to trace a moment of inner experience back through all the layers of the remembered, the imagined, and even the forgotten past which have condensed into its subjective resonance. But at the same time Freud assigns our basic motives to a portion of the self not directly apprehensible, an "it" and not an "I"; and in one vertiginous passage in *The Interpretation of Dreams* he maintains that consciousness is simply "a sense organ for the apprehension of psychical qualities," but that "pleasure and unpleasure . . . prove to be almost the only psychical quality attaching to transposition of energy in the inside of the apparatus."[2] Freud's later psychology of the ego allows him to reconcile this pessimism about consciousness with the manifest complexity of personality; still, we have come far from the notion of the soul as a self-apprehending essence.

The equivocalness which Freud introduced into psychology is curiously mirrored, for poetry, in Rimbaud. Rimbaud proposed an "alchemy of the word" in which—largely through an extension of Baudelaire's idea of synaesthetic correspondences—language could be made virtually consubstantial with consciousness. He "wrote silences and nights," "noted down the inexpressible," and "fixed vertigos." But his initial proposition, in the so-called "Lettre du Voyant," is that the rich, substantial self is dissociated, rooted in the unconscious, even chaotic. The conscious ego is at best something like the conductor of an orchestra; at worst, a mere internalization of received ideas.

> For I is an other. If the brass wakes up a trumpet, it isn't its fault. To me this is evident: I am present as a spectator at the blossoming of my thought . . . I give a stroke of the bow: the symphony stirs in the depths, or comes onto the stage at one bound.
>
> If the old imbeciles had not found only the false significance of the "I," we would not have to sweep away these millions of skeletons who, over an infinite time, have been accumulating the products of their one-eyed intelligence, proclaiming themselves the authors!

The poet cultivates himself by increasing his disunity, "through a long, immense and systematic *disorientation* of *all the senses*": "the soul must be made monstrous."[3] Yet Rimbaud came to believe that such a project must lead to madness; this may help account for his ultimate choice of silence (an alternative that has haunted many modern and contemporary writers).

As with Freud, there is in Rimbaud's work a kind of dialectic—increasing fineness of definition regarding the states of the self accompanying, even breeding, the suspicion that the self is unknowable, fragmentary, perhaps ultimately not there.

The paradox runs on; Sartre, Jung, Heidegger, R. D. Laing, the more profoundly skeptical sociological and deconstructionist thinkers, could all be adduced. In contemporary poetry, while we see only a little work that is indifferent to the question of selfhood, we see work emerging with equal force from both ends of the dialectic. The so-called confessional poets and their heirs are committed to a quest to define, and thereby perhaps to master, the pattern of individual character—the psychological Fates. The omnipresence of self-revelation in our perceptions, associations, actions is explored to its vanishing point. Other poetries, in one way or another, set themselves against the definable, the psychological self—whether by a contemplative, or Jungian, access to an archetypal self (Snyder, Bly, and, with reservations, Wright); or by a negative mysticism of withdrawal (Merwin and Strand); or by an engulfing sense of alienation, the self as shards of internalized social construction (the lesser figures of New York and Iowa surrealism, and, in a much more complex, problematic way, Ashbery). Finally, certain poets, perhaps the greatest, are capacious enough to contain the entire dialectic, as Freud and Rimbaud do. There is an immense interest in the shard-like, the random, in later Lowell; there is a (rejected but unkillable) Romantic vision of the transfigured self, confirmed and greeted by a finally intelligible world, at the heart of Ashbery's work.

I will begin here with the "confessional" enterprise and end with its less well-known current successors, devoting the middle chapters to the various poetries that reject, or endeavor to transcend, the psychological self. My concern has been to choose poets who embody the various stances or possibilities in their pure form, not to cover the field. Thus, the fact that there is no mention of, say, Merrill or Ginsberg—or that there is comparatively little mention of Berryman, Creeley, or Rich—in no way implies that these poets are less good, or less relevantly poets of selfhood, than many who are discussed at length.

My interest, however, is not merely in elucidating the underlying stance—and examining its advantages and disadvantages as a basis for poetry—but also in showing how contemporary styles, especially the more drastic and experimental ones, attempt a kind of equivalent for consciousness (as it is grasped, inevitably, under one or another theoretical presupposition). In analyzing these equivalences, I am strongly indebted to the treatment of mental atmosphere in a number of psychological theorists: Jung; the R. D. Laing of *The Divided Self*; Ludwig Binswanger and the existential or phenomenological analysts.[4] It is not that I find these theorists more adequate than the central Freudian tradition in their total, or genetic, account of human personality (quite the reverse, in fact). It is rather that they have in common with poetry an interest in describing the range and subtlety of feeling-tones, of inner atmospheres, in a given personality; and then, and only then, in drawing the correlations between these and the central issues of a life as they may be stated in other terms. (Freud, as we have seen, was reluctant to allow much qualitative range, beyond "pleasure and unpleasure," to the conscious mind. He admitted that he had never experienced the "oceanic feeling," and that his dreams were "less rich in sensory elements" than those of many people; and I think these facts help explain both the brilliance and the limitations of his focus on the content of association.)[5]

One final word: although the importance of subjectivism in the

development of contemporary poetry is almost universally acknowledged, there seems to be a certain resistance to making it the main
focus of critical scrutiny—especially an implicitly approving scrutiny. This resistance encompasses critics otherwise at opposite ends
of the spectrum: thus, a critic like Paul Breslin will fault the so-called
surrealist poets for an exclusive concern with "the inside of one's
own head," while a critic like Charles Molesworth will defend the
same poets against the "confessional" poets on the grounds that
their interiority is less idiosyncratic, less personal.[6] This common
bias arises not only because currently fashionable literary theory
emphasizes the negative half of the modern dialectic—the self as a
fiction, the labyrinth of mirrors—but also for ethical reasons. We all
tend to think of self-absorption as adolescent, "narcissistic"; to believe that the truly mature mind lives turned outward, in love and
work, toward the world of others. I could not, and would not wish to,
disagree with this finally. But it is half of a truth, not the whole truth.
We also live with and through the self, as long as we live. The energy
of original vision, at least in the arts, comes from within more than
from objective perception; empathy itself can be facilitated by self-
knowledge, as it is certainly impeded by self-ignorance. For many
people—particularly many, perhaps, of the kind of people who tend
to be drawn to poetry—true knowledge and true love of the world
do not arrive without the process described here in the discussion of
"confessional" poetry: the thoroughgoing yet critical self-absorption
that finally allows one to stand a little apart from the self, to see it as
an entity among entities. Thus, I see no need to apologize for regarding the self as one of the great human and poetic subjects; always acknowledging that the most adequate poetry of the self is
likely to be the most aware of its paradoxes, the least inclined to
freeze it by abstracting it from the totality of its relations.

2

"I AM THAT I AM"

The Ethics and Aesthetics of Personal Poetry

Much can be learned about the problems and triumphs of intimately self-revelatory ("confessional") poetry by considering the different ways in which it is read and judged. (Valid objections have been raised to the implications latent in the phrase "confessional poetry"—artlessness, theatricality, shame—almost from the moment it was first employed. I allow myself the term when referring to specific literary conventions of the 1960s, or to a thematic concern with disclosure or shock. Under other circumstances, I prefer the expression "personal poetry.")

It is important, for one thing, to recognize that this poetry seemed so controversial and problematic partly because of its position in literary history—its impact on minds brought up on the Impersonal Theory and the New Criticism's polemical overemphasis on persona (a doctrine whose value, surely, lies in making us aware that character-creation through voice occurs in lyric as well as narrative poetry, and not in suggesting that "I" in a lyric rarely means the author).[1] If either socially shameful disclosures or private names and facts had seemed inartistic to all ages and tastes, Catullus and Villon would not have come down to us as high points of literature.

Nevertheless, the personal poetry that emerged in the late 1950s does differ in degree from earlier poetry, in its tendency to make candor an aesthetic value and to suggest that complete self-definition is a sufficient and possible goal for lyric poetry. The result, for the critic, is not only to make judgment more than ever inextricable from a reaction to personalities but also to raise certain legitimate and unavoidable questions: the question of whether, and in what sense, "universality" is necessary to art; the question of whether a writer morally should—and psychologically *can*—tell the entire truth about himself to any audience. The recurrent *succès de scandale*—of *Howl, Life Studies, Ariel, The Dolphin*—merely point up a more pervasive problem; and yet evaluative criticism rarely acknowledges the full difficulty of setting its feet on firm ground. Negative criticism often relies on unexamined or *ad hoc* dividing lines as to what disclosures—or what attitudes toward those disclosures— are acceptable as literature. Laudatory critics, on the other hand, often proceed, as M. L. Rosenthal does in *The New Poets*, by establishing the latency of a "universal" moral bearing—asserting, for instance, that melancholic or paranoid fantasies are culturally representative, because of the still unabsorbed trauma of World War II, in which they were experienced as objective fact. There is much truth and importance to this point of view. Yet it sidesteps—and so leaves to personal bias—the question of whether intrinsic qualities, or methods, in the self-revelatory act make for success or failure in art.

It seems to me that this question must be dealt with before there can be an adequate formal criticism of personal poetry. But I am not sure we can, or should want to, approach it in such a way as to avoid moral considerations altogether. After all, some issues are both moral and aesthetic: the inherent seductiveness of the narrative "I," and its conceivable power to deflect certain perceptions in both writer and reader; the necessary but difficult distinctions between self-knowledge and self-dramatization, between authenticity and the aping of literary personae. Nor can we avoid the question of whether and how far disclosure in poetry presumes, and plays upon, an inevitable, however tenuous, social relation with a hearer.

I

It may be useful to begin our discussion by delineating two extreme positions on the implicit contract between writer and reader in personal poetry, and its moral implications. One position—the more classical and reader-centered—would be that the very act of writing about oneself presupposes something valuable or original or generalizable to communicate, and is therefore, in however oblique a way, a self-affirmation. Psychologically, this argument would claim that, in literature as in life, we rarely do anything in entire unawareness of its social consequences. The writer who claims to be unsparingly honest is already asserting a virtue, or a ground of interest, expected to transcend whatever is damaging in the revelation.

One danger in this argument is that, if pushed to an extreme, it tends to deny to personal art the disinterestedness—the wish to "do justice to" rather than "judge"—which we normally concede both to the high formal achievements of more objective art and to the moments of moral courage in our own internal self-confrontations. Another danger is that the argument offers little corrective to a critic's narrower notions of what is significant or generalizable. Perhaps in response to these dangers, another argument arises, one so centered on the writer and his own constant self-discovery in his writing that the possibility of negative critical response is rationalized very nearly out of existence.

Robert Duncan has advanced such an argument, in a piece responding to M. L. Rosenthal's criticism (in *The New Poets*) of the opening passage of Duncan's "A Sequence of Poems for H.D.'s Birthday":

> The young Japanese son was in love with a servant boy.
> To be in love! Dont you remember how the whole world is governd
> by a fact that embraces
>   everything that happens?

Rosenthal makes himself vulnerable by asking for a certain kind of universality: essentially, he implies a double standard of the offensively sentimental for heterosexual and homosexual poetry. But Duncan does not rest with attacking Rosenthal's prejudices. He goes on to justify the "girlish outcry" (Rosenthal's phrase) not only on the grounds that it "does get, very accurately, the tone of the actual dream I am drawing from" but that it is precisely its disquieting elements that determine the further direction, the need for analytic and formal resolution, of the feelings in the poem: "it is the very questionable pitch of the outcry, its being *'over-filld, more than was sensible,'* that gives resonance to the extremity of emotions to follow. The poem puts forward the unsurety it must go by—the urgency and lack of confidence in one—that gives its meaning into and finds its telling content reestablished in the counsel of the Mother in the dream. . . ." The hostile criticism in fact leads, in a tight circle, to the heart of the poem's subject—"It is part of the social reality back of my original dismay that the very shifts of feeling, verging, as they did, upon despised and outcast modes of adolescence . . . were sure to be seen as 'emptily facile' "—so that Rosenthal becomes, in a curious way, very nearly the coauthor of a poem he dislikes:

> The vividness of the reader's discomfort may have already entered the poet's imagination as he worked, even here, for the projection of possible readings is essential to his art, the art of a multiphasic message, a field of possible readings. . . .
>
> I have such a superstition of the existence of that field of feelings in which I work that there is not a passage that does not deepen the identity of my intention. Fabricator of identities, I feel betrayed as if caught in the act by every observation. Who can, as I pose him, be false to my own true self?[2]

Thus, Duncan would argue that at least in a certain kind of self-exploratory poetry (one informed by Olson's notions of "field," of "using the process") there are, as in psychoanalysis, no wrong turnings. Every statement, and every misstatement, reveals the self, and is a potential fulcrum for moving the forces behind it out into the light.

This audacious argument advances us a good deal, by its demand that the critic treat the poet's insights, feelings, and rhetoric holistically; and yet I resist its final plunge into relativism. Poetry cannot have quite the same economy as psychoanalysis; and even analysis is slowed by "resistances," though they can be put to use. It seems to me that there *are* wrong turnings, even in quite good poems: turnings into self-deception; into too easy reliance on the intellectual formulas of the time; into concerns which, though spontaneous and introspectively accurate, are nonetheless a dispersion of poetic energy. Finally, distinction and precision of language, though they may be misleading criteria when applied minutely to long or complex poems, when applied in the largest sense have everything to do with whether we feel a poem presents an individual consciousness, rather than merely a collection of attitudes and rhetorics.

In an attempt to bridge the two positions given above, I would emphasize that personal poetry, by its sharpened rendering of individuality, forces the reader beyond the externality of the normal functions of interpretation and judgment between people; and that this effect is no small part of its morality. To clarify this last point, let me invoke a confessional poem about exposure and judgment nearly four hundred years old, Shakespeare's Sonnet 121:

> For why should others' false adulterate eyes
> Give salutation to my sportive blood?
> Or on my frailties why are frailer spies,
> Which in their wills count bad what I think good?
> No, I am that I am, and they that level
> At my abuses reckon up their own:
> I may be straight, though they themselves be bevel;
> By their rank thoughts my deeds must not be shown. . . .

The sonnet begins as an extremely bitter counterattack against others' judgments (" 'Tis better to be vile than vile esteem'd"), and this passage might be read in the same spirit. But Shakespeare is defending himself on subtler and more philosophical grounds; he says "I may be straight," not "I am straight," and the difference is not merely rhetorical modesty. Rather, out of his bitterness, Shakespeare arrives at a fundamental human truth: that there is no Platonic form of ourselves, accessible to us or to others, by which we are good or vile, important or unimportant; there are only the hundreds of individual perceivers, each of them, like ourselves, limited to measuring others' natures by their own, able to "give salutation," with love or hatred, only to traits whose acquaintance has already been made within. Thus, one's tautological self-definition, one's "I am that I am," is irreducible, for all attempts to reduce it must proceed from equally self-referent centers. There is a touch of megalomania in the passage, as Shakespeare applies to himself the name of Jehovah; but perhaps it is more an ecstasy of freedom, even of participation, as he rises above the feeling that there is some external, superior Truth or Being to which others have a mysterious access but from which one is oneself mysteriously excluded. And if there is megalomania, it contains its own corrective, for the absolute faith that is taken away from others' judgments cannot then be returned to one's own; we must all be irreducible, whether that makes every one of us divine, or utterly helpless and fallible.

I think that all personal or confessional poetry aims at such a realization of a unique individuality and fate, and therefore at a similar transcendence of external judgments and categorizations (though not, of course, a transcendence of the moral sphere: the opinions others have formed of us, and particularly the harmful consequences of actions, remain ineluctably part of the material of selfhood—what must be understood and clarified).

The Great Work of the personal poet is to give an objective shape to his "I am that I am"—the atmosphere and phenomenology of his consciousness, the matrix out of which his world is continuously, involuntarily created for him, from which his slightest—and even his more considered—actions proceed with a more compelling logic than he can ever entirely grasp. To succeed in this work, the poet must be—at first, at least—uncompromisingly narcissistic. He is engaged in a sublime game, no less than the Valérian poet submitting to form; he gambles that because the self seems to have an intuited order, the more candid he is, the more he surrenders to the accidents and nuances of experience, the more significant poetic order will emerge.[3] But as my use of the terms "atmosphere" and "matrix" should suggest, his candor is not solely or even primarily factual; a consciousness has its rhythms, its imagery, its ways of apprehending materiality and the materiality of language, so that at some unattainable limit all the formal characteristics of poetry can conceivably become self-correlatives.

Of course, this kind of self-creation takes place, largely unconsciously, in any good poet; but only the personal poet sets it before himself as an absolute and sufficing goal. And because technique is seen as a self-correlative, in no other domain of poetry is the demand for originality so tyrannous. Nothing depresses us so much as a totally or unconsciously derivative personal poet revealing intimate facts—he seems to be committing a kind of suicide. At this stage, a poet can ill afford to take his own measure through the eyes of others, whether they be imagined moral judges or admired poets.

And yet, as the poet approaches success in his narcissistic endeavor of self-creation, he begins paradoxically to experience his self as if it were an external object—circumscribed, defined by laws, imbued with its own alien aura or flavor. More and more of himself becomes subject to ever broader judgments or prejudicial reactions, both others' and, at times, his own. He has indeed projected himself, cast himself into three-dimensional space. But from the reader's point of view—if the coherence of the poetic world has affected him at all—there is an involvement in the poet's self-creation which forestalls a return to the sphere of unsympathetic social judgments. The reader grasps intuitively how the same process, if he applied it to himself, could bring him to the same condition of psychic exposure. But neither can the poet return to the original indefinite narcissism of the familiar inner atmosphere. By this strange transaction, the poet has become at once subject, for the reader, and object, for himself.

It is this almost ritual process—of participation, yet also of objectification, and finally of transcendence of human isolation—that gives personal poetry its compelling power over us, more than the particulars of the given life. We feel a kind of tragic awe at entering into the inner language of a life, which is also its net of destiny; in that conjunction, we come close to the essential causes of human things. But we also learn a method or discipline of possible escape from the limitations of selfhood, and from the necessity of judging and being judged by others. Or, at the very least, we learn, in William Blake's terms, to judge "states" and not "individuals," by seeing how different states are built up out of the same basic human materials. (It is at this level that a deeper, earned universality rewards the reader who has refrained from demanding a shallow one.) The corollary to this argument is that we need not find the personality portrayed admirable, likable, or even in all ways interesting in order to have a full and pleasurable experience of personal poetry; although there is an unavoidable presupposition that the power to objectify sets the author's "real" self—morally, existentially, and in terms of the reader's interest—a few steps ahead of the "self" he has presented. We remain perfectly ready to be bored by poetic personality tics—the later Lowell's world-weary aphorisms, Berryman's fulsome praise of friends, Duncan's sacerdotal manners—when they are not being put to dramatic use.

Here I touch on the question so much belabored by Alvarez and others: whether the writing of personal poetry is in fact healthful and purgative for the poet—a kind of spiritual progress—or whether it can be almost the reverse, a destructive reopening of psychic wounds. Certainly the survival record of the first "confessional" generation is not enviable. But we should not rush to accept a new version of the doomed-poet legend without first exploring a marginally optimistic alternative hypothesis: that, insofar as literature has any direct relation to breakdowns and suicides, it is the half-completed rather than the fully completed self-objectifications that return to haunt the poet with redoubled destructive energy. Berryman is a case in point. A great deal of his gift lay in his inability to tolerate his literal self, his constant, comic flight into comfortingly excessive, unambiguous personae: Henry House, Henry Pussycat; the wise Black minstrel; the universal victim or mass-murderer. He is a curiously uninspired poet when conscious of speaking seriously, speaking as a whole man. Often he attempts to bluff the reader into taking vehemently uttered clichés for a sincerity beyond aesthetic criticism—even when his subject is as interesting, as well as moving, as the fate of Delmore Schwartz:

> This world is gradually becoming a place
> where I do not care to be any more. Can Delmore die?
> I don't suppose
> in all them years a day went ever by
> without a loving thought for him. Welladay.
>
> (Dream Song 149)

Berryman becomes a great poet at precisely the points where such straightforwardness is psychologically impossible for him. In the last Dream Song addressed to his father (384), if anywhere, we would expect complete confrontation. Instead, we get many indications of disunity and avoidance: the melodramatic shrillness, the superficially silly deflection of the father's hatefulness onto his profession ("I spit upon this dreadful banker's grave"), the absence of the word "I" after the second stanza, the inarticulate cries flying to comically opposite extremes ("O ho alas alas") and then continuing to punctuate the poem—

> and ax the casket open ha to see
> just how he's taking it, which he sought so hard
> we'll tear apart
> the mouldering grave clothes ha & then Henry
> will heft the ax once more, his final card
> and fell it on the start.

Berryman's meaning—which, as I read the last line, incorporates the pleasure of Zeus, the castration of the father, into the Sophoclean pleasure of never having existed at all—would be unendurable if uttered seriously; it is made, to my mind superbly, by being marred. But it does not then seem paradoxical (in hindsight, admittedly) that Berryman's conflicts and self-intolerance were not relieved by poetry.

What can be said of Berryman can be said still more emphatically of Anne Sexton, a more unconsciously theatrical poet. Sylvia Plath remains—because of the wholly finished quality of her best poems, and their increasing calmness toward the end—the strongest instance to be brought against the argument that full self-objectification is sustaining and purgative. But in her case one feels a peculiar, and as far as I know unique, short circuit between the artistic desire to complete the self by defining its laws, and the neurotic desire to complete the self by dying. This is a question that will be explored at length further on.

II

Robert Lowell's *The Dolphin* offers an ideal focal point for this discussion, not only because of the sharp moral controversy its indiscretions set off, but because of its explicit meditation on the problems of self-definition in poetry—a meditation necessarily elided in order to produce Lowell's great work of self-objectification, *Life Studies.* In *The Dolphin,* Lowell suggests that a writer can approach, but never quite reach, the limit at which self-analysis ceases to be self-flattery:

> Some meaning never has a use for words,
> truth one couldn't tell oneself on the toilet,
> self-knowledge swimming to the hook, then turning—
> in Latin we learned no subject is an object.

But the desire to overcome this limit preoccupies Lowell throughout *The Dolphin,* no doubt intensified by an awareness of being "vile esteem'd" both for the actions the book records—his divorce and remarriage—and for writing a book about them. (At times, indeed—in the final twist of twentieth-century self-consciousness—Lowell seems to fear that he acts as he does partly because he is writing about it: "I too maneuvered on a guiding string / as I execute my written plot.") Lowell's response to these problems sometimes takes the form of an almost masochistic attack on his own literary skills, "my perfunctory, all-service rhythms." But out of the attack grows a peculiar kind of self-transcendence. In "Summer Between Terms, 1"—a far from self-congratulatory poem, ending with a guilt-ridden image of "tomcats" that "find their kittens and chew off their breakable heads"—Lowell restates the problem in an outrageous pun: "Surely good writers write all possible wrong." He goes on,

It takes such painful mellowing to use error. . . .
I have stood too long on a chair or ladder,
branch-lightning forking through my thought and veins—
I cannot hang my heavy picture straight.

The special elevation of the ego created by the artist's self-descriptive obsession now becomes a dangerous, or at least a disorienting, eminence. The branch-lightning—an image wonderfully combining the force of immediate consciousness with its unresolvable divergences, its ambi- or multi-valences—merges, still more wonderfully to my mind, with the ambiguity of art, the vertigo caused by the height and the effort to balance the "heavy picture." The master of heaviness, of thunderous definitions and closures, discovers that this weight in itself defies gravitational alignment with the world; and his solution is to "use error," to hang the picture, as it were, at all of its wrong angles.

What bothers—and often bothers terribly—those readers who do not like the style of Lowell's sonnets is the fact that the lines remain heavy pictures and yet refuse to be hung straight. Adrienne Rich has complained that "this is poetry constructed in phrases, each hacked-out, hewn, tooled, glazed or burnished," but also that "at the moment when you thought Lowell was about to cut to the bone, he veered off, lost the thread."[4] These apparent flaws seem to me the result of a deliberate, peculiar honesty, in which Lowell uses his excessive (or at least old-fashioned) formal definitiveness to clarify the discontinuities in consciousness, the limits to the reality people can bear, the self-conscious mind watching and managing itself. To put it differently, Lowell attempts to represent action and reaction in his own psyche, to let each mood or insight endeavor to become absolute, to isolate or glaze itself, only to fall before the succeeding one. The great majority of lines are end-stopped, and turn on the lines preceding with a disruptive, often ironic force. The effect is a little like watching a film slowly enough to see the lines between frames; harsh and irritating, but with distinct advantages for self-scrutiny, particularly when contrasted with those surrealist styles whose fluidity tends to make of the unconscious, whatever its contents, a Peaceable Kingdom.

In its diction, too, *The Dolphin* is full of ambiguous triumphs of imitative form over the appearance of authorial control: the Victorian mellifluous vagueness used for disoriented states, journeys that "streak into the glitter of the blear"; the line "marching for peace with paranoia marching" given twice in succession in a spiral-staircase dream of indecision. Or consider the unpleasing mixture of metaphors in the passage about "truth" quoted above: unpleasing precisely because the poet is uncertain whether achieved self-knowledge would be an embryonic live thing, a fish in water, or excrement.

To some readers, these examples will seem mere lapses of taste. The objection might best be answered by a detailed look at the "Hospital" sequence, from which two of the examples come. It is, perhaps necessarily, Lowell's tour de force of using error, in which the question of artistic responsibility becomes a vehicle for the larger question of how responsible he is capable of being, or feeling, as a person.

The mental breakdown described in "Hospital" is brought on, as the poems themselves suggest, not simply by the recurrences of manic-depressive illness (in fact, controlled by lithium at this point in Lowell's career), but by a crisis of responsibility—the need to choose between the two women in his life. Perhaps for this reason, his most dramatic symptoms are hallucinatory displacements of impulses or actions away from his central "I." Even in saner moments, Lowell comments on this predisposition in himself:

> on walks, things nearest to me go slow motion,
> obscene streetlife rushes on the wheelrim,
> steel shavings from the vacillating will.

We may go one step further, I think, by invoking the insights of the existential psychiatrists—Ludwig Binswanger, Eugene Minkowski—who interpret psychotic symptoms as concrete representations of the loss of that sense of responsibility and engagement, of a continuous, piecemeal, but chosen "transcendence" or movement toward the future, which (following on Heidegger) they take to be the defining condition of healthy life.[5] When this synthesis of self and world collapses, distorted senses of time, space, and matter ensue. Time goes too fast, in the subject's flight from himself or his real circumstances, or else slows to a standstill, as the idea of significant change becomes unthinkable. What is dead and what is alive may become problematic; matter may be seen in the guise of trash or excrement, as the material of the subject's life comes to seem formless, or else predetermined—already part of the past. These formulations may help us see a powerful logic both in the structure of Lowell's "Hospital" sequence and in some of his literary "errors" there. In the first poem, for instance, the vagueness, the slime-luminescence, of the destination ("streak into the glitter of the blear") is not unrelated to the fact that it is the poet's shoes that "walk out" by themselves. Their "empty" autonomy signifies inversely his own lack of freedom: "They walk / the one life offered from the many chosen."

By the second sonnet, this kind of mechanical motion is going too fast for objects to be distinguished: "boys race the hooded highway lights untimed." (Are the lights "hooded," or is the highway itself a kind of womblike tunnel? Are the "highway lights" or the boys' headlights "untimed"? Since a straightforward version of the line was published in *The Review*—"boys race untimed along the hooded highway"—Lowell clearly made it difficult, in order to involve the reader in temporal and spatial disorientation.) The whole poem belongs to the realm of determinism and lapsed responsibility that Minkowski describes, in which everything is as if it were already past, and the world becomes trash, having lost all possibility of growth. "Person, place and thing," "violated" by the poet's writing or his behavior, "join the rubbish that predated nature." As the poet wanders in an erotically charged daze, trying "to find girls in the wide, white squares," the boys of his fantasy "tiptoe" through what is at once a car crash and a museum ("treasuries of smashed glass"), looking for fragments of masterpieces or dead bodies ("a lifelike hand or head"). At the end of the poem the poet is, somewhat to the reader's relief, "on bounds" in the asylum. But he now experiences a decelerated time, a duration-without-change, in which his own existence, or its metonymy, his writing, becomes undifferentiated and parasitic: his galley proofs "a sheaf of tapeworms, / sleek, untearable, interminable."

The next sonnet repeats the action of this one in more drastic terms. The poet dreams, now, not of a car but of a "taxi . . . changing into a van." He and his beloved are in back with the helpless cargo, the "rubbish" ("tan canvas-lapped bales"). The driver is far in front, invisible; but given the hints of sexual violence earlier, one is not altogether surprised to learn that he is "the man who assaulted you yesterday." Eventually, the driver himself relinquishes control, and moves back toward the lovers, his "step" causing the bales to begin to bury them. But at the end of the dream, it is the driver-"rival" who is dead; and the next sonnet carries the image of self-division to a grimly logical conclusion: "Did the beheaded wish himself in half? / He was so airily cool and free and high. . . ."

To be "dead," in this context, means to drop from dissociated "high" freedom (the mania of the "boys" or the driver) into the limbo of duration-without-change. The poet knows that his "rival" is not alive because "the same water washes in and out of the mouth." It can hardly be an accident that this same sonnet contains the attack on Lowell's "perfunctory, all-service rhythms." Lowell's artistic self-doubt, though sincere, makes a rich vehicle for his deeper distrust of his own psychic engagement with reality.

But the most sustainedly unpleasing rendering of limbo comes in the next sonnet, "Stairwell":

> Climbing from chair to chair to chair to chair,
> I dare not look the stairwell in the eye;
> its underpinning soils like carbon paper,
> each step up would stop an athlete's heart—
> the stairwell is hollow, bored, unbearable,
> the same six words repeating on a disk:
> marching for peace with paranoia marching,
> marching for peace with paranoia marching . . .

The jerky motion of the end-stopped lines; a child's image of futile and dangerous ascent; another image from writing, in which the impulse, as it is copied, becomes a soiling—all prepare for the nerve-grinding effect of the repeated phrase spiraling, like the staircase, endlessly through the same opposites. (These opposites, of course, embody the question which has brought the poet to his present stalemate: is he moving toward a better life—"peace"—or is he merely in flight from himself?) Yet even within this nightmare of blockage, its opposite is latent: because "hollow" has two meanings, emotional and physical, "bored" also suggests to us the "bore" of a gun—and a few lines later we find the decapitated man's head projected, "airily cool and free and high." In the succeeding poems, these two modes of feeling and of temporality (the dissociated violence of impulse and the standstill of guilt and doubt), like the poet's literal "double-vision," slowly converge. Looking again at his picture of "the beheaded," Sir Walter Raleigh, he is able to feel again the fine balance of the moment, in which danger can at least be met by artistic—that is, in the now familiar metonymy, any fully engaged—choice: "he isn't going to die, it's not been painted."

Thus, the sequence has a deeper logic in which "bad" or ungraceful writing joins with other sources of unpleasure—the nightmarish events, the tactile smudge and grit—in a phenomenology of psychic loss of control. Perhaps nowhere else in Lowell's work does the pain of madness become so tangible and immediate, to the reader who has not experienced it.

Let us look now at what some have considered a moral failure in the book—a failure which, however, can also be seen as an immersion in the subject, a transcendence of a false appearance of control. I refer, of course, to the poems based on actual letters from Lowell's ex-wife. With Lowell dead, there seems less point than ever in reviving the old controversy, except to mention that certain critics (notably Adrienne Rich in her piece, already cited, in *The American Poetry Review*) allowed their perhaps justifiable anger at Lowell's decision to publish when he did to spill over into an attack on the book itself as an inherently cruel elevation of art over life. Ironically, as it seems to me, it is the letter-poems that ensure the book the unresolved openness of life, allowing Lowell to say honestly, "my eyes have seen what my hand did." By representing his ex-wife by her own words, in poems where his own voice rarely intrudes, Lowell makes us experience her as a presence who cannot be answered, whose point of view will not fade into the customarily inclusive authorial one. I suspect that many readers will find her, at least on first reading, easily the most vivid and sympathetic character: a woman fighting bravely, without pride but with a clarity that seems better than pride (and yet tragic, as it clashes again and again with the poet's real need to live and talk by intuitive stabs). Concurrently—as I have already said—Lowell undermines the authorial prestige of his own voice in a number of ways, ending poems, for instance, not with the settled epitome of truth that the sonnet tradition calls for, but with a sudden influx of new, fleeting, often irrational feeling. Thus, the meditative "Summer Between Terms" ends on the self-lacerating tomcat image; "During a Transatlantic Call," on the other hand, ends with an abruptly resentful and cruel irony—"They tell me to stop, they musn't lose my money."

The narrative structure of the book heightens our sense of the unresolvable; for Lowell tampered with actual chronology in placing his return visit to New York—"at home and warm, / as if we had escaped the gaping jaws"—at the end, after the birth of his son, rather than in the middle. The effect is to make his crisis emotionally most acute when it is, pragmatically, resolved: "Some things like death are meant to have no outcome."

And yet, there is a certain coherence between the transformation in life described in *The Dolphin* and the transformation in art enacted in it. If the poet and his new love are, finally, as real to us as his ex-wife, despite a questionable dearth of dramatic presentation, it is because the things they have in common—their lability; their oblique, nerve-end way of assessing value; their enlarged capacities for boredom and for the sudden onrush of joy—*are*, in large measure, the style of the book. The descriptions of England and America serve, rather like Rome and Alexandria in *Antony and Cleopatra*, to delineate the metaphysical dimension of Lowell's choice. London is all detail and shallow perspective, worldly yet tender, an emblem of his beloved ("whole spirit wrought from toys and nondescript"), and of the sensual and existential present in which he found relief from the Puritan concern for last things. American landscapes, on the other hand, evoke what Lowell and his ex-wife seem to have shared: a tragic and disillusioned sense of what is really possible in life, combined with a sense of transcendence in living out not wholly satisfactory commitments. We hear twice of a shared fantasy in which the two of them are already dead, buried together on the inhospitable coast of Maine:

> once it was the equivalent of everlasting
> to stay loyal to my other person loved—
> in the fallen apple lurked a breath of spirits,
> the uninhabitable granite shone
> in Maine, each rock our common gravestone. . . .

The ethic, and its attendant sensibility, haunt Lowell on his return to New York. The "soaring," rectilinear architecture brings back both the old domestic atmosphere ("austerity assuaged with melodrama") and the febrile feeling of living constantly in public, emblematically ("a love of features fame puts up for sale"). The long perspectives become intimations of life in the long view, of inexorable laws, determinisms, retributions. "After London, the wind, the eye, my thoughts / race through New York with gaping coarse-comb teeth," he writes; and then,

> What shall I do with my stormy life blown towards evening?
> No fervor helps without the favor of heaven,
> no permissive law of nature picks up the bill. . . .

One of the forms under which Lowell fears retribution is aesthetic. In her unhappiness, his ex-wife flails him with their shared ethic of stoical commitment, and suggests that he will lose his talent by leaving her. Later, in her last attempt to win him back, she tries to reconjure a specific incarnation of that talent, his interest in tragic political drama in the 1960s: "Why don't you lose yourself / and write a play about the fall of Japan?" And Lowell seems to acknowledge that there is truth as well as bitterness here, that he has left certain artistic possibilities behind. He writes to his new wife, "we have not grown as our child did in the womb, / met Satan like Milton going blind in London. . . ." The creation of titanic ideas of good and evil, however realistically based, involves a distilling Platonism, a willingness to take an idea of a person for the person himself, which is not unlike the Platonism that holds that a turbulent, contentious marriage becomes a superhuman loyalty simply by being lived through to the end. (In fact, Lowell's most moving poems about this view of marriage, "The Flaw," "Near the Ocean," "Half a Century Gone," coincide exactly in time with his most heroic political works—"For the Union Dead," "Waking Early Sunday Morning," *Prometheus Bound*.) But there are consolations for the renunciation of the Miltonic:

> it's enough to wake without old fears,
> and watch the needle-fire of the first light
> bombarding off your eyelids harmlessly.

Of course, the imagery will not quite let us believe that any energy has really seeped out of this poetic universe. It has simply been redistributed, from the singular cosmic rebel back to the whole continuum of momentarily experienced consciousness from which the poet must, inevitably, have gathered him. This is not to say that Lowell ceased to be an important public poet. But I think that his concurrent public work, the rewriting of *Notebook* into *History*, bears out my statement. *History* is unique among poetical histories in that it continually flashes at us the raw materials of high drama, only to analyze them back into unyieldingly common problems: the channeling of sexuality; the fear of death and its relation both to tyranny and to art; the collective womb-image of the Golden Age. It is a book that makes us feel how much the desire for escape influences what most of us—even poets—commonly remember of the past.

III

In this brief treatment—burdened with a philosophical ulterior motive—I can only suggest one way of reading *The Dolphin*, and I cannot hope to make instantaneous converts to its merits. Its ideal reader (the only one, perhaps, who would like it quite as well as earlier Lowell) must read passages at once in their widest bearing, as one does with a novel, and microscopically, not presuming even the most displeasing tonality to be unintentional. But one need not be that ideal reader to feel that by his use of "error," aesthetic and ethical, Lowell presses on us—with fear, and a certain joy—how he cannot step outside either the immediacy of the present or the accumulated bearing, and the limitations, of his history and mental structures. In turning on himself, he casts himself into the round. I find this effect—which, for lack of a better term, I shall call a "reflexive mode"—in much of the better writing that has come out of the confessional period: in the magical effect of seemingly inappropriate humor on the work of Berryman and Ginsberg, neither at his best when solemn about himself; in the tricky perspective shifts behind Diane Wakoski's clarity; in the hesitant speech-emphases of Frank Bidart.

But perhaps one or two more specific examples—from poets who will not be discussed further here—will make it clearer what I mean by "reflexive." Robert Creeley, despite his very different literary background, resembles the later Lowell in his elaborate, sometimes energy-diminishing strategies for preventing his mind from saying more than his whole consciousness apprehends. In the first stanza of his poem "A Form of Women"—

> I have come far enough
> from where I was not before
> to have seen the things
> looking in at me through the open door

—does the second line mean that the previous state was a kind of non-being, or that it could only be located later, when the willful blindness that was its very essence was overcome? Whatever the meaning, the equivocalness of the starting-point makes the progress itself unsettlingly relative—a progress which, after all, consists in clarifying a hallucination, not in dispelling it. The same poem ends with a wish to be healed by turning outward:

> But I love you.
> Do you love me.
> What to say
> when you see me.

The open ending carries a great potential for freedom: the lovers face to face with each other, obliged to a response which the poem will not include or predict. And yet, at the same moment, Creeley's honest inability to write question marks casts doubt on the good faith of his wish, and suggests how much must remain closed and unfree— mired in heavy demand, anxiety, fatalism.

Since I have disagreed with Adrienne Rich as a critic, let me take as a final, parallel example a poem of hers that I admire greatly, "Song" from *Diving into the Wreck.* As the poem opens, someone asks the poet if she is lonely. Her sense of voyage and self-discovery wills that the answer be no; but some everyday human element obviously rebels, for, in her sequence of answers, the metaphors of journeying—though beautiful—become successively shorter and slower, until we arrive at this last stanza:

> If I'm lonely
> it's with the rowboat ice-fast on the shore
> in the last red light of the year
> that knows what it is, that knows it's neither
> ice nor mud nor winter light
> but wood, with a gift for burning

But the last line invites, demands the response that the gift of a wooden boat is not primarily for burning, but for traveling on water; that the illusion of burning is a "gift"—in the other sense—from loss and isolation, from the withdrawing sun of year's end. And yet, what is real burning but the separation of carbon from all its attendant elements—the type of that spiritual isolation, that withdrawal of sympathetic connection or interpenetration from the context or landscape, which the poet so strongly wills as the prerequisite for voyaging? I am tempted to read back into this poem that scorching withdrawal of sympathy which I felt in Adrienne Rich's review of *The Dolphin;* but my reassertion of the judging faculty hardly matters. For who has ever set out on a self-isolating quest without feeling how different getting someplace and merely flaring up with fullness of energy are in retrospect, and yet how alike, inextricable, they are in immediate experience? I am not arguing, in short, that the aspiration in Rich's poem—or, for that matter, in Creeley's—is rescinded by irony; the tone of both poems quite belies this. What their rhetorical or imagistic circularity does imply, though, is the impossibility of getting beyond the self enough to judge the self quite as fixedly as the will might desire. In this self-referentialness there is both possibility and limitation, perhaps because we are left a sense of the open space outside the circle.

It is through some combination of fullness or richness of rendering with this avoidance of false transcendence—of smugness, of embarrassment, of forced or pat conclusions—that the humbling yet liberating realization that "I am that I am" takes place, and is shared by the reader, in personal poetry. In this chapter, the emphasis has fallen on the avoidance of an unearned Olympian perspective, to the point that all of the examples have had a certain self-undermining element. However, I do not wish to preclude a tone of authority: some transcendence is, at least in experience, real; moreover, certain detached tonalities—the clinical thinginess of *Life Studies* comes to mind—testify to, rather than deny, the sense of self-entrapment. Sylvia Plath's passionately lyrical poetry of inner experience—to which we now turn, to explore the dimension of richness—is also, as we shall see, one of the most tragic poetries of the self unable to escape from itself that we possess.

3
REAL AND NUMINOUS SELVES
A Reading of Plath

What makes Sylvia Plath so different from Lowell—and, one often finds, more palatable to a certain kind of traditional reader—is precisely what makes her a promising subject for a deeper study of self-objectification. We return here to our earlier emphasis on consciousness as a phenomenology or matrix. For Plath almost entirely lacks the novelistic shallow-relief associated with the confessional poets as a group. We are much less concerned in her work than in Lowell's with fact, or with the flotsam and jetsam of actual thought; rather, with the intangible inner atmospheres—the cotton-cloud enclosures and "acetylene" levitations—of the self, and the private religion of larger-than-life restatements of its crucial predicaments which the self projects outward. We are at the level where ecstatic expansions of the "I," and the wish to be free of the implications of having an "I" at all, both come into play. And yet Plath's late poetry is also, inescapably, a very specific emotional autobiography; and many of its details acquire their full resonance only when a personal context is provided, whether by hints in the poems themselves, by interlocking passages in the novel *The Bell Jar,* or (though this is rare) by entirely extrinsic information. And this is not, I would contend, a weakness, except in a few local instances. In the large view, it gives Plath's work a tragic wholeness, a sense of the unity of mind, personality, and fate, the absence of which impoverishes certain easier poetries of self-transcendence or self-negation which we will consider later.

To put this in different and narrower terms, Plath's poetry takes place in the borderland where neurotic, even pathological experience coincides with experience traditionally described as metaphysical, existential, or religious. This accounts for no small portion of Plath's fascination; and legitimately so, for the mapping of this borderland is crucial to our very conception of human nature, and has preoccupied the most interesting and imaginative of the speculative psychologists since Freud—in particular, Jung, Laing, and Binswanger. (For this reason, the names of the first two, and more than a trace of the methods of the third, will appear often in the following pages.)

The aim of this chapter is to take a large or holistic view of Plath's poetry as an act of self-objectification. Most of Plath's critics seem to have felt unduly impelled to choose between a psychological and a metaphysical point of view.[1] I have tried, rather, to connect the two; but have felt impelled, for expository reasons, to divide the following discussion into two parts. The first is a study of the relations between the real and the numinous in Plath's more direct and interpretive renderings of her actual life—*The Bell Jar* as well as the later poetry. The second takes up the embodiment of mental atmosphere in style, syntax, and music, as it develops from the uneasy constriction of *The Colossus* to the dissociated strangeness of some of the last poems. In the holism I have spoken of, the two parts of the discussion will increasingly complement, even mirror, each other.

In the first section, I have tried to avoid even seeming to write a psychological biography of Sylvia Plath the person; or speculating about whether or not other people and events were as she portrayed them. There are times, however, when the strong possibility that they were *not* is itself part of a reflexive drama of self-entrapment in the poetry. In these and a few other crucial instances, I have availed myself of the information the biographers and memoirists have gathered—but always keeping the emphasis on what a psychologically sensitive reader might feel from the writing itself.[2]

I

Almost everyone by now knows at least the broad outlines of the Freudian self-analysis Sylvia Plath made so central to her work: the immense impact of the father's premature death; the mother's tightly controlled response, experienced as unfeeling, which both abrupted the normal process of mourning and confirmed the daughter in what she rather enjoyed calling her "Electra complex"; the failed marriage, interpreted in hindsight as an effort to "make a model" of the father; the constant, and finally overmastering, fascination with a death which would be both reunion and revenge.

There is, however, a striking contrast between the dark halo of myth and melodrama that surrounds this story in the poetry, and the emotional impoverishment of its literal *mise en scène*, as presented in *The Bell Jar*. There, what confronts us is the mildly antiseptic world of the marginally established middle-middle-class: the Depression family's inability to leave the economic point of view out of sight for long, combined with the Nordic family's reluctance to express emotion. The idea that a quantification of basic human needs robs them of aesthetic or affectionate quality—so central a notion in *Ariel*—enters *The Bell Jar* by way of a satire on family mores: "It's not that we hadn't enough to eat at home, it's just that my grandmother always cooked economy joints and economy meat-loafs and had the habit of saying, the minute you lifted the first forkful to your mouth, 'I hope you enjoy that, it cost forty-one cents a pound,' which always made me feel I was somehow eating pennies instead of Sunday roast."[3]

A suggestion of Jung's may help us build a bridge between the two worlds of Plath's writing. For Jung, one of the signs of neurosis, and still more of psychosis, is a confusion of personal with archetypal figures. Though an archetype may be generated by an aspect of someone's—say, a mother's—actual personality, it quickly acquires a life of its own, rendering accurate perception of the individual henceforth impossible: "The child's instincts are disturbed, and this constellates archetypes which, in their turn, produce fantasies that come between the child and its mother as an alien and often frightening element. Thus, if the children of an overanxious mother regularly dream that she is a terrifying animal or a witch, these experiences point to a split in the child's psyche that predisposes it to a neurosis."[4] The neurotic is thus in one sense blessed with an escape from the banalities of life, into what Jung himself calls the "treasure" of profound, intense, fertile collective ideas; but in another sense cursed with an interfering screen between him and the true personalities of others. Therapy may, paradoxically enough, involve an intensification of the archetypal image until the patient realizes that it cannot possibly fit a living person—as in Jung's case of the woman whose dream-image of her doctor grew more and more godlike as her transference was, in fact, dissolving.

The ambivalence in Jung is one that Plath would discover for herself; for her archetypal world—though a "treasure" by contrast to the emotionally flattened atmosphere in *The Bell Jar*—itself quickly took on a petrifying, life-denying quality. To begin to understand this, we must try to trace connections, of the kind Jung suggests, between the literal and the numinous versions of the story.

Archetypally, Plath's father is represented either as godlike but fragmentary, protean, inaccessible ("The Colossus," "Full Fathom Five"), or else as the dark father, the Nazi and torturer. That this latter image is archetypal, the biographers, I hope, have made clear enough: in life Otto Plath, far from being a Nazi, left the Kaiser's Germany partly because he was a militant pacifist. Possibly the image stems from Plath's early anger at her father as a Prussian "autocrat";[5] yet her longing for him is so evident, in *The Bell Jar* and elsewhere, that one's mind is drawn more to the traditional etiology of masochism. In place of what is really feared—abandonment, indifference—malignity or persecution is substituted, both because it implies concern, or at least involvement, intention, on the part of the other, and because it constitutes a very high degree of presence. Nothing is so unlike the inaccessibility of a corpse as the intrusiveness of a tyrant, a jailer, a torturer. In an oblique way, "Daddy" seems to acknowledge all this. At a point in the poem when the Nazi theme has reached a pitch of hysterical inarticulacy ("the brute / Brute heart of a brute like you"), the father's real image suddenly comes to mind, and there is a comic incongruity:

> You stand at the blackboard, daddy,
> In the picture I have of you,
> A cleft in your chin instead of your foot

The speaker seems suddenly half-aware that the fantasy image needs defending, and the true grounds of reproach—as well as a much more loving underlying feeling—slip out:

But no less a devil for that, no not
Any less the black man who

Bit my pretty red heart in two.
I was ten when they buried you.
At twenty I tried to die
And get back, back, back to you.

The father's negative omnipresence, while it conveys a truth about the state of obsessive mourning, also expresses an unappeased wish on the part of the hurt little girl whose voice can still be heard here.[6]

In a similar way, the dark mother of the poetry is both opposed and connected to Plath's more realistic picture of her mother. The archetypal mother, a moon-goddess strongly weighted toward Hecate, is at once Plath's Muse and an embodiment of her deepest sense of purposelessness ("the 0-gape of complete despair") that turns the world to stone. In *The Colossus*, De Chirico's "Disquieting Muses" (another version of the same figure, "bald" like the moon, and three in number, like the Fates, the Furies, or the Triple Goddess) are insistently contrasted with the poet's real mother, their daemonic force defeating her overweening confidence in reason and the will-to-optimism. But beneath the contrasts, a connection insists itself: the Muses are sent by an "illbred aunt" whom the mother has "unwisely" kept "Unasked to my christening"; their faces are "blank as the day I was born." Finally, an accusation bursts out:

And this is the kingdom you bore me to,
Mother, mother. But no frown of mine
Will betray the company I keep.

The Bell Jar might supply us with the grounds of the connection. There, the mother's concern for appearances and her stoical practicality strike the daughter as an inhuman, and unfeminine, obliviousness to subjectivity and feeling. By not inviting the "illbred aunt"—that is to say, by not acknowledging a shadow-self in herself or anyone else—she becomes incapable of truly maternal understanding and support. Like De Chirico's mannequins, she is "eyeless" and "mouthless," in the simple old sense of *see no evil, speak no evil*; her head is a "darning-egg" in that it is filled exclusively with businesslike, daylight concerns. (In "The Moon and the Yew Tree" this comic image of a rigidly assertive woman, turning away from bodily femininity, rubs off a little onto the moon-goddess herself:

The moon is no door. It is a face in its own right,
White as a knuckle and terribly upset.
It drags the sea after it like a dark crime. . . .

A parallel passage in "Three Women" confirms the menstrual implication. In a curious nook of symbolic thinking, the moon's absolutely regular period, the tide, becomes a proof of her sterility—that is, her lack of generative warmth.)

In *The Bell Jar*, the reproaches against the mother grow bitterest where the father's death is concerned;[7] and this too registers in "The Disquieting Muses," in a curious way. The "Mother, mother" of the penultimate line echoes—even in its positioning—the ballad "Edward, Edward," where these words are spoken by a son who has killed his father at his mother's urging. Where Edward tells his mother to "beir" the "curse of hell," Plath insists that her mother "bore" her to an infernal "kingdom" whose female powers are the reverse of life-sustaining. But when, at the end of "The Disquieting Muses," the poet herself opts for stoicism and social pretense, she repeats the mother's actual choice, and thereby draws the real unholy trinity (of mother, self, and Hecate-like Muse) into ever closer unity. Poems like this one, and "The Moon and the Yew Tree," convey a worry about feminine identity which cannot—at least in any simple way—be reduced to a response to social pressures in the 1950s. Even Plath's courageous, often-quoted aspiration to be a "triple-threat woman" becomes a little terrifying in the light of "The Disquieting Muses."[8] It not only reveals an unconscious assimilation of herself to the Triple Goddess; it also suggests a fear that any competence in a woman, even domestic competence, may be fundamentally aggressive, and a destructive force.

Plath's feeling of connection to immensely powerful negative numina thus both expresses and compensates for a deep sense of lack, of the unsupportedness of her identity. The numina have, as we shall see, a fateful way of reappearing whenever adult love relations are at issue. But the sense of unsupportedness in itself would be likely to predicate a terrible constriction in the possibilities of relationship. The relevant doctor here is not Jung but R. D. Laing; and a number of critics—notably David Holbrook and Jan B. Gordon—have pointed out how many aspects of Plath's poetic world parallel his formulations. (Most conspicuously, there is her persistent imagery of being turned into an object, and dismantled, by the understanding or the emotional claims of others.) What Laing describes, in *The Divided Self*, is an "ontologically insecure" kind of personality, whose basic experience is that "identity and autonomy are always in question," that one's very being is qualitatively weaker than that of the outside world.[9] In this situation, the reality of other people is experienced as a threat, in two ways: "engulfment" (the fear of losing one's identity in the other if one is loved or understood) and "petrifaction" (the fear of being put to use, made into an object, by others, and even by the very fact that one exists as a datum in others' minds). As Laing points out, the fact that people are often treated impersonally in everyday life is peculiarly frightening to the ontologically insecure; and yet true intimacy is no safer. Against both dangers, the easiest defenses are to hide oneself from view, and to turn the other person into an object first. The former can be accomplished by a consciously insincere compliance, and ultimately by the creation of a "false self," a surface personality designed precisely to prevent the expression of any authentic feeling. (Much can be said about the "false self" in Plath; but for the moment let us content ourselves with noting how, in "Fever 103," a new self is generated to meet each new lover, each new threatening demand—

Not you, nor him

Not him, nor him
(My selves dissolving, old whore petticoats)—

so that both can be discarded together in the ascent to a bodiless "Paradise" of the true, inner self. Laing, too, describes this as the ultimate goal, and illusion, of the ontologically insecure personality.) The other defense—turning the other person into an object—is accomplished either by an active preference for mechanical relationships, or by a contemptuous intellectual understanding of the other.

How these Laingian anxieties and defenses, and the proneness to archetypal visitation, come together to distort and limit the possibilities of relationship can be seen if we trace the course of the image of the dark father or demon-lover through *The Bell Jar* and into the later poetry. Esther, in the novel, instinctively turns away from the idea of a love based on an open sharing of troubled feelings (as in the episode with the Southern boy, Eric), and tries to content herself with her mechanically conventional courtship with the eventually despised Buddy Willard. Yet her imagination always goes out most vividly to mysterious strangers: foreigners, "Constantin and Socrates and Attila and a pack of other lovers with queer names and off-beat professions" (p. 80); or the affable but conspicuously lonely proletarians—a prison gatekeeper, a sailor—whom she encounters, and fantasizes about, during her depressed wanderings. From the Laingian point of view, the remoteness of these men already makes them objects (Esther thinks of one of them, Constantin, as a "bright, unattainable pebble"—p. 89), and thus incapable of reifying her; from the equally pertinent Jungian one, it opens them to becoming vehicles of archetypal presence. For there is a third series of mysterious men, who really merit the term "demon-lovers." The most important of these is the melancholic Peruvian Marco, who nearly rapes Esther on her last night in New York. Marco's refusal, from the moment they meet, to let Esther cross his wishes in the slightest way provokes a curiously ambivalent reaction in her. Dancing with him, "moving as he moved, without any will or knowledge of my own," she comes closer to the language and the feeling of erotic self-abandonment than she does with anyone else in the book: "I let myself blow and bend like a tree in the wind." She concludes that she can "see why woman-haters could make such fools of women"; they are "like gods: invulnerable and chock-full of power" (pp. 112–113). Even after the attempted rape, the sense of a secret understanding between the two persists. It occurs to Esther to steal Marco's diamond in retaliation, thus fulfilling his own worst fantasy about her; it does not occur to her to turn to anyone else for help. When he daubs blood onto her cheeks, she cannot bring herself to wash it off; it is "touching, and rather spectacular . . . like the relic of a dead lover" (pp. 118–119).

The demon-lover motif returns when Esther determines—out of prudence, as she tells herself—to lose her virginity with "somebody I didn't know and wouldn't go on knowing—a kind of impersonal, priestlike official, as in the tales of tribal rites" (p. 240). The lover she finds, Irwin, is subtly unhuman, an *Übermensch* set apart not only by his Don Juanism, but by his agelessness ("the pale, hairless skin of a boy genius"), and his precocious mastery ("a full professor at twenty-six") of mathematics, an abstract discipline inaccessible and, when she is in other moods, repellent to Esther. Irwin is not cruel, but bloodletting enters the scene unbidden; Esther hemorrhages uncontrollably after intercourse, believes she is dying, and has to be rushed to a hospital emergency room. Neither Esther nor the structure of the novel will quite accept this as a simple, if rare, medical accident; clearly, the "rite" has found its proper epiphany. This epiphany parallels the imagery of passion as blood loss in *Ariel* ("The blood flood is the flood of love"; "The blood jet is poetry"); and it is definitively restated in the vampire mythology of "Daddy."

This mythology confirms the Laingian presupposition that intimacy saps one's limited stock of vital forces, threatens one's very being. But, by a deeper logic, if men are the undead, it means that they are the dead: the "dead lover," the dead father, returning in his death-denying disguise of omnipotent will. To find love a negative, obliterating experience is thus to feel reunited with the father. Insofar as the "blood flood" signifies menstrual blood, it is also to become one with the barren moon-goddess, the evil father's consort.[10] In this overdetermination, we come very near the core of the masochist theme in Plath's work.

"Daddy" represents a vengeful literary assimilation, after the separation, of Plath's marriage to the same complex, and the same ritual. To reproduce the (masochistically transformed) image of the father, she has chosen a man for his dominating, sadistic qualities, regarding even his sexuality, like Marco's or Irwin's, as a torture instrument:

> And then I knew what to do.
> I made a model of you,
> A man in black with a Meinkampf look
>
> And a love of the rack and the screw.
> And I said I do, I do.
> So daddy, I'm finally through.

And yet the opening premise itself ("I made a model of you") implies the possibility that she has merely imagined him this way, or else made him this way by her will to respond only to this element in him; and thereby has, in a sense, destroyed him, or at least the relationship ("If I've killed one man, I've killed two"). It is, after all, the destruction of the model that makes the voodoo rite of exorcism effective. There is a burden of guilt as well as abusiveness to this passage, which can only be glossed over if it is to be read as a straightforward attack on the husband's character.[11] Rather, the poem, here as in the passage quoted earlier, wavers near the Jungian therapeutic point at which the archetype becomes so inflated that it can no longer be imposed on a living, or even a dead, person. If the separation is not completed, it is perhaps because the archetype is occasioned by an absence, not a presence; so that, grim as it is, it alone offers the possibility of connection. As Holbrook has pointed out, the concluding rhyme-word "through" means not only through with the father in his vampire disguise, but through to the father where he actually is—in the grave.[12]

It should be clear why—without denying Plath insight into the social harmfulness of supermasculinity as an ideal—I disagree with a radical feminist interpretation of her work. Its burden, on the more intimate level, seems to me not sexual "oppression" but the ambiguous attractions a more-than-human Other may hold for ego weakness in either sex. Plath's writings describe a complex of feelings in which (as in the masculine Madonna complex) the other sex does not easily 'scape whipping. If men are figures of indomitable will, they are morally beyond the pale—as in the lines from "Three Women": "It is these men I mind. . . . They are jealous gods / That would have the whole world flat because they are." But if they are not gods, the note of sexual contempt for "small" men quickly becomes audible. It was Plath's strength, and a good deal of her despair, that she realized—if not precisely this—the possibility that deep conflicts among her conscious and unconscious values and wishes might have made her unhappiness almost inevitable. When the same governing image, the hook that cannot touch without injuring, is applied in 1962 to her own unconscious uses for others—

> I am inhabited by a cry.
> Nightly it flaps out
> Looking, with its hooks, for something to love
>
> ("Elm")

—as, a year earlier, to the conventional utilitarianism of what passes for normal affection—

> My husband and child smiling out of the family photo;
> Their smiles catch onto my skin, little smiling hooks
>
> ("Tulips")

—the whole question has been raised onto the disturbingly universalized philosophical plane which is the true ground of *Ariel*.

It is high time, then, to consider Plath's vision of reification as a philosophy. "The Applicant" is its central, if enigmatic, treatise. There, the basic premise seems to be that the impulse to love can spring only from an ontological incompleteness as radical as a missing limb:

Do you wear
A glass eye, false teeth or a crutch,
A brace or a hook,
Rubber breasts or a rubber crotch,

Stitches to show something's missing? No, no? Then
How can we give you a thing?

By the same grim logic, to be loved is to risk becoming the other
person's prosthetic part, petrified by the Medusa gaze of need: "A
living doll, everywhere you look." What is the nature of this seemingly ultimate ontological lack? There is really no clear answer, but
imagistically the lack is reformulated three times: as an empty hand
(loneliness); an empty head (this may be simply a sneer at the—masculine—"you," but it also suggests the impossibility of an inner life
that does not feed on the outside); and finally as nakedness—our
common human vulnerability before death and the material world.
Marriage, it would seem, defends even against the latter, by making
a part of the outside seem reliable, even symbiotic with the self:

I notice you are stark naked.
How about this suit—

Black and stiff, but not a bad fit.
Will you marry it?
It is waterproof, shatterproof, proof
Against fire and bombs through the roof.
Believe me, they'll bury you in it.

The problem with this sort of marriage is that its very function-
ality—and also the fact that it limits, and so defines, the self—infuses
it with a deathly rigidity; makes it, in fact, a coffin. (It is, as Holbrook's commentary makes clear, hard to be sure that this passage
really refers to the companion and not to the false self. But as we
have seen in "Fever 103," the latter arises so immediately in the presence of the former that there can easily be some ambiguity of reference.) The idea that companionship enables one to ignore one's
ontological jeopardy seems to underlie Plath's peculiar joke about
anniversary metals:

Come here, sweetie, out of the closet.
Well, what do you think of *that*?
Naked as paper to start

But in twenty-five years she'll be silver,
In fifty, gold.

Through the companion, time is turned into a possession, which appreciates in value rather than dwindling as death nears. Marriage thus becomes a kind of preventive magic. But the illusory value of gained time would seem to nullify the erotic value of the young lover—somewhat as the taste of pennies excluded that of beef. This is not to deny that the passage has other meanings: a feminist one, critical of the male demand for an unremitting object-like pleasingness in women; perhaps a Freudian one, in which "Naked as paper" reveals an under-theme of sexual desensitization. (It is often hard to separate themes of sexual distaste from those of depersonalization in Plath.) But it is the constant suggestion that reifying relationships are ontologically necessary that gives "The Applicant" its peculiar and terrible coherence.

For it is not only in actual human relationships that our defenses against death become, in turn, deathly. Intellectual or scientific understanding is another dangerously attractive extension of the instinct of self-preservation. On the surface, it promises to translate identity into a form that is indestructible; coded "in mathematics," the child's "pure leaps and spirals" ("The Night Dances") may "travel / The world forever." But in fact, so translated, the gestures "Lose themselves"; for the establishment of universally valid paradigms or laws reduces the individual and his experience to a mere instance or consequence, without independent ontological grounding. In *The Bell Jar,* Esther says of her required physics course—one feels, without hyperbole—"it was death." It appears to her a quite literal deconstruction of the world of things: "What I couldn't stand was this shrinking everything into letters and numbers. Instead of leaf shapes and enlarged diagrams of the holes the leaves breathe through and fascinating words like carotene and xanthophyll on the blackboard, there were these hideous, cramped, scorpion-lettered formulas" (p. 37). Plath's rejection of conventional religion has the same ground-theme as her rejection of science. If a divine consciousness had voluntarily created the world, that consciousness would be guilty of a supreme sacrifice of means to ends, experience to design:

> All the gods know is destinations.
> I am a letter in this slot—
> I fly to a name, two eyes.
>
> ("Getting There")

Nor does the vision of reification exhaust itself with the conscious activities of the human mind. Plath's imagination, with its almost schizophrenic concreteness, discovers the possibility of being turned into a thing, dismantled, made to suffer violence, in nearly all the processes of living. Actions can be seen as things (as are, after all, the photons which carry them to our consciousness), in which case living in time becomes an endless series of losses, indeed of mutilations:

> So your gestures flake off—
>
> Warm and human, then their pink light
> Bleeding and peeling
>
> Through the black amnesias of heaven.
>
> ("The Night Dances")

This process can be seen in active as well as passive terms. Then, in a fantastic metaphorical extension of the idea of the "eating game," the idea that life lives only by destroying other life, any action in relation to a thing becomes an attack on it:

> The engine is killing the track, the track is silver,
> It stretches into the distance. It will be eaten nevertheless.
>
> ("Totem")

Finally, the relation between consecutive reified actions can be seen as additive rather than subtractive. But in that case, the sinister conclusion—reached in the stoical "Berck Plage" as well as in the suicidal "Edge"—is that one is only "complete" when one is dead.

A final corollary is that time itself can be regarded as a fragmentation and reification of the individual; and the awareness of time as an aggressive act of the machine-ego. Perhaps Plath was aware of Freud's speculation that the consciousness of time was, at some primordial point, a choice on the part of an ego overwhelmed by the accumulation of stimuli, when she wrote, against the celebration of a birthday, of "the million / Probable motes that tick the years off my life,"

> You are silver-suited for the occasion. O adding machine—

> Is it impossible for you to let something go and have it go whole?
> Must you stamp each piece in purple,

> Must you kill what you can?

("A Birthday Present")

But in Plath's version of the argument, to be aware of life moment by moment is to "stamp" and "kill" it; the world is only "whole"— unfragmented by use or intention—when it is "let . . . go," in Enlightenment or, more probably, suicide. Analogously, as "The Applicant" reaches its terrible conclusion, it becomes clear that the lack, or "hole," is consciousness itself; the intolerable machine-companion is not only the surface self, not only the lover, but anything that fills consciousness—that is to say, the world. "You have a hole, it's a poultice. / You have an eye, it's an image." And so the argument reaches the Other Shore of a nihilistic mysticism.

In thinking about this system of ideas, we cannot afford to lose sight of the person for whom it became necessary. Out of all the divergent memoirs of Sylvia Plath, two impressions emerge repeatedly: that of hyperactivity, preternatural vividness, and that of an incommensurate "other-directedness," conventionality, lack of spontaneity, a false self. The history of her precociously focused but undiscriminating ambition is too well-known to repeat at length: the straight A's, even in courses she hated; the forty-five submissions to *Seventeen* while still in high school; the guest editorship at *Mademoiselle* . . . Her letters have only one tonality, an ingenue's star-struck hyperresponsiveness, even at moments when we know from *The Bell Jar* that she was experiencing horror or a numbed inability to feel. Yet she did not always fool people; and sometimes, indeed, left them puzzled that she should choose a persona so much more cramped than her mind. Her college roommate was reminded of "an airline stewardess"; her supervisor at *Mademoiselle* had "never found anyone so unspontaneous so consistently"; Robert Lowell remembered a "maddening docility"—maddening, because her real "patience and boldness" in literary matters were perfectly evident from her poems.[13] The two themes, will and convention, weave back and forth in her attitudes toward sex and love—though, to be sure, it is harder to judge of the life than of the art. Her praise of Ted Hughes as "very simply the only man I've ever met whom I could not boss" is at once frightening, in the implied view of love as a power struggle, without mutuality or quarter—and terribly conventional, in its sense of the appropriate outcome.[14] (Readers will differ, of course, in how far they would place the blame for what is distasteful in these traits on society—the American Girl image to which even the tinge of sado-masochism is not foreign—rather than on Plath herself. I can only say that what impresses me is the absence of any internal, or even realistic, sense of balance. Plath met and more than met every de-mand she could conceive of—as though convinced that the world would destroy her at the slightest sign of weakness; but also as if needing to press outward, to release a paranoid aggressiveness—the "triple-threat" theme. Finally, conventionality could be dispensed with more easily than this counterimplosive stance toward life, as Butscher makes clear in his embarrassing but significant chronicle of Plath's phase of female Don Juanism—it is the only adequate phrase—following her breakdown.)

When such a person justifies becoming suicidal by a philosophy of Buddhistic quietism, a horror of the mechanical and mechanizing self that acts and desires, part of what is going on has to be an invol-untary, unconscious, but still essentially moral Day of Judgment on her particular self.

To put the matter a little differently: Plath is distressed, metaphys-ically, by the idea that the quality of experience vanishes when it is seen as an instance of abstract and universal laws; yet she is dimly aware that the ritualistic quality of her unconscious and the manipu-lative quality of her persona have exactly that effect on the surface of her life. When Esther contrives to escape from the intolerable re-quired physics course by pretending to love it, and then sits in her auditor's seat writing poetry instead of notes and basking in the teacher's "sweet little appreciative smile" while she thinks of his voice as "only a mosquito in the distance" (p. 38), what has effec-tively happened is that the lesson of physics—the secondariness of appearances to formulas—has been vindicated in the far more cen-tral area of human contact and mutual respect. And the world "shrinks," morally, as it did metaphysically: the teacher to a bug; Esther's poetry to a stage prop; "intellectual maturity"—for which Esther is complimented by the Faculty Board—to a refinement of manipulative compliance. It is no wonder that when Esther remembers the episode she wants to beg the teacher's forgiveness; or that it is at this moment that she is first compelled to undermine her declarations of ambition by a "hollow flatness" in her voice.

The reader may find it surprising to speak of a suicidal breakdown as being in any sense "moral"; but both Laing and Jung could be adduced as witnesses in favor of such a point of view. Laing speaks of the "breakdowns" of certain patients as a casting off of the false-self system—a determination to express their true experience, even if it is an experience of vacancy—which he sees as in a sense creative. Jung speaks of the unconscious as seeking wholeness by generating an opposite to whatever is unbalanced in the conscious self, especially in the persona: "A man cannot get rid of himself in favor of an artificial personality without punishment. Even the attempt to do so brings on, in all ordinary cases, unconscious reactions. . . . To the degree that the world invites the individual to identify with the mask, he is delivered over to influences from within. . . . An opposite forces its way up from inside; it is exactly as though the unconscious suppressed the ego with the very same power which drew the ego into the persona."[15]

These formulations give a compelling—if incomplete—logic to Esther's breakdown in *The Bell Jar*. Esther's unconscious self-judgment really begins in New York, where she is forced to connect her best ambitions with the crudest kinds of promotional image-building; while, always in the background, the execution of the Rosenbergs suggests that a terrible scapegoat ritual is needed to maintain society's collective narcissism. Esther's first "mad" action is a repudiation of the self that belongs, or wants to belong, to the New York environment: she throws the new clothes she has bought off the roof of her hotel. From then on, "the unconscious suppresses the ego" in more and more central ways. It suppresses reading and writing, the grounds of Esther's substantial achievement; then eating, the shameful greed which, earlier in the book, she is inclined to blame both on the poverty of her background and on its deadening, quantifying spirit. The final privation, sleep, is more mysterious, more intimately related to the sense of existential futility—the repeated actions of life becoming absurd in the face of continuous consciousness. "It seemed silly to wash one day when I would only have to wash again the next. . . . I wanted to do everything once and for all and be through with it" (p. 135). But Plath's recurrent metaphor for this symptom is suggestive: it is that the nights ceased to exist. They were raised like shades, or "snapped out of sight like a lizard's eyelid" ("The Hanging Man"). It is not only in Jungian writings that the phrase "daylight world" connotes practicality, directed thinking, action in relation to the world; or that "shadow"—"the most beautiful thing in the world" to Esther (p. 155)—means the uncharted interior of the self. In a certain sense, the symptom, with a terrible poetic justice, locks Esther into the world of the persona which she has overvalued; demonstrates that the persona's acts become meaningless without a periodic infusion from underneath. And by placing the only available darkness before birth and after death, the symptom prepares the final assault against the ego: it argues the necessity of suicide. And yet even while succumbing to the argument, Esther remains curiously aware that the target is not her biological life but her existential stance: "It was as if what I wanted to kill wasn't in that skin or the thin blue pulse that jumped under my thumb, but somewhere else, deeper, more secret, and a whole lot harder to get at" (p. 156).

It is difficult to discuss the theme of suicide in Plath adequately, because it becomes to such a degree a vehicle for the whole positive side of her mysticism—for a kind of Beatific Vision. The two are not identical, philosophically or psychologically; but they meld, in an experience too overdetermined, all-embracing, all-satisfying, ever to be disentangled. We might call the experience the journey into the sun. It is adumbrated in several poems—"Getting There," "Fever 103"—and its supreme formulation comes in "Ariel"; but for our present purposes the prose version in *The Bell Jar* offers a greater opportunity to identify and separate the strands of motive.

Esther's mystical moment comes when she risks (or, at least, thinks she risks) her life by taking an advanced ski run when she has only begun to learn the rudiments of skiing from Buddy Willard. In retrospect, the episode seems to her a punishment of herself—and also, since she feels the impulse to say "Buddy Willard made me break that leg" (p. 90), of Buddy—for what has gone wrong in their relationship. In prospect, it looks more like an unconscious, or symbolic, attempt to overcome the unbridgeable distance between them: he is signaling to her from the bottom of the ski run; she "measure[s] the distance" and momentarily glimpses "a smooth white path from my feet to his feet" (p. 101). But when she actually plunges—savoring "the thought that I might kill myself"—Buddy is replaced as a goal by the sun:

> It hung over the suspended waves of the hills, an insentient pivot without which the world would not exist.
>
> A small, answering point in my own body flew towards it. I

felt my lungs inflate with the inrush of scenery—air, mountains, trees, people. I thought, "This is what it is to be happy."

I plummeted down past the zigzaggers, the students, the experts, through year after year of doubleness and smiles and compromise, into my own past.

People and trees receded on either hand like the dark sides of a tunnel as I hurtled on to the still, bright point at the end of it, the pebble at the bottom of the well, the white sweet baby cradled in its mother's belly. (p. 102)

The sun, here, is clearly something very much like the Indian Atman, the Self/Void, the qualityless, self-sufficient but "insentient" Being which alone sustains all contingent existences. (The earlier description of the hills "stall[ed] at my feet" suggests an impatience with material presence, which is no doubt relieved by the later vision of the hills as "suspended waves.") To move toward the sun is to cast off the false selves ("year after year of doubleness and smiles and compromise") and isolate out the pure, essential self which is also, unfortunately and necessarily, a self-against-the-world, "saintly and thin and essential as the blade of a knife" (p. 103). This theme recurs insistently in the poems—"Fever 103," "Getting There." But to move toward the sun is also to incorporate the world, as the "inrush of scenery" suggests. And it is to be incorporated; for it is—in Esther's explicit understanding, not through any imposed Freudian gloss on the oceanic feeling—a return "into my own past. . . . to . . . the white sweet baby cradled in its mother's belly." It is, in short, a return to the one known human condition in which identity *is* connectedness; where the twin pains of isolation and insecurity on the one hand, and awkward, cold, manipulative connection on the other, can never arise. The journey is even the discovery of an ideal beloved, for the "pebble" repeats a phrase Esther uses while watching the most attractive of her demon-lovers, the interpreter Constantin, asleep: "bright, unattainable pebble at the bottom of a deep well" (p. 89). (The reified quality of the image reflects Esther's despair, but also its roots in her tendency to petrify where she fears petrifaction: the passage with Constantin follows a gloomy meditation on how women are "brainwashed . . . in some private, totalitarian state" by marriage.) In short, in the journey to the sun all the values held to be irreconcilable in life—love and freedom, monistic unity and uninfluenced, uninfringeable selfhood—come together.

Finally, the journey, though it is seen as the reverse of birth, is also—by the feeling of accelerating motion through a "tunnel"—inescapably a memory, or fantasy, of birth.[16] Later in the novel, Esther would like to think of her recovery from her breakdown as "being born twice" (p. 257).

David Holbrook is of course right to maintain that if Plath killed herself believing literally that suicide amounted to birth, it was a "schizoid" and not a mystical phenomenon. But that is no reason to deny Plath access to the profoundly creative meaning that the concept of "second birth" has in William James and Erik Erikson—where it is applied, particularly, to the experiences of young people who, like Plath, feel profoundly unfulfilled in the identity given them by family, culture, and class. And indeed, the whole question of whether Plath's experience is to be seen as genuine mystical experience or as pathological fantasy has come more and more to seem to me a matter of both-and, not of either-or. (The reader to whom both-and seems an impossible or senseless answer might consider Ludwig Binswanger's discussion of suicide in "The Case of Ellen West"—a remarkable analysis of how a schizoid personality can formulate and even attain a universally valid image of human completeness, but only, thanks to the distorting power of the psychosis, in the act of preparing for self-destruction.)

Certainly Plath's vision of Atman, of a Universal Self behind, prior to, larger than, all individual existences, is one of the great religious archetypes. The further experiences—of turning to God as a lover; of finding a "pivot," a "still place" ("Getting There") at the center of all motion; of interpenetration with the cosmos; of second birth—are the component experiences of most mystical visions. They have come to many people—St. John of the Cross, Eliot, Whitman, among others—as healing experiences, making the permanent frustrations of life tolerable, and great accomplishment possible. And yet, in Plath, the experiences are unquestionably skewed—skewed by the fact that the pure self never ceases to be a self-in-opposition, "the blade of a knife"; by the corresponding fact that objects and other people are felt to be obstacles, "stalled" in one's path; and finally by the feeling of psychic unsupportedness—whatever its origins—that makes her place the sustaining Atman so uncompromisingly outside of, before, conscious life. And it is fairly clearly these skewings that make the imagined possibility of dying a necessary—though not a sufficient—precondition of the mystical voyage.

But as we say this, we should remember that we do not really know enough about what elements of skewing, or intrapsychic compensation, may be found in life-sustaining, and even in collective, mystical formulations. In a passage in *Philosphies of India*—particularly fascinating, if one comes upon it while thinking about Plath—Heinrich Zimmer suggests that Indian mysticism's emphasis on the absolute as nothingness, nonselfhood, be seen as a compensatory motion, balancing the almost exclusively social character of the Indian concept of selfhood—prescribed, down to the smallest details, by caste, sex, and profession.[17] In such a case, one might choose to see the movement of negation as essentially preparatory—the true archetype of the Self, as Jung or Blake would have seen it, arriving only when all overbalances are compensated.

In the poems of *Ariel*, Plath attempted, more than many readers have realized, to preserve her life by disentangling the positive from the negative strands of her subsuming experience. In particular, she tried to separate the vindictive motives for self-destruction—after her separation from Ted Hughes—from the archetype of rebirth. In one of the bee poems, "Stings," the bees—previously identified with ordinary women, "Honey-drudgers"—pursue a man, "a great scapegoat," and essentially sacrifice their lives to misrepresent him, reshape him into an evil version of himself:

> The bees found him out,
> Molding onto his lips like lies,
> Complicating his features.

It is hard not to read this as a commentary, before the fact, on the image of Hughes created by "Daddy" and, implicitly, by the suicide itself. But, for the moment, Plath detaches herself from this impulse sardonically: "They thought death was worth it, but I / Have a self to recover, a queen." Even the famous "Death & Co." is instructive in this respect, in its singling out of two ("of course there are two") deathly persuaders. The first—though terrible and voracious enough—is essentially the Thanatos of *Beyond the Pleasure Principle*, the wish for death that arises from the strain and the limitations of biological individuation. He "tells me how badly I photograph" and "exhibits / The birthmarks that are his trademark." He is linked with the inward gaze of mystical monism, though, curiously, with a particularly life-affirming monist: his "eyes are lidded / And balled, like Blake's." (The incongruity is, however, rather grimly resolved by Plath's own statement that it was Blake's death mask she had in mind.) The second figure stands for the self-destructiveness that Freud rightly saw as an inversion of Eros. The glamor of dying becomes essentially autoerotic ("Masturbating a glitter"). "He wants to be loved"—that is, he suggests that death can both simulate and compel (as the old saw goes, "They'll be sorry") the love that is missing in life. It is only when the two figures, Eros and Thanatos, act together on the poet that "Somebody's done for."

And it was only, it would seem, when the two became indistinguishable—and equally beautiful—in Plath's mind that suicide could no longer be resisted. As it is presented in "Edge," suicide is a supreme ritual, condensing myths of apparently opposite meanings. (We are reminded of how often, in her writings and letters, Plath had expressed a need to invent rituals—for being deflowered, for marriage, for leaving an insane asylum—a need that seems related to her hatred for an experience that was repetitive and fragmentary in its meanings, her wish to "do everything once and for all.")

The "Greek necessity" of "Edge" is fairly clearly that of Medea, who killed her two children to take revenge for her husband's infidelity. But this Medea's infanticide and suicide are seen as loving and benign:

She has folded

Them back into her body as petals
Of a rose close when the garden

Stiffens and odors bleed
From the sweet, deep throats of the night flower.

"She" is furthermore equated with Christ on the cross, by the two conspicuous echoes of *perfectum est*. This curious quality of feeling would seem to rest, personally, on the conviction that to be reunited with one's mother's body is a supreme good; theologically, on the sense that the believer who eats Christ's body—like a nursing child—is similarly incorporated into eternity with Him, "preserve[d] ... unto everlasting life" in the words of the Book of Common Prayer. It is a frightful, but in its own way an extremely logical, condensation of opposite feelings. But a normal perspective on it seems to register in the poem only in the words "The illusion of a Greek necessity." Or perhaps it registers, too, in the last line, in the sense that the white moon-goddess has presided, from a distance, over another "dark crime," another act of black magic and of negative and therefore sterile Eros: "Her blacks crackle and drag."

To end this discussion where it began, then, we might say that Plath, in Jung's phrase, "drowned in an eternal image"—the "fixed stars" reflected in water which, in Jung's iconography as, I think, in "Words," represent the numina perceived intrapsychically in the absence of a credible religious framework.[18] But we should then add that that is the moral Plath chose to draw. In life, the pressure of immediate circumstances; her care to save, not kill, her children; the indications that she perhaps hoped to be rescued herself—all tell a more confused and human story of impulsiveness and ambivalence. But as an artist, Plath's grand theme was perhaps the intrusion of the simplicities of the unconscious—paralleling, in the odd way we have seen, the reductiveness of the persona—onto the self trying to lead an integrated life, within itself and with others; and it was on this note that Plath chose to end.

II

Very near the core of Plath's strictly poetic genius is her ability to create in the reader a trance-like, floating sensation—at once vividly attuned to, and alienated from, the outside—which must have played a very important role in her own experience of the world. In my case, at least, this was the strongest initial appeal of the poetry: it was exhilarating, no matter how often the reviewers told me that it should be "depressing," "pessimistic," or "tortured." It now seems to me that a great deal of the power I felt lay in metrics and sound-patterns, and in a peculiarly subtle mastery of pacing. Let me illustrate first, therefore, with a passage which produced this trance-like effect in me, despite the fact that it contains no particularly striking *trouvailles* of diction:

> Over your body the clouds go
> High, high and icily
> And a little flat, as if they
>
> Floated on a glass that was invisible.

("Gulliver")

The first line, ringed with *o*'s; the second, with three accented long *i*'s in the first four syllables, trailing off, as the sound itself does, to long *e*: the element of incantation is clear enough. (Nor is the still greater visual predominance of the letters *o* and *i* insignificant. These letters are, I think, symbolic for Plath: zero and one; female and male; the full/void and the utterly separated, purified "I.") But it is in the third line that the genius for pacing appears. With the qualification "And a little flat," the state of dissociated freedom comes to seem slightly dangerous, or, at least, unreachable. The vowel sounds themselves flatten; and the peculiarity of the rhyme with the preceding line (assonance on the first syllable; eye-rhyme on the second; and the particular bizarreness of a spondee rhymed with a pyrrhic) gives a sense of straining to get past an obstacle. Then, the very word that poses the threat ("flat") is occupied from within by the tonic *o*, and we and the poem "float" into the freedom of a new stanza.

Often such musical analogies seem the most adequate to describe Plath's use of imitative pacing. (Interestingly enough, Plath was indifferent to music until she began writing the poems in *Ariel*, when she became fascinated with Mozart and, especially, Beethoven.) Consider the beginning of a much finer poem, "Ariel" itself:

> Stasis in darkness.
> Then the substanceless blue
> Pour of tor and distances.

The two near-spondees, rhyming, balanced around the insignificant pivot "in": a line could hardly contrive to have more "stasis," less forward movement to it. Moving ahead another five syllables, a hypothetical second line completes itself with the third occurrence of the rhyme—falling, yet again, on an abstract word denoting a privation of quality or presence. Thus, "blue" enters like the declaration of a second theme: because it is a quality; because it is formally unexpected; because it is only the second long vowel in the poem. The theme expands instantaneously, in a "pour" of long-vowel assonance and rhyme, then curiously sinks back under the first theme, as the velocity of the bolting horse melts concrete objects to an abstract blue of "distances."

This little sonata already contains the essential action of the poem. The second theme, of velocity, intensified quality, intensified selfhood, will be developed around the symbolic long *i* and the related long *e*, in what must be one of the most aurally spectacular passages in English poetry since Dylan Thomas:

And now I
Foam to wheat, a glitter of seas.
The child's cry

Melts in the wall.
And I
Am the arrow,

The dew that flies
Suicidal, at one with the drive
Into the red

Eye, the cauldron of morning.

As in the mountain vision in *The Bell Jar*, the "I" is "honed" against the sun until it is "saintly and thin and essential." It is thrust to the end of the line, against unconditioned space; underscored with ideas of purification, expansion, intensity, and above all speed and daring ("White / Godiva," "unpeel," "seas," "child's cry," "flies," "suicidal," "drive"). But finally, at the crisis, "I" metamorphoses into "Eye," fuses with the cosmic, impersonal awareness, or sheer Being, of the sun itself.[19] Specific identity—like specific perception in the opening stanza—"melts" in the "cauldron" of its own acceleration, back to a formless monism.[20]

I have dwelt on this poem not only because it is a tour de force, but because its melding opposites reveal a side of Plath's ontological vision peculiarly relevant to her stylistic development. In a certain sense, as we shall see, the opening stanza we examined so laboriously contains the plot not only of "Ariel" the poem but of *Ariel* the book.

The philosophical vacillation between motion and stasis runs through all of Plath's late writing. Where one poem yearns for a "still place . . . Untouched and untouchable," another insists: "Perfection is terrible, it cannot have children." "Years" scornfully dismisses the attractions of a "great Stasis"—

O God, I am not like you
In your vacuous black,
Stars stuck all over, bright stupid confetti.
Eternity bores me,
I never wanted it.

—and asserts a contrary preference:

> What I love is
> The piston in motion—
> My soul dies before it.

But surely, in the reader's mind, this piston is uncomfortably close to the "engine / Chuffing me off like a Jew" in "Daddy"; while in "Getting There," "The gigantic gorilla interiors / Of the wheels" are themselves "The terrible brains / Of Krupp," "The silver leash of the will"—the power-obsessed, reductively scientific late-capitalist (and masculine) culture frequently under attack in *Ariel*. But they are also the element of indomitable will in the poet herself. In a less well-known poem, "The Courage of Shutting-Up," the "black disks" that (echoing a phrase in "Getting There") "revolve, like the muzzles of cannon" are the recording disks of the poet's brain, driven by vindictiveness against her husband, "Loaded . . . with accounts of . . . Bastardies, usages, desertions and doubleness." By the end of "Getting There," the train has become indistinguishable from the speaker's "skin / Of . . . old faces," the false self; and the image of an "engine" has this resonance in a number of other poems (" Stings," "Totem").

Finally, one also notes in "Getting There" that the wheels are thought of as divine precisely because they are not free: "Fixed to their arcs like gods." And this brings us to the really important point: that the most crucial ideas, death and divinity, freedom and law, will not stay relegated to one side of the division. When Plath says of the piston, "My soul dies before it," one might sense that the Elizabethan meaning of "die" is in play, and thus the familiar theme of sexual masochism, submission to the dark father. But later in "Years" the feeling is grounded more deeply, in a realization that the wish for an absolutely unchecked, exhaustive expression of energy is a hurtling toward death, like the ominous wish "to do everything once and for all" in *The Bell Jar*. It is also a wish that goes beyond human capacity, so that it brings back the idea of divinity; and the new year becomes

> a Christus,
> The awful
>
> God-bit in him
> Dying to fly and be done with it

In other words, the initial premise in "Years" that the choice of motion is a choice in favor of life, and against the supernatural, is no sooner set forth than it must be inverted. Motion itself is deathly and divine. As in the first stanza of "Ariel," the two extremes inexorably converge.

What this system of unsatisfactory—and, finally, equally nihilistic—opposites implies, on a psychological level, is an inability to conceive of an even interchange between the self and the world, neither side overbalancing the other. For Plath—as a great deal of evidence, poetic and biographical, suggests—there were only two possible stances toward life. I have called them "will" and "convention," but that does not really state the matter adequately. Like the Secretary, the most depressive of her alter egos in "Three Women," Plath draws into close conjunction the idea of merely responding to life's demands, the idea of spatial and temporal fixity, and the sense of underlying meaninglessness:

> I shall not be accused by isolate buttons,
> Holes in the heels of socks, the white mute faces
> Of unanswered letters, coffined in a letter case.
> I shall not be accused, I shall not be accused.
> The clock shall not find me wanting, nor these stars
> That rivet in place abyss after abyss.

One can, then, be held in place by reality—"reality" meaning the world of objects *and* the social mask *and* poetic convention *and* the laws of one's fate, the "fixed stars"—and so threatened with slowing to a depressive standstill. Or one can continuously, consciously keep ahead of all these things, by a hurtling pace of living and writing, by the imposition of fantasy on reality, by violence acted or suffered— "death hurdle after death hurdle topped," in Lowell's melodramatic but suggestive phrase. But this too is a kind of unfreedom, and brings its own horror of the "engine"-self. Perhaps this is why having children was so terribly important to Plath: it and perhaps art are the only ways of keeping ahead of oneself in time that confirm, rather than fragment, one's integral humanity.

For the stylistic equivalent of being held in place by reality, we have only to look at Plath's early development. Plath often concedes obliquely that it was as difficult for her to be born as a poet as as a person. Her practical mother and her hired teachers could not teach her a sense of rhythm; only the mother's evil double, the Disquieting

Muse, did. I do not, in fact, believe that Plath was ever truly indifferent to sound values; but she was capable of rendering them unfluid to a degree that amounts to a kind of negative genius. What gives the poems in *The Colossus* a claustrophobic feeling is not the fact that they are set pieces, almost all visual description; or that the morals are tidy (they aren't always); but that one moves forward in the poems so slowly and effortfully. Many of the shorter lines seem to aspire to the condition of having no unstressed syllables at all—

> Goat-horns. Marked how god rose
>
> ("Faun")

> Tablets of blank blue, couldn't,
> Clapped shut, flatten this man out.
>
> ("The Hermit at Outermost House")

—while in more elaborated forms the spondaic quality tends to undermine the governing cadence, producing rather torpid and glutinous lines like "Bellied on a nimbus of sun-glazed buttercup" ("Watercolour of Grantchester Meadows"), or the choppy quality that mars the complicated stanzas of "All the Dead Dears." This style does, of course, have compensating advantages. It bears a distant relation to Pound's revival of alliterative verse forms; and, as in Pound, the reward is often a sense of the gritty obtrusiveness of the object—the wonderful dead snake, for instance, whose belly is "Sunset looked at through milk glass." This is, in short, no "academic poetry," correct and mild-spirited. It is the expression of a mind so obsessed with issues of will and stubbornness, with the obstructiveness of the material world, that it could call a hurricane a "collusion of mulish elements"; the only mind, perhaps, that could have invented such a combination of the vivid and the inert.

It is not, however, insignificant that Plath did very readily adopt the "academic" genre conventions of her time; or that those conventions called for the externalization of emotion in a landscape or spectacle, a spatial location; or that she wrote the poems, as Ted Hughes has described it, "very slowly, Thesaurus open on her knee . . . as if she were working out a mathematical problem," in a handwriting "like a mosaic, where every letter stands separate."[21] All of these facts, even the handwriting, have a common element psychologically: a submission to the given, a refusal of forward or self-generated motion.

It is hardly news at this point (but nonetheless true) that the poems in *The Colossus* that do show marked forward movement and fluidity of pacing, an unforced conversational voice, deal most commonly with familial anger ("The Colossus," "The Disquieting Muses") or a mesmeric fascination with suffering ("The Thin People," "The Stones"). It is generally these situations—violence acted or suffered—that break the deadlock with reality, and empower the second phase, the manic keeping-ahead-of-experience characteristic of *Ariel*. The hurtling momentum of the most famous of the later poems has often been remarked on, as have some of the technical qualities that contribute to it: the incisive, exclamatory conversational voice; the run-on, comma-spliced sentences broken over short lines; the irregular but richly overused rhymes, culminating in the nursery-rhyme repetitions of "Daddy."[22] In quieter poems, too, the reader is kept tautly aware of quickenings and slackenings of pace. The characteristic two- and three-line stanzas—cultivated, in *The Colossus*, as exercises in difficult rhyming—now function as a kind of musical measure, a fixed unit against which an often subtle drama of long and short lines, long and short sentences, may take shape. (A simple instance would be the end of "Berck Plage," where it takes the children one sentence and four stanzas really to see the funeral; then takes the author one two-sentence stanza to draw her grim conclusions.) We have already seen the virtuosity Plath could rise to when these resources were blended with her strongly developed sense for onomatopoeia and sound-pattern. Her destructive Muse had only to teach Plath a sense of rhythm—to teach her, that is, her own need to control the tempo of experience—and she was, almost overnight, one of the masters of pacing in modern poetry.

But it is not only pacing that makes us aware of a tense contest between mind and reality in *Ariel*. It is also a matter of rhetoric, of how the poems attack the subject. The poems in *The Colossus* generally do not. The subject is there, and the speaker is located in relation to it, by loaded description or else by plain statement. The poems in *Ariel* have a method at once more active and more tentative. They proceed by explicit acts of definition ("This is the sea, then, this great abeyance"; "This is the light of the mind, cold and planetary"). They proceed by questions, questions which tend, slightly paranoiacally, to generate other questions without the pretense, even in punctuation, of waiting for an answer ("Why is it so quiet, what are they hiding?"). They proceed, too, by an offer of alternatives, sometimes made explicit in a question ("It is shimmering, has it breasts, has it edges?"), sometimes merely implicit in the doubling of images ("These lamps, these planets / Falling like blessings, like flakes"). Doubling can also take the inverse form of a simple repetition of crucial words or phrases ("Love, love"; "things, things,"; "I let her go. I let her go"). Sometimes this expands into a litany-like repetition-with-variation, dramatizing at once the ceaseless activity and the obsessive sameness of the thought:

> What is the name of that colour?—
> Old blood of caked walls the sun heals,
>
> Old blood of limb stumps, burnt hearts.
>
> ("Berck Plage")

All these techniques keep us aware of language as a reaction to, an absorption of, the shocks of reality (and thus of a mind imposing itself, but aware of its self-revealing isolation). In this sense, the poems enact their own making; they are what is called "poetry of process," but without the loss of tension, of external precision, which that concept can imply in less anxiety-ridden poets.

The extended image-chains, the surrealist cadenzas, which are one of *Ariel's* defining features, present the same paradox: they are obsessive and helpless from an intrapsychic point of view; yet aggressive, multiplicative, centrifugal—a kind of escape velocity—where the givenness of outside reality is concerned. They can certainly be bewildering. One may be reading about a sleeping baby—"the drenched grass / Smell of your sleeps, lilies, lilies"—then cross a stanza-break to

> Their flesh bears no relation.
> Cold folds of ego, the calla,
>
> And the tiger, embellishing itself—
> Spots, and a spread of hot petals.
>
> The comets
> Have such a space to cross,
>
> Such coldness, forgetfulness.
>
> ("The Night Dances")

One learns to read these image-chains as one grasps how—far more than with most surrealist poets—they are fueled by characteristic ambivalences, unresolvable contradictions of feeling. Here, for instance, the thought of "lilies" (the repeated word, I think, a sign of an effort of self-persuasion, as in "With excessive love I enamelled it / Thinking 'Sweetness, sweetness' ") brings out an underlying uneasiness at the fact that the child's flesh has become wholly separate from her own. This theme is elaborated in moral terms as "cold" egotism and then as narcissistic sexual flaunting (always a sensitive topic in the late poems). In this poem, there is a resolution, or at least a surcease: with the "comets" (linked, by sound, to the "hot petals"), the absolute separateness of our beings and desires, grasped as a universal condition, moves the poet to empathy rather than fear; and the current of "normal" maternal feeling is restored.

Whether, beyond their psychological verisimilitude, these improvisations help or hurt the structure of the poems has to be a matter for delicate *ad hoc* judgments. For me, this one—by the very unpredictableness of the movement of revulsion—deepens the sense of isolation in the poem. The longer, more confused series of transvaluations in "Fever 103," however, seems to me uneconomical, and a defect.

As Edward Butscher and others have seen, the momentum of this phase of Plath's writing—and especially of the famous poems of anger—represents, on the whole, a will to life and health. By pressing back against the pressure of reality—vengefully externalizing the sources of evil, but also, as A. Alvarez has said, insisting on willing her own suffering—Plath defended herself against the dangers of engulfment and dependency, and experienced herself as active and autonomous.[23] (This is not to mention the simpler proof of solidity inherent in creative energy itself.) But if this were all Plath had done, the poems might be less interesting than they are, being essentially misrepresentations clung to in desperation. But this was not all; Plath was very conscious of creating fictions or dramas, and thereby of externalizing (and, we must assume, hoping to exorcise) her own motives as well. For me, the most remarkable thing about the angry poems is that while they are, as Alvarez says, "unforgiving," they are not unfair, in that they make the ambivalent feelings behind them, and the need to manipulate an unacceptable reality, so plain that we accept the statements about others as emotionally inescapable but not, therefore, as true. In this, the poems perfectly exemplify what I have tried to define as a "reflexive" mode.

Earlier I suggested how "Daddy" seems to me to undermine its own fictions, to rule out a clear allocation of blame. Let us look now at the emotional dynamics of a somewhat more complicated, many-leveled poem, "A Birthday Present." On the surface or "unfair" level, the poem seems to argue that suicide is the only way not to "kill" life, but to have it (in two senses) "go whole." The "you" of the poem, presumably Ted Hughes, is an "adding machine," lacking in "nobility" or true compassion, because he wants to prevent the speaker from taking her life.

Beyond the obvious paradoxes, there are two difficulties with this argument. The first is that the "present" only becomes death in the course of the poem. It is the Angel of the Annunciation before it is the Passion of Christ. At the beginning, as the characteristic jabbing questions circle around it—"It is shimmering, has it breasts, has it edges?"—it is something far more indefinite. It has the "shimmer" we associate with unfixity, but also with living substance. It may be round or sharply delimited, nourishing or cutting, female or male. It is as if we were thrown back to a child's first tentative movements—of recognition, distinction, reliance—toward the outside world. (Perhaps, incidentally, it is only the contrast with "breasts" that makes me take "edges" as male; but later aggressive phallic images accrue—"a tusk," "a ghost-column"—and the annunciatory angel is, after all, an impregnator as well as a messenger from God.) There is also a vacillation between megalomania and self-deprecation in the speaker's attitude toward herself. If the gift may be "enormity," a sign of divine favor vouchsafed to a suffering saint, it may also be "small," suited to the chastened status of someone who has nearly given up on her own life. (And so the idea of suicide enters the poem, somewhat insidiously, as a danger safely past, which leaves the speaker grateful for life on the humblest terms.) In sum, we know that the present will somehow give, or define, the meaning of the speaker's life; but it seems to do so in quite contradictory ways.

The second difficulty perhaps arises only if one knows—as admittedly one does not, directly, from the poem—that Plath and her husband were separated when the poem was written, and that she entertained definite, but diminishing, hopes for a reconciliation. In this light, her desire for him to give her a birthday present, however "small," and her vision of the two of them eating dinner beside it, have a poignantly simpler meaning. And her reproach to him—"Is it impossible for you to let something go and have it go whole?"—becomes an ironic projection, since it is she who cannot let him go, cannot affirm her life on self-sufficient terms. To put the matter a little differently, his reasonable anxiety that she not commit suicide stands in, becomes a scapegoat, for his truly intolerable refusal to give himself, his love. This, after all, is the one gift that "only you can give . . . to me"; death can come from herself, or from a million accidental causes. (But, of course, she does want death to come "only" from him, in the sense that she wants him to bear the blame:

> I know why you will not give it to me,
> You are terrified

> The world will go up in a shriek, and your head with it,
> Bossed, brazen, an antique shield,

> A marvel to your great-grandchildren.

If the surface sense here is that he cannot share her passion for the subsuming moment, the under-sense is that—as both of them understand—one of the goals of her suicide is to petrify the meaning of his life, turning him into a medieval monster out of one of his own poems.)

By the same token, death becomes a way of never losing contact with him. In this context, to choose a knife as the means of suicide is at once an act of poetic justice—identifying the criminal—and an expression of sexual longing. (The choice of stabbing is unique to this poem, and would seem to go against the distaste for messy deaths expressed in *The Bell Jar*.) At the end of the poem, the knife does "not carve, but enter" (a word rarely used for stabbing, frequently used for sexual penetration), and its entry leads to immediate parturition, the birth-separation of the universe. To notice these things is not to deny the mystical dimension—the subsuming moment, in which the self realizes the universe by purging it of subjectivity, of selfhood—which has been so ably charted by Richard Howard, among others.[24] It is, however, to double these meanings with darker psychic ones, in which death at once symbolically recovers the loss—of a lover, and of future children—and takes vengeance for it.[25] It is also to leave the "present" finally mysterious (as the syntax itself does: "If it were death . . ."), with the mystery of what is truly satisfying in life; or perhaps one should say the mystery of what—which of the great experiences, love or death or the pride of parenthood or the initial fluidity of the infant's landscape—places one in an ultimately significant relation to the world beyond one.

It is the inability not to register the convergence of contradictory motives, combined with the sense of the final mysteriousness of desire, that gives this poem, and some others from the same period, the quality of tragic action rather than special pleading. Is it this same lack, or subversion, of the useful defenses of the closed mind that made the poems finally of little therapeutic use to their author? Or does the problem—as an existential analyst might see it—lie deeper, in the very splitting of ontological tempi which helped rush Plath's clarity ahead of any natural rate of emotional growth? (I myself find Alvarez's comparison of the stance of the poems to "manic defense" solider than his attack on the idea of catharsis per se.)[26] Whatever the reason, I think every reader must have felt that at a certain point in *Ariel* the hurtling anger, impatience, and energy in the voice begin to flag. Perhaps the turning-point is "Years"—written in mid-November 1962—in which the preference for motion over stasis is argued and yet, as we have seen, subtly undermined. After that, the tempo slows. Oracular statements replace the questions, the probings, the alternatives. Images are lingered over longer and more tenderly; but the spaces between them—syntactic and conceptual—widen. There are ambiguities of perception, and ambiguities of emotional tone. Instead of the earlier sharp tension between mind and world, there are moments when everything seems to blur into everything else. There are other moments when the concern is rather with a total loss of contact with reality: the sheeted mirror, the paralytic lying like a "Dead egg . . . Whole / On a whole world I cannot touch," the "riderless" words that run "Off from the center like horses." This is a poetry of the dissolution of the ego—perhaps one of the most accurate and interesting such poetries we have; in it, the principle of stillness again triumphs, though in a wholly new way.[27]

"Totem" may serve to illustrate both the difficulties and the fascination of the very late work. The title concedes the difficulty, for Plath intended it—according to the note in the new *Collected Poems*—to suggest a totem pole, "a pile of interconnected images"—but with the interconnections, as the word "pile" implies, left largely to the reader's imagination.[28] But I cannot help suspecting that Plath was also thinking of Freud's *Totem and Taboo*, in which totemism is connected to the killing and eating of a primal father. For the poem is perhaps best summarized as an extremely depressed meditation on the idea that all life lives at the expense of other life—an idea carried to an absurd extreme in the opening lines: "The engine is killing the track, the track is silver, / It stretches into the distance. It will be eaten nevertheless." As the poem develops, this paradigm is applied to questions of religious and intellectual sustenance:

Let us eat it like Plato's afterbirth,

Let us eat it like Christ.
These are the people that were important—

Their round eyes, their teeth, their grimaces
On a stick that rattles and clicks, a counterfeit snake.

The uncertainties of emotional stance are, I think, evident. Is it a reverent act to eat Plato, or does the brutal double sense of "afterbirth" convey scorn for his notions of immortality and preexistence? Is the tone of "the people that were important" wistful (*if only anyone were*) or satiric (*it all boils down to ego*)? Is it the living who devour the dead, or is it the dead, with their conspicuous "teeth," who gain immortality by preying on the living? Or is the last image really an image of death itself, the grinning skull that devours everything? In the image that follows, the horrifying apartness of the predator is identified with what should be its opposite, the apartness of mystical vision, which sees through the particular to eternity or nothingness:

Shall the hood of the cobra appal me—
The loneliness of its eye, the eye of the mountains

Through which the sky eternally threads itself?

Dimly, one senses that both of these things are part of the speaker's vision of herself, perhaps because of the association of "madness" with another universally feared animal a few lines later: "I am mad, calls the spider, waving its many arms." It is, again, very hard to specify the meaning of this strangely jocular line. Is it that madness is a theatrical gesture; that it is a breaking apart into multiple selves; or that it is merely a beholder's misunderstanding of the all-too-natural horribleness of the one self? Whatever it is in itself, "in truth it is terrible, / Multiplied in the eyes of the flies." The flies ("like blue children") are perhaps Plath's own threatened children, doomed to see her distorted but ubiquitous, as she has seen her own mother and father.[29] But the ending of the poem seems to dismiss the question of accurate or inaccurate perception, personal or cosmic reference; for the "infinite" itself has only one meaning, "the one / Death with its many sticks."

A poem with so fluid a sense of outside and inside, truth and fic-tion—with so many "short circuits and folding mirrors"—poses ob-vious and large-scale problems for the reader. Still, for me at least, the poems of this period have a dramatic power comparable to that of the more aggressive, more externally articulated poems earlier. Perhaps this power lies in the baleful unarguableness of depressed perceptions; or perhaps, conversely, in the fact that such perceptions are sometimes more transparent to the world than expectant or angry ones. There is, in these poems, a new—or newly intense—tone of wistfulness, a leaping out of context to hold on to evanescent beauties: the "beauty of drowned fields" in "Totem," or the balloons "we live with / Instead of dead furniture,"

> Guileless and clear,
> Oval soul-animals,
> Taking up half the space,
> Moving and rubbing on the silk
>
> Invisible air drifts,
> Giving a shriek and pop
> When attacked, then scooting to rest, barely trembling.

The insolidity, the nonresistance to shock, of this beauty may well trouble the reader. It suggests that within the psyche, too, there is no holding center, and the gentler feeling-states may simply vanish when the angry or suicidal ones come forward. Still, the tender ap-preciativeness is genuine; there is no paranoiac sense of beauty as a deceit, or an assault on the psyche. The anthropomorphisms in these poems ("Dawn," "Kindness," and "the spider" speaking) have a childlike conspicuousness that conveys mainly the poet's yearn-ing—yet her inability—to believe in and draw sustenance from a common symbolic language. Almost the greatest sadness in the poems lies in the fact that objects can produce in us a sense of posi-tive negation just by their unimaginable inactivity, like the won-derful telephone "digesting / Voicelessness" in "The Munich Mannequins."

Nevertheless, the tendency toward a complete severance of rela-tions with the outside is clear from one of the poems from the last week of Plath's life, "Contusion." The "dead egg" is now tangent to the world at only one point, a point of response to injury. Elsewhere there is a pervasive numbness—a numbness associated, by "The color of pearl," with the idea of death as an aesthetic "perfection." The next two stanzas recast the same idea in different imagistic terms. The vaguely vaginal imagery of the second (the "pit of rock" where "The sea sucks obsessively") suggests that the injury is still sexual loneliness, but at the same time subsumes that longing under earlier, less appeasable oceanic ones. With its next reshaping, the image passes beyond any object that clearly exists in the world—

> The size of a fly,
> The doom mark
> Crawls down the wall

—though the feeling of helpless fascination before "doom" is clear enough; and we see a little further thanks to the allusion to Emily Dickinson's "I heard a fly buzz when I died," and the (possible) suggestion of a countdown before a missile is fired. The last stanza tells us what really we already know: that all search for connection or correspondence on the outside—including metaphor itself—is on the point of ceasing.

> The heart shuts,
> The sea slides back,
> The mirrors are sheeted.

Here our own consideration might cease, if the last poems, "Edge" and "Words," did not bring us to a further meaning of stasis too little emphasized hitherto: that of pattern, aesthetic "perfection," psychic determinism, law and the "fixed stars." Law is always, as we have seen, an ambivalent concept in Plath's writing. In science, it is repellent; as ritual, archetype, "Greek necessity," it is hypnotically attractive. It, rather than freedom, is the privilege of the gods. And as the Nazi becomes the truly desirable love-object, the professor of higher mathematics becomes the ritually obligatory seducer. And— in the physics class, or in Irwin's apartment, or in "Edge"—law is always, in some sense, "death." From this vantage point, Plath's surface hatred of the impersonality of process and scientific law seems in part a reaction formation not only against her own potential manipulativeness, but against the impulse to suicide.

The later Freud might not have found any of these equations particularly surprising. In *Beyond the Pleasure Principle*, the existence of a compulsion to repeat even unpleasurable experiences is the principal evidence for the conservative character of the instincts, and thence for the hypothesis of a death-instinct. But needless to say, when the equation of pattern and death appears in an individual as an emotional given, not as a theoretical conclusion, the possibility of its abstract validity does not lessen the need to look for personal determinants—the most important of these, surely, being the father's death, which seals up in itself the usual goal of repetition, the world of early childhood. Perhaps the most tragic equation is the one, evident in "Edge," between death and the completion of an aesthetic pattern, artistic "perfection" or "accomplishment." It is the more tragic because it helps explain the lack of normal defenses against the intolerable coalescence of contrary feelings which is the chief merit, precisely, of Plath's most dynamic poems. As in the first stanza of "Ariel," the extreme of motion becomes a stillness.

Are we to conclude, then, that poetry itself, for Plath, belongs finally to the realm of law, the inhuman, and death? A number of elements in our experience of the poetry rightly prejudice us to reject this conclusion as over-simple. One is the real and exhilarating momentum of the poems; another, the vivid presence of particular things and—as Robert Pinsky has pointed out in a brief but brilliant discussion of "Poppies in July"—the peculiar independence allowed them. [30] From a biographical point of view—since Plath was always ambivalent about law—her statement that she felt "absolutely fulfilled" while writing, and the occasional comparisons of writing to childbirth, the paradigmatic positive action, reinforce this impression.[31]

It seems more accurate to compare poetry not to death but to the moment of courting death, which, so often in Plath's work, does bring a kind of absolute fulfillment. Stéphane Mallarmé—another poet whose dissatisfaction with materiality and the present moment has been judiciously and persuasively connected with the early death of a parent[32]—spoke somewhere of the pleasure of poetry as the "vibratory near-disappearance" of the world of things. Plath's masterly concentration on tempo, on the dynamics of her mind's absorption of reality, accomplishes this difficult balance; and makes us—like Esther on the ski-run—feel the "inrush," the implosive pressure of reality, momentarily as a joyful increase of vividness. Which is to say that for Plath, as for many poets, poetry is a kind of sacred space, not quite in real experience, where contradictions elsewhere felt to be irreconcilable—vitality and perfection, ecstatic self-assertion and the otherness of the world—coexist, and the psyche feels momentarily whole.

A final word is perhaps needed on the kind of universality Plath laid claim to directly, by incorporating World War II and the death camps (and the atomic bomb) into her own story. Irving Howe and others have felt this incorporation to be unjustified, hysterical, even immoral.[33] The first point to be made is that the public dimension is in fact part of the self-portrait, and not a separate issue. It is a psychological fact that melancholic temperaments, once they hear of certain kinds of terrible events, cannot stop thinking of them, or cannot separate them from themselves—as one's skin will freeze instantaneously to a cold enough piece of metal. (We see this in *The Bell Jar*, in Esther's obsession with the execution of the Rosenbergs.) All of the confessional poets have been particularly interested in the events that elicited this reaction in them: in Lowell's case, the subtle cruelties of tyrants who were artists *manqués*; in Berryman's, theatrical mass murders. Their implicit premise has been that if the hidden element of attraction in the obsession is once unearthed, it will teach us something about why it occurs to human beings actually to do atrocious things. The neurotic artist makes his own personality a bridge between the surface innocence of social life and the eruption of horror. (The gap between the two evidently troubles most of the confessional poets—Lowell speaking of "the chafe and jar / of nuclear war" considered as a conversation piece; Berryman contrasting his own sense of diffuse, unverifiable guilt with the clear framework that an age of afflictions and dogmas gave Mistress Bradstreet.) The connections arrived at may, of course, be more or less successful, more or less melodramatic. But Howe's article shows no awareness of this more general confessional ambition, an ambition which creates its own standards of proportion, and makes Howe's more literal ones somewhat beside the point.

It is true that some of Plath's psychopolitical formulations are simplistically superior: for instance, the passage in "Three Women" which attributes all cruelty to the will to "flatten" in masculinity and in abstract thought, ignoring her own ambivalence about these things. It is also true that one must sometimes read very carefully to disentangle her from that peculiarly contemporary sentimentality that imposes a paradigm of "victimization"—hence a black and white morality—on the trickier, grayer modalities of common psychological pain. But finally Plath's stance is more guilty, more involved, than this. Her psychically weak life was lived under the aegis of humanly narrow ideals of being "good" and "successful" which are often thought of as characteristically German (and American). Out of this life, she drew a nexus of themes—sacrifice; purity; scapegoating; depersonalization and counter-depersonalization; the grandiose archetypalization of the self, and of heroes, and its implicit underside, the wish for a surcease from individuality—which have a great deal to do with the appeal of totalitarian ideas. These connections are drawn quite firmly in some of the better, quieter poems touching on the Nazi theme—for instance, "Mary's Song," where the "same fire" of purification in which the "Sunday lamb . . . Sacrifices its opacity" and becomes "A window, holy gold" also consumes "the tallow heretics" and "the Jews." It is unclear how far Plath consciously connected these mechanisms to her own specific personality, how far she saw them as necessary consequences of the condition of having or being a self at all, as it is set forth in "Totem" or "The Applicant." But there are times when the personal connection flashes out weirdly and wonderfully in her imagery—as in the prose statement where she speaks of "big business and the military in America" as if they were herself and Ted Hughes, a "terrifying, mad, omnipotent marriage."[34] (In a different way, Plath's sense of psychic invasion by negative numina is positively sublimated in her sane fear of nuclear fallout, "mercuric atoms," thalidomide.) Thus, as with Lowell, though less consciously, confession is the basis and measure for the understanding of public motives; the things that terrify Plath outwardly are the same things that terrify her in herself; and for the reader, the two converge in a coherent, if narrow, insight into the psychic appeal of evil.

4

LANGUAGE AGAINST ITSELF
The Middle Generation of Contemporary Poets

Sylvia Plath's poetry often expresses a desire to leave the personal sense of self behind, to attain to some mode of being that is conscious yet impersonal, transparent, the "eye" of "Ariel," the newborn universe at the end of "A Birthday Present." Yet her poetry remains a personal poetry, because it represents that wish itself as rising from a matrix of individual and social history, and also, perhaps, because it despairs of fulfilling that wish in life. Other poets of Plath's generation have tried to realize and inhabit a larger than personal—in some cases even a larger than human—mode of selfhood, which for them becomes the paradigm of health. Galway Kinnell has given the theme an extreme, and now rather notorious, formulation, speaking of a progress inward "until you're just a person. If you could keep going deeper and deeper, you'd finally not be a person either; you'd be an animal; and if you kept going deeper and deeper, you'd be a blade of grass or ultimately perhaps a stone. And if a stone could read, [poetry] would speak for it."[1] If this inverted hierarchy savors a little of the Freudian conservatism of the instincts that resists life and evolution, Gary Snyder's essay "Poetry and the Primitive: Notes on Poetry as an Ecological Survival Technique" offers us a conservatism that is deeply, though ahistorically, humanistic: "Poetry must sing or speak from authentic experience. Of all the streams of civilized tradition with roots in the paleolithic, poetry is one of the few that can realistically claim an unchanged function and a relevance which will outlast most of the activities that surround us today. Poets, as few others, must live close to the world that primitive men are in: the world, in its nakedness, which is fundamental for all of us—birth, love, death; the sheer fact of being alive."

In poetry written under such premises, the personal self is underplayed not out of shame, or an Impersonal Theory, but because it is seen—as in Rimbaud—as internalized history. Snyder writes, "Class-structured civilized society is a kind of mass ego. To transcend the ego is to go beyond society as well. 'Beyond' there lies, inwardly, the unconscious. Outwardly, the equivalent of the unconscious is the wilderness: both of these terms meet, one step even farther on, as *one.*"[2] The truly important educative experiences become, then, experiences of unlearning: empathy with animals, primitive and peasant cultures, the wilderness; a reacclimatization to solitude in nature; the evocation of a Jungian collective unconscious through meditation or surrealism. And so a new (and at the same time an old, a Wordsworthian) repertory of characteristic subjects is established.

I

With this attitude toward the ego comes a special and in some ways hostile attitude toward language itself. Most of these poets share the view that language is one of the most powerful agents of our socialization, leading us to internalize our parents', our world's, definitions, and to ignore the portions of our authentic experience—the experience of the body and of the unconscious—that do not express themselves directly in verbal terms. (The poets I chiefly have in mind are James Wright, Robert Bly, W. S. Merwin, Snyder, and Kinnell. But the impulse toward the primitive, and away from language, affected many if not most of the poets who were in their thirties during the 1960s—notably Denise Levertov, A. R. Ammons, Robert Creeley, and Adrienne Rich, who in fact coined the famous phrase "the oppressor's language.")

The essential project, then, is to force language to transcend itself.

These poets desire not a *mot juste*, but a word we can hear meant by the entire man who speaks it, his heart, lungs, and musculature as well as brain and voice box. Galway Kinnell speaks of "breaking to a sacred, bloodier speech"; James Wright of "the pure clear word" and "the poetry of a grown man." Wright defines this "grown man" in terms that are characteristically bodily, proletarian, and of the dream life, as well as anti-verbal:

> The long body of his dream is the beginning of a dark
> Hair under an illiterate
> Girl's ear.

When Snyder, in the essay quoted above, follows on Charles Olson in laying great emphasis on the breath, he gives it an almost mystical significance, as locating man in the physical world and in his own full self. It is "the outer world coming into one's body," and "with pulse ... the source of our inward sense of rhythm"; while "the voice, in everyone, is a mirror of his own deepest self" (pp. 123–125).

The reasons for the emergence of this shared poetic at this particular time are obviously complex. Some, no doubt, belong to literary history. All of these poets began writing in the early 1950s, at a time when most accepted poetry was orderly, cerebral, and, through the influence and the very sophistication of the New Criticism, a little codified; and some (Wright and Merwin, and, to a degree, Kinnell) had early successes in this mode. (Snyder's more Poundian skills, on the other hand, went unappreciated—in Eastern circles, at least—because of his identification with the "Beats," until sometime in the 1960s.) In one sense, then, these poets distrust rational organization and literary convention because they had to fight their wars of poetic identity against an overvaluation of these things. But one cannot ignore the larger history, the fact that this was the first generation to confront concentration camps and the atomic bomb, the fully revealed destructiveness of civilized man, while still growing up, before private values had had a chance to solidify. Like many other people in the 1960s, these poets came to hold, at least briefly, the scathing view of our collective moral history expressed by Kinnell in *The Book of Nightmares*:

> In the Twentieth Century of my trespass on earth,
> having exterminated one billion heathens,
> heretics, Jews, Moslems, witches, mystical seekers,

> black men, Asians, and Christian brothers,
> every one of them for his own good,
>
> a whole continent of red men for living in unnatural commu-
>   nity
> and at the same time having relations with the land,
> one billion species of animals for being sub-human,
> and ready to take on the bloodthirsty creatures from the other
>   planets,
> I, Christian man, groan out this testament of my last will.

For this generation, the search for values before and behind civilization became an "ecological survival technique" in deadly earnest;
and (also for the first time in recent history) there were tools other
than Fancy available to the task, in modern anthropology and depth
psychology. When Snyder defies at least fifty years of taste by calling Rousseau's Noble Savage "one of the most remarkable intuitions
in Western thought" (p. 120), his choice of words is worth pondering; what was once considered a myth, whether appealing or
noxious, is now seen as an inspired scientific hypothesis, opening
new areas of exploration and discovery.

   If "to transcend the ego is to go beyond society as well," we might
well begin our stylistic consideration with the "I" of the poet. The
poets we have been concerned with up to this point—Lowell, Berryman, even Plath—intend a descriptive "I," a voice we recognize
complexly as we do a friend's, a social ego at its richest and most individual. Their "I" seldom begins a poem; it arrives politely late,
surrounded by phrases that cast back its idiosyncrasy, intelligence,
tone, like so many mirrors. The "I" beginning, on the other hand, is
ubiquitous in Wright ("I am bone lonely"; "I am delighted"; "I
woke"), and not uncommon in any of his contemporaries. But more
remarkable is the shared penchant for putting the "I" in the simplest
of possible sentence structures, pronoun plus active or linking verb,
with no modifiers before or between. The "I" becomes numb, neutral, universal: a transparency through which we look directly to the
state of being or feeling. (Snyder, on the other hand, prefers to omit
the pronoun entirely—following on Pound and the ideogram.)

   The preference for simple sentence structures is not limited to
first-person utterances. With these poets, no matter how wild or
surrealistic the content becomes, the syntax tends to remain clear
and enumerative. When Robert Bly describes the kind of free-

associative poetry he desires, his metaphors are of motion from point to point, acrobatic enough, but still essentially linear: "a leaping about the psyche," "that swift movement all over the psyche . . . from a pine table to mad inward desires."[3] This constitutes a strong break with the hitherto dominant mode of irrationalist poetry in English (that of Hart Crane, Dylan Thomas, et al.), which, following from Rimbaud and Mallarmé, tends to suspend or confuse the normal syntactic flow, and create spaces for mystery and free association between the words themselves. Perhaps it is the location of the mystery *in* language, or in an operation performed on language, that repels a poet like Bly; better, for him, that the true complexity of feeling perish unuttered than that it become ambiguously intertwined with the studied complexity of the intellect.

But there is a strictly literary, as well as a psychological or epistemological, aspect to the search for simplicity. These poets are Wordsworthian questioners, bent on isolating the poetry in poems from all that serves essentially mundane ends: to prepare or seduce the reader, to shield the writer from anticipated criticisms, aesthetic or moral, to move the poem mechanically from place to place. Beginnings and endings in these poems are as abrupt and direct as the grammar is simple. There is an implicit aversion to all rhetorical devices which set an image in an "improving"—or even an interpretive—perspective; the image is intended to flash, like a spontaneous mental picture, and is usually coterminous with the line. Indeed, the whole aesthetic of "rendering" is suspect for these poets; its necessarily overburdened descriptions seem cold and predictable, its theory a rejection of the spontaneity and subjective validity of feelings. Often, these poets deliberately reinstate the outlawed nineteenth-century vocabulary of feeling and awe: Wright is devoted to the words "lovely" and "strange," Kinnell to forbidden abstractions like "infinite," "reality," "nothingness." (There is a similar forthrightness about human loves and loyalties, a refusal to let the fear of sentimentality—which after all implies forced emotion—interfere with deep commitments.) Perhaps it is all summed up in the mannerism—frequent even with Merwin and Kinnell, poets whose natural breath-unit is as long as Whitman's—of placing a single word alone on a line. There could be no clearer statement that the artifice in poems is finally peripheral; the poetry must, and can, spring from "the pure clear word," the meant word.

These generalities will acquire more substance if we examine particular poems. Let us look first at James Wright's famous and enigmatic "Lying in a Hammock at William Duffy's Farm in Pine Island, Minnesota."

> Over my head, I see the bronze butterfly,
> Asleep on the black trunk,
> Blowing like a leaf in green shadow.
> Down the ravine behind the empty house,
> The cowbells follow one another
> Into the distances of the afternoon.
> To my right,
> In a field of sunlight between two pines,
> The droppings of last year's horses
> Blaze up into golden stones.
> I lean back, as the evening darkens and comes on.
> A chicken hawk floats over, looking for home.
> I have wasted my life.

The relation of the "I" to this poem of almost pure sensation is self-evidently problematic: two quite impersonal occurrences, followed by a statement so deep as to seem nearly universal—all the more so, perhaps, because it is a quotation from another poem, Rimbaud's "Song of the Highest Tower" ("J'ai perdu ma vie"). The critic A. Poulin has misidentified the source as the last line of Rilke's "Archaic Torso of Apollo" ("Du musst dein Leben ändern"), but there is reason in his error: Wright's last line, like Rilke's, forces the reader to go back and relive the previous, the apparently objective, part of the poem in order to come to terms with it.[4]

One notices first the sleep of the butterfly: how entrusted, how pliable it is, "Blowing like a leaf in green shadow," possessed of the stillness of a plant or even of a metal, "bronze." It is an image of being wholly at one with one's world; and this quality persists into the following lines through the subtle harmonizing of time and space ("the distances of the afternoon"), the sense of the cowbells as a musical measure of both. ("A field of sunlight" is another, subtler blending of categories—physical object and light—which also has the effect of making the world seem closer, more intertwined, more real.) The image of the horse droppings offers a far more complicated, but still serene, sense of temporal process—one involving continuity ("last year's"), transmutation into mineral permanence ("golden stones"), but also beautiful consumption ("Blaze up"). Insofar as one can paraphrase at all, the poem sees in a process—even a decay—that is continually productive of new beauty, the kind of visionary perfection we habitually associate with permanence alone. I suspect a Freudian undercurrent, too, in the fact that such an important position in the poem is given to dung; Wright could hardly help being aware of the theories which associate our early feelings about our own feces with the development of the categories—so crucial to our sense of being a part, or not a part, of the physical world—of subject and object, beauty and ugliness, saving and losing.

It is the evening and the chicken hawk that toll Wright back to his sole self. The verb "floats," with its sense of indefinite location in time and space, itself contrasts strongly with the harmonious centrality of almost everything else in the poem; then, we are told that the hawk is "looking for home." But the hawk, presumably, will find its home easily (perhaps this is why "floats" suggests buoyancy, as well as indefiniteness); whereas the human consciousness the hawk brings to mind can know the feeling of being fully at home in the physical world, fully alive, only at such brief and special moments as the poem records. Such moments seem possible, too, only when the human world is remote; the house in the poem is empty. Thus, it is the very specialness of the moment that gives birth to the sense of a surrounding waste.

If Wright's poem, though novel in some respects, in others remains assimilable to Romantic prototypes (Rilke or Keats), Gary Snyder's "Trail Crew Camp at Bear Valley, 9000 Feet. Northern Sierra—White Bone and Threads of Snowmelt Water" is both harder and more deeply alien to Western poetic practice:

> Cut branches back for a day—
> trail a thin line through willow
>   up buckbrush meadows,
>   creekbed for twenty yards
>   winding in boulders
>   zigzags the hill
> into timber, white pine.
>
>
> gooseberry bush on the turns.
> hooves clang on the riprap
>   dust, brush, branches.
>   a stone
>   cairn at the pass—
> strippt mountains hundreds of miles.

    sundown went back
        the clean switchbacks to camp.
    bell on the gelding,
    stew in the cook tent,
    black coffee in a big tin can.

By virtue of the omitted pronoun, the poem plunges us emphatically into activity, work, rather than detached consciousness. But the succeeding lines are verbless and choppy, a delicate mimicry of the worker's extreme concentration on his task, the narrowing horizon of his senses, his almost arrested movement. The effect is so strong that, in the last line of the first stanza, a mere preposition of forward motion (coinciding with a return to the original margin) produces a kind of rushing sensation.

And yet this day of minute labor all serves to bring Snyder slowly toward a vision that is its complete opposite, as bare, unlimited, sublime as the labor is detailed, focused, concrete: "strippt mountains hundreds of miles." We are not told Snyder's emotions on encountering this sight; but if one is alert to the music of the poem, there is a quality of caught breath slowly released in the enclosing sibilants of the line. The pass marks the end of Snyder's task; he now returns in moments over the trail it has taken him all day to clear ("switchbacks" is thus a sort of pun). He returns, also, to the world of detail, but detail now irradiated—as we sense from the languorous *rallentando* of the last three lines—with exhaustion, hunger, accomplishment, the taste of the upper air.

It may have occurred to the reader that the pattern of Snyder's poem very strikingly resembles that of a religious experience. Trails are like Ways; hence Snyder's occupation suggests a process of meditation or spiritual exercise, clearing the path from temporal life to the moment of Enlightenment—the sudden dropping away of the phenomenal world in the contemplation of the infinite and eternal, All and Nothingness. The ending of the poem reflects equally age-old processes: the return to the world, the heightened awareness of reality paradoxically following on the awareness of its opposite, the insight that the Way Up is the Way Down. Yet we should be wary of saying that the events in the poem symbolize such an experience; they *contain* the experience, as a Zen koan does, even if the content is to be unlocked only by subsequent meditation. From a Zen point of view, skillful and concentrated work, which tends to fuse the categories of subject and object, being and doing, is a kind of spiritual exercise which can lead to Enlightenment; and this Enlightenment would be no less itself for arriving through a sudden vista of mountains. (Symbolism in the usual sense presupposes a hierarchical arrangement of kinds of experience, categories of consciousness; and it is this presupposition that I think Snyder's Zen sensibility would wish to exclude.)

For all their wish to transcend the ego, these poems do imply that the self can be centered, can know itself, within a moment of experience. Indeed, it is because the attunement to the moment, to the outside world, is so complete that what is at the center seems not an individual but a universal self. Such poems, though their subjects are seemingly small and cool—rhythms of day, night, and the seasons; work, pleasure, and rest—are essentially epiphanic and religious. (They are also ethical, in their suggestion that we may be more truly alive in these cool moments than in the grander ones of intellectual or emotional crisis.) There is a love of, or a fulfilling connection with, the particular that makes these poems as distant from the skeptical, baffled, or alienated poems—also hostile to the ego—which we will consider later, as they are distant, in another direction, from "confessional" poems.

Many, perhaps most, of the surest achievements of this generation so far belong to the very short, very pure genre we have been discussing. Some of the best, besides the two I have analyzed, are: James Wright's "Twilights," "To the Evening Star," and "Today I Was So Happy, So I Made This Poem"; Galway Kinnell's "La Bagarede"; Robert Bly's "The Clear Air of October"; Merwin's "Watchers"; and many, many poems by Snyder, but I will mention "Fire in the Hole," "Burning the Small Dead," "The Levels," and "For a Stone Girl at Sanchi." The question remains, however, how such a style can move beyond the moment of attunement to a fuller spectrum of psychic life, not to mention social and political life. To deal with this question and to begin to evaluate, we must turn to a perhaps overdue consideration of the individual poets and of their larger visions and structures.

II

Gary Snyder is the most remarkable personality among these poets, and the most famous, through his association with the ecology movement. In the face of the disasters likely to ensue from growing populations increasingly dependent on fossil fuel or nuclear technology, Snyder has presented himself as spokesman for a "great Subculture" which, throughout history, has periodically reinvented the small community, based on directly affectionate bonds between the members and a sense of affectionate interdependence with the environment, as an alternative to the efficient order of the State. Snyder has devoted much of his life to the study of this Subculture, as he finds it here and there in history: in American Indian culture and folklore; in the communal Christian heresies; in Tantrism and Zen Buddhism (he spent several years as a novice in a Zen monastery in Kyoto). But he also finds his Subculture in us: not only in those who are in fact commune dwellers, but in those who—as "nomadic engineers and scholars . . . scoring in rich foundation territory"—unconsciously perceive ourselves, in relation to society, as "again, hunters and gatherers."[5] Snyder would have us go farther in this direction, gathering back into the self, and into more limited communal contexts, the sense of psychic sufficiency we have learned to need to buttress with possessions, with constant social excitement, with the civilized illusion of omnipotence. In his latest complete book, *Turtle Island*, Snyder mingles a somewhat Thoreauvian poetic treatment of the psychic value of simplification (Snyder and his family live in relative isolation in the California Sierras) with direct social advocacy in prose. Whatever the practical value of his proposals for worldwide economic/ecological reform (to my unexpert eye, they seem remarkably sane and undictatorial; for that reason, it is hard to imagine how they would be implemented), Snyder also has a darker kind of consolation to offer us: his conviction that cultural continuity and a sense of human worth can survive the most cataclysmic changes in our outward modes of living.

This conviction in Snyder undoubtedly owes a great deal to his training in Buddhism, a system which suggests that the world has been destroyed and created time and again, but that the One is, in potential, completely present in all creatures at all moments. In the 1960s Snyder showed little enthusiasm for Marxist revolution, but he obliquely answered the academic liberals who turned conservative in the supposed interests of culture by saying, "The traditional cultures are in any case doomed, and rather than cling to their good aspects hopelessly it should be remembered that whatever is or ever was in any other culture can be reconstructed from the unconscious through meditation."[6] In the 1970s, when the violent change in the air seemed more economic than political, Snyder changed little; his poem "The Dead by the Side of the Road," in which he answers the useless killing of animals by machines by making ingenious use of the bodies, as if he had killed them himself, shows the same combination of creative joy and fatalism, the attachment-and-detachment of the religious man.

This double perspective on the world can be seen even in Snyder's most objective and Poundian lyrics. "Trail Crew Camp at Bear Valley" has it; but it comes clearly to the surface in a poem like the lovely "Burning the Small Dead." Here, an unsettling wideness of reference is first conveyed by the title—completed with "branches" only at the second line, and initially more likely to suggest the cremation of human or animal bodies. The hint is confirmed as the poem broadens its frame, in time and space, from the burning branches, through their history ("a hundred summers / snowmelt rock and air"), to the mountains under them, themselves volcanic, creations of fire; then to the stars of which planets are made. All the levels coalesce in the final image of "windy fire," so that the last completion of the title could easily be "Burning the small dead / stars." The poem at once dwarfs and aggrandizes all its particulars, disorienting us as the famous koans do. Finally, it reduces the universe to one infinitely metamorphic substance/process (a line of thought that belongs equally to Buddhism and to Heraclitus).

Snyder's dance above yet within experience is marked formally by the peculiar persistence of rhyme within his free verse—one of those signatures of what Eliot called the "aural imagination" that so often distinguish true poets from mere writers using lines and stanzas. In Snyder's case, what we find is a kind of syncopated rhyming: off-rhymes altered each time they recur, so that "stone" / "clams" / "time" / "doorframe" is not an unusual sequence (in "Burning the Small Dead" it is "air" / "Sierra" / "Ritter" / "Altair" / "fire"); or the odder habit of rhyming the beginnings and endings of adjacent lines. This habit says, in effect, what the encircling lines of "East Coker" and *Finnegans Wake* say; and says it, often, with all the airiness of a children's round—as in "Fire in the Hole," where, after the dynamiting (which, like the vista of mountains in "Trail Crew Camp at Bear Valley," takes stanzas to prepare for and is over in an instant), we hear:

> strolld back to see:
> hands and arms and shoulders
> free.

But along with this airiness, it is important to notice (the more so, since Snyder is often turned into the kind of invariably reassuring guru we Americans are prone to invent for ourselves) how large a part waste, separation, and grief play in his subject matter. I am thinking not only of his famous but, by his own declaration, atypical "This Tokyo," in which "freedom is a void," and all consolations from Dante to "the candy heaven of the poor" are reduced to egotism, "the comfort of the US for its own"; but of the poem about "the full warm brilliance of the human mind" in the eyes of the children of Arunachala, who "die or sicken in a year" while religious ascetics live for centuries nearby; the poem about failing to recognize the photograph of an old girlfriend, though responding to the expression, "tender, / Calm, surprised"; or

> The glimpse of a once-loved face
>   gone into a train.
> Lost in a new town, no one knows the name.

Hearing this poem ("What Do They Say"), one realizes that another dimension of Snyder's quick connections, his skewed, syncopated rhyming, is a grieving over transience. Even the round-rhyme of beginnings and endings can express the impossibility of any adequate response:

>   lone man sitting in the park
> Chanced on by a friend
>   of thirty years before,
>   what do they say.
> Play chess with bottle caps.

The sense of pointless persistences and repetitions, of wasted feelings—though often put in the mouths of accusing female personae, the anima as a destroying Kali—is a crucial aspect of Snyder's imagination: the "absolute zero" at which only the "fossil love" of his deepest monistic experience still manages to burn.

If Snyder's love poems often have such haunted elements, he is nevertheless remarkably at ease—undistorted by shame, boastfulness, or cruelty—in his poetry of sexuality. The finest, though not the most typical, of these poems is "The Bath" from *Turtle Island*. It is perhaps the one contemporary poem which adds new territories of feeling to the tradition of humanist sexual prophecy (that is, prophecy about sex as a discovery or affirmation of a greater human identity) inherited from Blake, Whitman, and Lawrence. Snyder's criticism of Christian (or, more generally, Western) thought has always been that it makes so much of the fate of the universe depend on human, and especially neurotic sexual, guilt and compensation ("low-order Tantric phenomena"). In "The Bath," Snyder goes to what Freud considered the root of the problem, individually and historically—the incest taboo and the family romance. As he observes himself, his wife, and his son reacting to each other's bodies in the sauna, Snyder seems—in the words of his Zen teacher—to "become one with the knot itself, til it dissolves away."[7] His discovery, one might say, is that to regard incestuous feelings either as a horror in themselves, or an interference with later relationships, is to fail to understand the fundamental equality of persons and events and the interpenetration of all beings. The father entering the mother sexually, and the child entering the world; the child drawing milk from the mother, and the mother drawing pleasure in "jolts of light" from the act of nursing—are all the same event, "flows that lifted with the same joys forces," a joy inherent in the reshaping of substance by which the universe exists. The continuity between the mother's love for men and her love for her sons, between their love for her and their later love for other women, is a further instance of this reshaping, not a threat to it. *This is our body*, the poet reiterates, stressing that we cannot avoid the common ownership; and the last time the refrain is repeated in the poem, "our body" has come to include "The Great Earth," itself a mother whom we must both separate ourselves from, and love. Snyder's sexual prophecy thus includes his ecology—appropriately, since Snyder elsewhere argues that the need to control wild nature can be an externalization of sexual repression. And both the psychology and the ecology rest on Snyder's Buddhism—on his sense of the simultaneous complete reality and unreality of the world of multiplicity. In the poem preceding "The Bath" in *Turtle Island*, Snyder draws a playful genealogy of Matter and the Mind by the repeated incest that Milton thought worthy only of Satan, Sin, and Death.

It is often when such playfulness and mystical insouciance are in evidence that Snyder's handling of public subject matter is most authoritative and memorable. Few readers, I think, will forget the passage in "For the West" that begins

> Ah, that's America:
> the flowery glistening oil blossom
> spreading on water—

and ends

> as it covers,
>   the colors fade.
> and the fantastic patterns
>   fade.
> I see down again through clear water.
>
>   it is the same
> ball bounce rhyme the
>   little girl was singing,
>   all those years.

An embittered involvement, on the other hand, tends to lead to surprisingly weak, unimaginative editorializing:

> Death himself,
>   (Liquid Metal Fast Breeder Reactor)
>   stands grinning, beckoning.
> Plutonium tooth-glow.

This will hardly convince those who think nuclear technology a worthwhile risk, nor does it (as Snyder's prose occasionally can) expose a pathological component in their reasoning; it boils down to simple name-calling. It is unfortunate, though understandable, that Snyder writes more often in this vein (and in an opposite, over-sweet primitivist vein) as his view of the United States grows bleaker.

All the same, the scale and coherence of Snyder's vision call up our old image of the poet as world-historical figure (Yeats, Eliot, Lowell), in a way that none of the other poets treated in this chapter quite do. But when one compares Snyder with the great, one immediately feels that his works are a smaller portion of his Work than theirs are. There is a remarkable evenness of quality, but there are far fewer self-surpassing quantum leaps in the presence of extraordinary themes. Perhaps this is, in part, intentional; Snyder has often supported the idea, popular with 1960s radicals, that the "major poet" is a myth fostered by bourgeois competitiveness, and that future poets will write, with less premeditation, for an immediate communal context. I find such a view suspect, insofar as it obscures the fact that the fullness of one's own powers is often accessible only through search and courtship, in poetry as in mysticism. But I am not sure that Snyder's ideas entirely circumscribe his achievement. Small poems can be more perfect than large ones, and his—thanks to his redirection of the Poundian inheritance—are among the most crystalline now being written. And he has, for years, been promising a long poem, called *Mountains and Rivers Without End*; when completed, it may render my mild reservations about his accomplishment quite obsolete.

III

The stripping-down to the image and the simple sentence which we encounter in Robert Bly and James Wright has both much and little in common with Snyder's austerities. For Snyder, a Poundian program of glass-like clarity suits a central calm as detached from emotion as from the categories of reason; Bly and Wright, on the other hand, aim at the recovery of a repressed feelingful self, in all its forthrightness and vulnerability. In many of their innovations, one feels a gauntlet flung down to the reader's notions of poetic decorum: the half-humorous, half-arrogant titles ("Depressed by a Book of Bad Poetry, I Walk Toward an Unused Pasture and Invite the Insects to Join Me"; "Johnson's Cabinet Watched by Ants"); Bly's peppery exclamation points; the short numbered sections which may—as in one poem by Wright—consist only of something like "I look about wildly." There can also be a deliberate courting of anti-climax, as in this section-ending from Wright's "Stages on a Journey Westward":

> It [snow] sounds like the voices of bums and gamblers,
> Rattling through the bare nineteenth-century whorehouses
> In Nevada.

This is the hostility to rendering I have spoken of. The starkly informative concluding line-fragment seems to cry out: Isn't this enough? Does one need to describe the spittoons? (And yet Wright may, with characteristic trickiness, be hedging his bets, hoping that the Spanish meaning of "Nevada," *snowy*, will drift hauntingly across our minds.)

The willful, programmatic side of the enterprise overwhelms Bly's poetry more often than Wright's, perhaps because Bly has less gift for the auditory side of poetry, perhaps because he is less helplessly emotional by temperament. Almost all his ecstatic passages give the impression of someone coercing his own feelings—witness "If I reached my hands down, near the earth, / I could take handfuls of darkness!" or "Oh, on an early morning I think I shall live forever!" Bly is at his best as a local poet of the Midwest, when—as in "The Clear Air of October"—the sense of the immanence of the absolute distills slowly out of his love and fear of the engulfing spaces and seasons, without a conscious forcing. He is also very moving in his later, quiet poems about depression, aging, the fear and the acceptance of death.[8] I shall return in the next chapter to Bly's influence on younger poets; but here it seems more fruitful to concentrate on the sometimes mysterious grounds of Wright's greater—though uneven—success in the same mode.

Wright's emotionalism, in fact, long antedates both his association with Bly and his (never unambivalent) commitment to free verse. His teacher Theodore Roethke would seem to be the source, insofar as one is needed, of his liking for soft-focused Tennysonian modes; consider the early poem "Autumnal":

> Soft, where the shadow glides,
> The yellow pears fell down.
> The long bough slowly rides
> The air of my delight.

In such a passage, one feels the eye submitting to be guided by the ear, as (in a deeply rooted human equation) thinking is guided by feeling. The last line, indeed, proclaims a solipsism of "delight," in which the feeling not only shapes but creates, engulfs the perception.

Though the immediate influence of Roethke quickly vanishes, at all stages of Wright's career one finds cadence shaping and carrying statements that would sound self-indulgent put as plain prose:

> I have gone forward with
> Some, a few lonely some.
> They have fallen to death.
> I die with them.

("Speak")

It is in Wright's imagery that emotionalism finds its own kind of precision, even of rendering—in that special body of imagery that developed (under the influence of Georg Trakl and of Latin American poets) along with the formal innovations Wright shares with Bly. To call this imagery "surrealist" is to oversimplify considerably; for it is far too consistently beautiful, or else gothic, for the fidelity to the unconscious that surrealism advocates—as is, to judge by Wright's translations, Trakl's own imagery. To see how Wright's imagery works on us—what is, in fact, rendered—let us look, from a structural point of view, at a particularly beautiful and subtle example, the opening of "Twilights":

> The big stones of the cistern behind the barn
> Are soaked in whitewash.
> My grandmother's face is a small maple leaf
> Pressed in a secret box.
> Locusts are climbing down into the dark green crevices
> Of my childhood. Latches click softly in the trees.
>   Your hair is gray.

The secret, enclosed spaces, the gateways to the underworld, become, as the stanza progresses, both physically narrower and more clearly intrapsychic: from the cistern with "big stones" to the "secret box" to the entirely imaginary door suggested by the latch-like clicking of branches in the wind. The haunting last sentence then sets the whole scene at an infinite distance, in an irretrievable past. But at the same time, there is another imagery accumulating, one of saturation ("soaked in whitewash") and of preservation through compression (the "pressed" leaf). The passage has—as in canonical surrealism—Freudian underpinnings: the reentry into childhood experience seen as a return to the womb. But it seems more important to point out that what is described is less childhood experience itself, than the way it continues to exist in the poet's mind—difficult of access, outside normal dimensionality, dense with being. That is to say, Wright's imagery, like his art generally, is often essentially gestural: it calls up not the thing itself, but a quality or value it has for the poet. That Wright's subtleties are of this order makes them hard to defend against the (sometimes fair) charge of gorgeous but schematic, and unsolid, Romanticism. And indeed, Wright seems almost to have courted such confusion. The notion that value needs to be protected from objectivity—from uninvolved perception or judgment—is implicit in many of his most persistent and characteristic images: the intricate hidden structures, "cities / Of moss," "hallways" in a diamond or a leaf; the twilights; the famous image of the evening star as a "Beautiful daylight of the body" that tells the animals "The open meadows are safe."

I have said of Snyder that his Work seems greater than his works, for all their fineness; and the same could be said of Wright. The overbalancing element, here, is the epic sense of place. Like Faulkner or Sherwood Anderson, Wright aspires to be the "sole owner and proprietor" of half-imagined places as detailed and populated as the real ones on which they are based. His landscape, at times, stretches as wide as "the sea, that once solved the whole loneliness / Of the Midwest"; but essentially it is his native southeastern Ohio, where the fatality and exhaustion of Eastern Europe repeat themselves in towns named for the supercorporations, beside the river that is at once Indian sacred place and "Tar and chemical strangled tomb." Wright's immense sympathy with those who have failed to transcend the regional Fates—a group wide enough to include Warren G. Harding as well as the murderer George Doty—adds to his claims as representative and bard (although it is sympathy, with all that implies of covert identification, and not empathy, as Robert Hass has pointed out in an excellent essay).[9] Yet Wright earns comparison with Faulkner at least insofar as he, too, makes his place seem peculiarly central to the beauty and evil of America, the tragic logic connecting excessive promise to premature old age. Wright's epic ambitions stand behind (and complicate our responses to) his seemingly bare reliance on emotion; and I do not think Wright is unconscious of that fact. His most confident private namings (unlike Lowell's, say, or Frank O'Hara's) tend to be little dramas, in which his duties to others, his duties as a witness, seemingly overpower his literary judgment:

> And Jenny, oh my Jenny
> Whom I love, rhyme be damned,
> Has broken her spare beauty
> In a whorehouse old.
> She left her new baby
> In a bus-station can,
> And sprightly danced away
> Through Jacksontown.
>
> Which is a place I know,
> One where I got picked up
> A few shrunk years ago
> By a good cop.

("Speak")

(It is, however, indicative of Wright's trickiness as a rhetorician that the announced failure—really merely a postponement—of the rhyme only draws our attention to the greater artifice of the inversion, "a whorehouse old," with its Blakean moral resonances.)

Two Citizens is at once the fullest version of Wright's regional myth, and a second watershed in his stylistic development, in which rhetoric becomes decisively more important than imagery. We can learn a good deal about the rules of this deceptively simple new style by paying close attention to the epigraph, taken from Hemingway's "The Killers":

> "Well, bright boy," Max said, looking into the mirror, "why don't you say something?"
> "What's it all about?"
> "Hey, Al," Max called, "bright boy wants to know what it's all about."
> "Why don't you tell him?" Al's voice came from the kitchen.
> "What do you think it's all about?"
> "I don't know."
> "What do you think?"

We learn, first, that we are going to hear a great deal of American lingo, of speech whose main point is not to convey information; that this speech will bear on us more insistently through an empty-seeming poetry of repetition; and, finally, that we will be made to guess at the (often nasty) incidents behind it, and so, to a degree, lose our innocence regarding them. More than ever, Wright's is a poetry of exaggeration, of expletive, of extreme and fluctuating emotional stance (characteristic endings: "And if I ever see you again, so help me in the sight of God, / I'll kill you"; "I love you so"). Part of the value such rhetoric has for Wright is cultural: it is a kind of emotional sound barrier through which American males break into tenderness, when they are taught both to admire and to need toughness. But along with the overemphasis there is always, as I have suggested, mystery. Tender as well as cruel stories are left half-told. The poet repeatedly makes explicit a sensitive, inhibiting relationship to his own act of expression ("I am almost afraid to write down / This thing"; "This poem frightens me / So secretly, so much"). Images are no longer opalescent and precise, but forced into vagueness by a multitude of contexts. Thus, the lines

> I have brought my bottle back home every day
> To the cool cave, and come forth
> Golden on the left corner
> Of a cathedral's wing

refer at once to the location of Wright's lodgings, to a painting he has seen, to drinking, and to lovemaking ("the heavy wine in the old green body"), as well as picking up a generalized wing symbolism from elsewhere in the book. The story of Jenny, the heroine of *Shall We Gather at the River*, thins to a strange parable about making love to a tree, behind which we sense older parables never explicitly mentioned—the fall of Adam, the Crucifixion and "Saint" Judas, and most particularly the story of Apollo and Daphne, of art compensating for a disastrous romantic miscalculation.

The philosophy behind these tactics becomes clear in the best single poem in the book, "Afternoon and Evening at Ohrid." Here, language seems initially master of reality: the lovers' ignorance of Serbo-Croatian stands not only between them and the landscape, but between them and each other. But later, reality—physiognomy, perception—seems capable of instantaneous transformation into language, and, moreover, into private signals:

> She wandered ahead of me, muttering to herself
> That language of grief, the mountains and water that are always
> A strange face, browned at the end of summer.
> Ahead of me on the mountain path, my browned love told me clearly:
> Come to me and love me clearly with the thinning shadow of the turtle.

At the end of the poem, there is this interchange:

> What is your name,
> I said.
> I love you,
> She said.

Names, in short, are relationships, not fixed labels; so that language and the reality it refers to come into being together, with the relation. And it is only by entering a relation—while having to guess at a name—that the reader is admitted into the world of the poem. These premises allow Wright to invent a complex style, adequate to emotional and cognitive ambiguities, without abandoning his generation's distrust of the "meddling intellect" and its dissections. The protective impulse previously expressed in the imagery passes into the language itself.

Two Citizens is, oddly enough, a kind of successor to the Jamesian "international novel," which measures America against Europe. At the beginning, in "Son of Judas," we get—instead of the old identification with the outcast—a Blakean critique of the possibilities of good and evil in a society that presents no real counterforce, political or religious, to acquisitive greed:

> Where Mark Hanna and every other plant
> Gatherer of the grain and gouging son
> Of a God whonks his doodle in the
> United States government of his hand.

(Throughout the sequence, masturbation and adult heterosexuality are used as loose, but sufficiently clear, metaphors for degrees of recognition of otherness in societal behavior.) But Wright's anger is directed at his own class, as well as at the capitalists. In Yugoslavia, he comes to the—hardly original, but seriously felt—conclusion that poverty is not necessarily morally degrading in a rooted society, where ideas of acceleration, progress, and novelty (including the idea of sex as a mere hierarchy of sensations) do not fill the cultural air. Remembering, by contrast, a sex crime he witnessed in his youth (a poetical screen-memory, one suspects, for whatever is most dreadful in the Jenny story), he utters the ultimate American sacrilege: "I Wish I May Never Hear of the United States Again." His change of heart comes, ironically enough, through a love affair with an American woman that seems to begin in Yugoslavia. As he learns to prefer a love that has room for separateness to the exploitative mode (Mark Hanna) and even the projective or emanative one (his Daphne, the "Jenny sycamore"), he realizes that rootedness is precisely this inner experience of a commitment prior to judgment—and is perhaps more valuable where it exists without cultural reinforcement. A host of illustrative memories now come back from his childhood—of the men who "Wanted to be in love and give good love / To beautiful women, who weren't pretty"; of his teachers and friends; and even, finally, of himself, overcoming his adolescent disgusts to act as midwife to a cow. And it is finally his own helpless, rooted connection to America that brings him home.

The experimental style of *Two Citizens*—which, despite his later misgivings about it, remains the basis of Wright's most interesting work up until his death—confirms his position as a great innovator, the only one in his generation who (like Eliot or Lowell) changed the possibilities of American poetry more than once. His ultimate stature as a poet is a harder question. That someone of his temperament and projects should often have been a sentimentalist, is almost a tautology. One can hardly expect that posterity will be as indulgent as some of Wright's contemporaries have been to passages like

> I wish to God I had made this world, this scurvy
> And disastrous place. I
> Didn't, I can't bear it
> Either
>
> ("To the Muse")

—or to the outrageously easy compassion that allows him to equate the American vandals who have "scarred" their names on the stone of Chartres with the builders of Chartres—

> In our own way we hewed the town mayor
> Among the several damned
>
> ("Names Scarred at the Entrance to Chartres")

—or to the equally easy scorn of

> The soul of a cop's eyes
> Is an eternity of Sunday daybreak in the suburbs
> Of Juarez, Mexico.
>
> ("The Minneapolis Poem")

Wright's triumphs as a social or moral poet usually occur when ambivalence—or the acting out, or through, of ambivalent feelings—takes the place of what would be irony or balance in a more classical writer. Sometimes this happens in the imagery. In the first Harding poem, for instance, the equivocal picture of small-town America ("the chiropractors' signs looming among dead mulberry trees"), and the refiguring of the central tree image, from the beautiful honey locusts to the nightmarish "The cancerous ghosts of old con men / Shed their leaves," act out Wright's inability to disentangle Harding's populist attractions from his potential corruption. Sometimes, on the other hand, the poet becomes a dramatic character, involved, buffeted, confused, as in "Ars Poetica: Some Recent Criticism," which begins, "I loved my country, / When I was a little boy," and ends—having found no person or memory to settle on with unmixed love—in the violence of bafflement: "Ah, you bastards, / How I hate you." Such daring strategies are Wright's way of correcting his weaknesses entirely on his own terms; of saying things neither dishonest nor objective. They show—as does Wright's use of inarticulacy, and the gestural quality of his work generally—a deep affinity with the method I have called "reflexive" in the personal poets. These aspects of Wright, which have tempted me, twice, to use the word "trickiness" in reference to him, are less often noticed than his innovative simplicities. But I suspect they will be talked about a great deal more before we begin clearly to separate his good, and even great, work from what was praised as "sincere" merely for voicing common nostalgias.

IV

Two other poets must be considered more briefly. If James Wright is the most lyrical of the poets treated here, Galway Kinnell is the most energetic. He attained early fame with his very ambitious poem "The Avenue Bearing the Initial of Christ into the New World," which is still arguably as good as anything he has written. It can remind one of Crane and early Lowell in its sonority, but more of *The Waste Land* in its ability to include a seething cauldron of urban sensations, of randomness and ugliness, yet hold its own poetic shape. What it lacks, however, is a controlling or interpretive vision, beyond mere awe at the weight of humanity, the "instants of transcendence" and the "oceans of loathing and fear." At the rare points where it tries to conceal this lack through rhetoric, the poem becomes abruptly stagey.

Both the strengths and the weaknesses here are prophetic for Kinnell's later work. He continues to have the most over-vaulting and Marlovian style of his contemporaries, but it is a double-edged advantage, since his share of the generational directness, and his personal fondness for metaphysical clichés, make any hamming more obvious, and less likely to be mitigated by surrounding beauties, than it would be in a poet like Crane. On the other hand, his later poems succeed in uncovering the real feeling behind the Avenue C poem and making it, itself, the subject. It is the sense of a violent, impersonal, unseemly energy behind life, stunning the ego and bringing both "transcendence"—because it makes a continuum of the personal self and the cosmos—and "loathing and fear," because it is inseparable from the threat of change and death, "the pre-trembling of a house that falls." In poem after poem, Kinnell re-suffers one identical ordeal, accepting death in order to be able to accept life, and concomitantly—like his Thoreau in "The Last River"—accepting cruel appetites in order to accept his full animal being and to avoid a crueller sadomasochistic simulacrum of spirituality. At times, the acceptance seems as negative as that, at least; but at other times it has its own special serenity, as at the end of "La Bagarede," where "the seventh / of the Sisters, she who hid herself / for shame / at having loved one who dies, is shining."

Kinnell's form has not altered substantially since his second book, just as his central experience has not. It is a sequence of generally very short, always numbered free verse units; the isolations some-what take the place of rhetoric in conferring a brooding intensity on details; and the poet is free to move quickly from himself to nature to vignettes of other lives, while keeping our primary attention on the pattern that moves us into terror and out again into some form of resolution. Kinnell's poetry has a very narrow range of purely per-sonal experiences. He can really handle only those that touch directly on his cosmic vision—passionate love, being with the dying and the newly born, the vulnerability of political imprisonment in the South—but of these he writes extraordinarily well (offhand, at least, I can think of no poetry about the first year of life better than that in *The Book of Nightmares*). But one looks in vain, in Kinnell's po-etry, for the personal roots of his own vision and his repeated self-trial; though I am struck by the recurring theme of self-hatred, the special self-hatred of the large man presumed to be brutal by others, to be imprecise and blundering by himself—as it appears, for instance, in his discussion of his size at birth ("It was eight days before the doctor / Would scare my mother with me"). But I have dwelt too much on limitations, not enough on what makes the poetry convincing, remarkable—those frequent moments of stunned sensation in which human beings turn into force and object, and nature into embodied metaphysics, before our eyes; in which a tear is

one of those bottom-heavy, glittering, saccadic
bits
of salt water that splash down
the haunted ravines of a human face

and the dawn happens so: "The song of the whippoorwill
stops / And the dimension of depth seizes everything."

W. S. Merwin's very presence in this chapter is testimony to the pervasiveness of the crisis of values we have been discussing. For there is nothing naturally concrete, or earthly, about Merwin's sensibility; it is rather ethereal, and tends—like Northrop Frye's, or Robert Graves's—to find its music in the apprehension of orderly ritual patterns behind temporal events. The sense that the archetype, the purely repetitive element, is more real than the individuating circumstances is as clear in a poem on "Spring" from *The Moving Target*—

On the water the first wind
Breaks it all up into arrows

The dead bowmen buried these many years

Are setting out again

And I
I take down from the door
My story with the holes
For the arms the face and the vitals

—as in the early "Dictum: For a Masque of Deluge": "A falling frond may seem all trees. If so / We know the tone of falling." It is therefore the more remarkable how Merwin's poetry has developed toward the same tactics as his contemporaries' (the simple, quasi-narrative sentence, the isolated word, the numb "I"); toward the same loyalties, political and symbolic; and above all, toward the same stress on the inadequacy of language:

My blind neighbor has required of me
A description of darkness
And I begin I begin but

Indeed, Merwin in his later poetry rejects language more radically than his contemporaries do, reducing it to the mere gesture of beginning, or an inarticulate cry. And concurrently what is gestured at seems less and less a distinct though pre-verbal creaturely state and more and more an uncreated, mystical or nihilistic, Void. One wonders how far this line of development in Merwin can be attributed to his initial etherealness; how far, on the contrary, to a fear that there is more mere literariness to be purged in his own beginnings than in his contemporaries'. In some of his best poems we find a savage sense of how one can be distorted by one's ulterior motives, by the wish for others' approval, which we have not found elsewhere, for all the distrust of civilization. Thus, the speaker of "Lemuel's Blessing" calls on his totem, the wolf, to deliver him from his own dog-like nature:

> From the ruth of approval, with its nets, kennels, and taxidermists;
> It would use my guts for its own rackets and instruments, to play its own games and music;
> Teach me to recognize its platforms, which are constructed like scaffolds;
>
> From the ruth of known paths, which would use my feet, tail, and ears as curios,
> My head as a nest for tame ants,
> My fate as a warning.

At the end of the poem, the poet seems to value only the undifferentiated aspiration, or "cry," at the heart of his work, and is almost eager to jettison what is more tangible:

> Let my ignorance and my failings
> Remain far behind me like tracks made in a wet season,
> At the end of which I have vanished,
> So that those who track me for their own twisted ends
> May be rewarded only with ignorance and failings.
> But let me leave my cry stretched out behind me like a road
> On which I have followed you.

Perhaps—as with Sylvia Plath, who was a friend of Merwin's—nihilism is the last refuge of a self too afraid of its own readiness to comply with, and to use, the expectations of others, if it engages itself with the outside.

But one would not be doing justice to Merwin if one ignored a political dimension more extreme, in his work, than in that of any of his contemporaries. Many poems in *The Moving Target* and *The Lice* —notably the stunning litany "For Now"—treat a coming nuclear war not as a possibility but as a fact. In the light of this, one can hardly blame Merwin for conceiving his relation to visible things as continuously elegiac; or for regarding the enterprises of cultural sublimation and self-justification—including story telling and so, implicitly, poetry—with a bitterness comparable to that in the more extreme pronouncements of the New Left (see, for instance, "The Students of Justice" or "Caesar"). The grounds of Merwin's stance are therefore complex, and his great talent (especially for the music of poetry) is beyond question. Nevertheless, his gnostic tendency to oppose the pure self to the entire world of specifics has introduced a darker theme into the generational project, one whose influence we will consider at length farther on.

It is hard to evaluate these poets, as a group, in comparison to their predecessors. More distance may be needed before we can intelligently measure the cost of renouncing so many of the enhancements, the structures, the tacts of earlier poetry, against the qualities of consciousness—the poets might say, of being—rendered newly, or at least more sharply, articulate through their daring. It does seem to me, however, that all of these poets have gone through an unusually marked crisis of confidence in mid-career, in which their poetic self-definition—being so highly ethical to begin with—tempted them to exchange a problematic aesthetic merit for an imperishable moral one, and to allow themselves self-repetition with the same excuse a first-grade teacher has: the lesson is not yet adequately learned. (Perhaps the political climate of the late 1960s played a role, with its promise of an immensely enlarged, but less literary, audience sympathetic to the poets' collective vision.) In any case, the books published around 1970, when the poets were in their early forties (Wright's *Collected Poems*, Bly's *The Light Around the Body*, Snyder's *Regarding Wave*, Kinnell's *The Book of Nightmares*, Merwin's *The Carrier of Ladders*) become more ambitious ideologically, but at the same time more given to abstract self-explanation and to formula. Few are free of the kind of moral pomposity, the self-importance about the act of writing, regardless of the aesthetic value of the result, evident in Wright's

> If you do not care one way or another about
> The preceding lines,
> Please do not go on listening
> On any account of mine.
> Please leave the poem.
> Thank you.

or in Kinnell's bombastic peroration:

> The foregoing scribed down
> in March, of the year Seventy,
> on my sixteen-thousandth night of war and madness,
> in the Hotel of Lost Light, under the freeway. . . .

The most cogent and successful of the ideological or prophetic books produced in this period seems to me to be Snyder's *Turtle Island*—it, too, weakened by preachiness, but given weight by the quality of such central poems as "The Bath" and "The Hudsonian Curlew." Later in the 1970s the didactic impulse seems to have receded, though at some cost to the level of ambition—witness the return to fine but small-scale nature epiphanies in Merwin's *The Compass Flower* and in some, though not all, of Bly's recent work. James Wright alone managed, before his premature death in 1980, to reinvent the very premises of his style, in order to encompass a more capacious and public subject matter in a more dramatic and, in some sense, objectified way.

   Individual declines and recoveries aside, there is something of the tightrope act about this generation's work, even at its best. On the far side lies the real choice of silence, or of some purely physical or gestural art form. On the near side lies a kind of routine rhetorical religiosity—visible, already, in the slacker work from the early 1970s—in which the pre-verbal state is asserted, rather than conjured up, and the anti-verbal doctrine serves mainly to relax critical standards. The danger that asceticism regarding language may modulate into sheer lassitude will be considered in the following chapter. Perhaps a poetry at once so exploratory and so denuded could be written only on the very edge, or hinge, of such a crisis of cultural self-confidence as we have been going through. It requires a very special combination of love and hatred to succeed in making language do exactly what, by one's own definitions, it cannot.

5

"SURREALISM"
AND THE ABSENT SELF

Over the last ten years, one has more of a sense of a single period style dominating the work of emerging poets than at any time since the 1950s. Or perhaps it is just that this period style, like the post–New Critical style of thirty years ago, seems a peculiarly disturbing one, in the range of intellectual and emotional experiences it excludes. I have had almost innumerable occasions, as a reviewer, to offer examples of what I mean by this period style; let me preserve, here, two counterbalancing triads, one from the end of the decade in question, one from near the beginning. In 1982 I reviewed the winning volumes for 1981 from three of the major contests, and had the eerie feeling, at times, that they could all have been written by the same person. Here is "Little Memoir," from Jonathan Aaron's *Second Sight*, Anthony Hecht's selection for the National Poetry Series:

> I went to parties
> to persuade myself it was useless
> preparing for emergencies,

but people kept talking about
the season's emptiness,
the weather's delay. So
I returned to my apartment,
sold everything, and listened.

This comes from "Border Town Evening," by the Yale Younger Poet, David Wojahn:

Facing the leather-goods window,
he's come to himself in the glass. . . .
It's the moment when he wants
to touch the face of the man there,
who so resembles him in this light.
But he turns away toward home.

Here, finally, is a passage from the title poem of Denis Johnson's *The Incognito Lounge*, Mark Strand's choice for the National Poetry Series:

Every bus ride is like this one,
in the back the same two uniformed boy scouts
de-pantsing a little girl, up front
the woman whose mission is to tell the driver
over and over to shut up.
Maybe you permit yourself to find
it beautiful on this bus as it wafts
like a dirigible toward suburbia
over a continent of saloons.

Before discussing these examples, I would like to quote another three, from 1974, both to establish the duration of the phenomenon and to suggest something about its literary line of descent. These were culled, almost at random, from a single issue of *The American Poetry Review*. The first is by Lucien Stryk:

Beyond the sycamore
dark air moves
westward—
smoke, cloud, something
wanting a name. . . .

This is by Richard Schramm—

> how can I tell you
> of the lost differences
> drawing away in tepid light dawn
> until dusk. . . .

And this comes from a poem by Gary Thompson ironically entitled "I Am Changing My Life at 5:30 in the Morning":

> and my old face
> is still pressed against the glass
> staring out
> from two unexplored caves where the eyes
> should have been.

It isn't so much technique that makes these six poets so similar (though it is noteworthy that most of them use heavily enjambed short lines, and that only Denis Johnson finds anything approaching blank verse compatible with his attitude toward his subject matter) as it is a quality of voice and vision. There is the same low-key anomie and discouragement—though never passionate despair—in all these writers. If they write about what Binswanger called the *Umwelt*, nature, they write of nameless "differences," cloudy "tepid" things that reshape themselves without sharp outline or contrast, and that cannot be described. If they write about the *Mitwelt*, society, its most deadened, commercial, ritualized aspects are made emblematic almost of life itself, or else (as in Jonathan Aaron's poem) become Kafkaesque intimations of the uncanny. If they write about the *Eigenwelt*, the self, it is the self of the mirror, whose "resemblance" is so tantalizingly there yet unrevealing, whose eyes are hollow containers or else "unexplored caves." On whatever level, it is taken for granted that the successive experiences of life will be blurred, interchangeable ("Every bus ride is like this one"). Any investment of value or strong feeling comes to seem, as in Denis Johnson's poem, a quixotic indulgence. If, as Christopher Lasch has argued, the dominant emotional malaise of our time is a narcissism whose hallmark is not that it finds the self exciting, but that it never finds anything beyond the self exciting enough, then surely this is the poetry of that narcissism.[1] Its protagonists, one feels, are out of touch with themselves in proportion as they feel their world does not generate, or offers no purchase to, the big emotions—whether of love or of resistance, rage—that make us sure of who we are. Here we come to the nadir of the contemporary poetry of the self, in a poetry that finds the personal self sterile, perhaps even not there, yet can posit no escape from it either by plunging into a fertile collective unconscious or by taking an interest in the outside world.

I

It is an ironic fact that this anti-epiphanic period style has been produced and fostered largely by enthusiastic younger admirers of the middle generation, the so-called "new surrealists." (My second set of quotations will give a good idea of the "new surrealist" style at its lowest common denominator; its more famous exponents include Mark Strand, Charles Simic, James Tate, Larry Levis, Richard Shelton, William Matthews, and Gregory Orr.) The irony lies, first, in the contrast between the anti-epiphanic mood and "surrealism" itself—the original surrealism of André Breton, who believed that his program could lead to "solving all the principal problems of life," because its free-associative method, like that of psychoanalysis, would release dangerous and energizing repressed material from the unconscious.[2] But there is also a contrast with the work of the middle generation, which—though its imagery is too codified, as I remarked with respect to Wright, to be "surrealist" in Breton's sense—still aims at epiphanies of energizing contact with nature or with the preverbal portions of the self. So it is puzzling how so different a vision generated itself, in so short a time, among writers profoundly influenced by the middle generation, as well as by the ideals of the original surrealists.

The answer, I would suggest, may be found in the rigidification of three tendencies of thought in the middle generation—concerning philosophy, politics, and selfhood—whose extremeness was already, perhaps, an invitation to a poetry of allegory rather than of experience. In particular—and in marked contrast to Breton's basic confidence in language, his delight in the "extraordinary verve" he found in automatic writing—the middle generation's doubt of the capacity of language to get past the ego to the inner self has grown almost into a fear of the pollution of the inner self, by the ego, through language. Our surrealists are always on the brink of believing that silence is superior to any expression, and their poems tend to trail off—rather than end—in service to that principle. One cannot read a page of Merwin without encountering the praise of "silence" ("the owner of the smile") and the sense of the impossibility of discursive revelation ("This letter that vanishes / If the hand opens"). Charles Simic makes "my voice" a figure of insane conservative authority, "the mad captain / Thrown in chains by his suffering crew." Mark Strand can only reassure his listeners "that the lies I tell them are different / from the lies I tell myself," or, still more minimally,

> that breath is a mirror clouded by words,
> that breath is all that survives the cry for help
> as it enters the stranger's ear
> and stays long after the word is gone
>
> ("Breath")

This anti-verbal aspect of contemporary surrealism has been discussed at length and brilliantly in Robert Pinsky's *The Situation of Poetry*. Pinsky is inclined to treat it as a logical extreme of a "nominalism" prevalent in our poetry at least since Williams— "nominalism" being the medieval term for the philosophy which holds that individual particulars alone are real, and that general categories, abstract nouns, are no more than convenient fictions.[3] Pinsky's argument is a very elaborate and sophisticated one, and cannot be summarized adequately here. I would disagree with it only insofar as I would distinguish sharply between an epiphanic "nominalist" like Snyder—for whom the specific object and the specific moment remain adequate vehicles for the deepest spiritual meaning, even if words do not—and anti-epiphanic poets like Merwin and Strand, for whom all vehicles of meaning quickly become as suspect as the linguistic ones. Their implicit philosophy, I would say, is the Way of Negation, gnosticism, or Manichaeanism—whatever one wishes to call that doctrine according to which both conceptual thought and the world of the senses are a treacherous illusion, separating the spirit from itself and from God. A poem like Merwin's rather eloquent "Habits" essentially makes all conscious life—even dreaming—the devil's property:

> Even in the middle of the night
> they go on handing me around
> but it's dark and they drop more of me
> and for longer

then they hang onto my memory
thinking it's theirs

even when I'm asleep they take
one or two of my eyes for their sockets
and they look around believing
that the place is home

(How strange a thing intellectual fashion is, that a generation that still finds Eliot too fastidious and incorporeal will swallow this whole!)

The spiritual value of such a stance is obviously beyond the scope of this discussion. But surely there is a psychological and an artistic danger in its staticness. If all concrete realization is a betrayal of spirit to habit, there is little point in following any new insight, intuition, or association through what can only be the suicide of its valuable elements; and the self loses the possibility of being changed by experience, even the most inward experience. Only a repeated gesture of quest, a repeated purgation of false meaning, is possible. At its best, this mode—far more than the opposite mode of incarnation or epiphany—prompts Yeats's protest: "What, be a singer born and lack a theme?" At its worst, it can cover any number of defensive reasons for wishing to leave one's potentialities indefinite.

Of course, not all of the younger surrealists share the ascetic inclinations of Merwin and Strand. For many of them, the direction of transcendence is downward, into the body, the lives of plants and animals, the earth. The masters are Bly and Wright; and the numinous has at least reliable images, if not reliable words. Still, since poetry is a verbal art, the problem of articulacy remains. And Bly, at least, is not as far from Merwin as might first appear. He talks a good deal about Blakean energy, but he manifests it mainly as frenetic anger; his spiritual voice is heavy, speaking of drowning and burial in stanzas that are quickly over. But Richard Howard has put this a great deal better, observing that there is a "characteristic Bly contract, a stipulation that in order to escape a living death, *i.e.*, a life which is no more than life in a dying body, the self must renounce its very principle of individuation, must invite death into the body not as a mere nothing at the end but as a positive force throughout";[4] and that, in consequence of this contract, "There is in the very *façon* of all these poems, in their repetitions and slacknesses, in their organic fatigue that would send them into the ground for repose . . .

there is here a numbness or torpor, an inertia so new to art, which by
its traditional nature is the celebration of energy, of mastery, that
Robert Bly himself is not always certain of its accommodation in his
utterance."[5] As D. H. Lawrence advised, Bly's followers have listened not to the teller but to the tale. Nor, alas, have they failed to
inherit the uncertainty about "accommodation in . . . utterance."

For, whatever force it may accrue when pursued out of personal
need, the philosophy of inarticulacy is surely unpromising as a literary convention. In the epigoni, the writing about stagnation sometimes remains sharp, because the precursors have in fact defined "an
inertia new to art." But the writing about the numinous tends to be
lazy, stale, and falsely grandiose, because the precursors have established that active imagination here isn't worth the trouble. To choose
one example among many, Robert Mezey's "New Year's Eve in Solitude" begins with some vividness:

> Night comes to the man who can pray
> only on paper
> He disappears into paper
> with his old mouth shaped to say no
> and his voice is so tiny

But when Mezey comes to what is really to be desired, all he can
offer is a "nothing" in which a "bright child . . . shines," and this
conjuration:

> cover my eyes and I will see them
> those companions clothed from head to foot in tiny fires
> that I said goodbye to when I first opened my eyes
> Give me my robes of earth
> and my black milk

Only one of these images required any seeing with the mind's eye;
the rest come untransformed out of a vast vague modern storehouse
of archetypal rhetorics, the Christian, the Freudian, the Lawren-
cean/chthonic. (Mezey, of course, is not alone in this fault; even
Charles Simic will end a poem with such empty verbiage as "Its ritual and secret life / Where I wish to be anointed.") The weakness
seems to me a logical consequence of the philosophy. We cannot
pretend to know what the gods look like, and at the same time repre-

sent ourselves as entirely helpless in the face of stubborn flesh and useless mind. If there is no slightest thread, no umbilicus, we can follow back from our present situation toward the archetypes, the archetypes become mere allegory.

Side by side with such banal visions, oddly, one often finds a proliferation of far-fetched ones, all the more like "conceits" because they are usually framed as similes or personifications. Many readers will know at once what I mean, but let me offer—again, rather randomly—two examples, from Herbert Scott's *Disguises*: "Snow covers the earth like a uniform, / tracks crossing like berserk buttonholes" and "branches of trees snap / at one another, and do not apologize." The monotonous overtness of the tropes preferred can be ascribed, in part, to the middle generation's reaction against New Critical subtleties, of which buried or implicit metaphor is one of the chief. And yet when this apparent candor of form contrasts so strangely with the artificiality of the content, the effect—whether intended or not—is a kind of parody of imagination itself. The similes seem to insist that symbol making is a conscious, and a self-conscious, process, while the mere conceitedness of the comparisons denies it any exploratory value—and thus, willy-nilly, we are back to the anti-projective epistemology of Merwin and Strand.

If philosophy imposes limits on the power of language in the new surrealists, so too does a kind of politics—a continuation, in less fruitful terms, of the populism and primitivism, the anti–high-culture stance, of the middle generation. The flattened "I," in the earlier poets a gesture toward pure creatureliness, has become more social in its meanings. Robert Pinsky has summed it up beautifully by alluding to "the 'cool' of high school in the 'fifties" and "one-of-the-guys surrealism" (a tag phrase which suggests one reason why this is not surrealism: a poet constantly preoccupied with not losing his cool, and so losing face in front of "the guys," could not carry out Breton's program of psychic risk, of courting the unconscious).[6] Pinsky goes on to show how the new surrealists use jokes, vulgarity, and ultracontemporary references to leaven the Romanticism of their gnostic transcendence. His best example is from William Matthews: "Sleep is my radio and all / its news is true." I would offer Larry Levis ("I hear the wind pick up bad breath / through American storm fences and old iron") or else Charles Simic: "I piss in the sink / with a feeling of / eternity." This comes from a dreadful poem called "The Garden of Earthly Delights"—the delights consisting in the banal if not disagreeable behavior of the poet's friends at a party:

> Gary owes $800 to the
> Internal Revenue. Roger says
> poetry is the manufacture of lightning-rods.
> José wants to punch his wife
> in the mouth.

I dare say such a poem of self-congratulation has been written for every hip circle in the country aware of anti-art, but it is beyond me why a poet of Simic's talents should bother to write it, even if he does dedicate his second book rather widely: "To all my friends."[7]

Many diverse phenomena testify to the same wish to submerge individual in group identity, to the point of near-anonymity. There is the ever-increasing number of poets who publish under their nicknames—a trivial point, perhaps, but a nickname is often the gift of a peer group, whereas one's full name is one's own from birth. There is the vogue of literary imitations of pre-literate forms: riddles, fairy tales, litanies, Asian figures, translations from the Quechua. There is the vogue of teaching schoolchildren to write poetry, and the astonishing fact that otherwise lively poetry journals devote many pages to the results. To be fair, some of these enterprises can be rewarding and vivifying; but often they are destructively superficial. William Stafford's account in *The American Poetry Review* of the composition of his "People of the South Wind" is a woeful example of how sheer mental doodling, guided by *idées reçues,* can be equated with primitive thought, simply because both are different from civilized intellectual planning.[8]

One effect of this anti-intellectualism is a relative indifference to the whole technical aspect of poetry. Aside from the leavening jokes, visual imagery—privileged as the "surreal" element in poems—is just about the only element on which any imaginative ingenuity is expended. Formal meter is rare, but so is any organic relation between form and specific content, of the type recommended by Williams and his followers. Rather, the line breaking proceeds according to quite rigid conventions: either it follows the grammatical divisions of the sentence, or else one encounters a column of enjambed lines so even that they could have been measured with a ruler. One has the feeling that what the middle generation undertook as a rather special challenge—the avoidance of those aspects of technique that the New Critics had been particularly good at analyzing—has turned into a tradition of negligence.

I think there may be a relation between the folksy anti-intellectualism and anti-individualism of this poetic stance and politics in a larger sense. Paul Breslin has argued, in a fascinating essay, that the new surrealism is the product at once of the ideals of the 1960s—primitivism, a distrust of cultural rationalizations and superstructures—and of the profound political discouragement of the 1970s, the despair of any active manifestation of these ideals.[9] This discouragement, Breslin says, led to an excessive turning toward a Jungian, ahistorical inner self; I would say it may have led to an attenuated sense of having a self at all. The New Left, unlike the new surrealism, was individualistic, at least insofar as it called the individual to a project of judging and transcending his entire cultural conditioning. And as Breslin observes, "in the heyday of the New Left this [confessional poetry] was the poetry that seemed representative. It was around the time when the New Left began to collapse that confessional poetry went out of fashion and the new poetry came in."[10] (And, in fact, the poetry that remained militantly political through the 1970s—mostly Black or feminist poetry—is, whether for good or bad, much closer in style to confessional poetry than to the new surrealism.)

It is at times possible to detect a theme of political impotence—the loss of the public capacities of the self—involved in the theme of the attenuation of the self per se. Richard Shelton, a poet who can praise silence and absence with the best of them when writing about the inner life, writes in a more moving but almost masochistic strain about political powerlessness—as in his poem to the saguaros about to be cut down for "The New Road":

> I have stroked them until my hands
> are bloody, but what comfort
> can I offer? They are doomed
> and I am tired of being human. . . .

Even Pinsky's remark about "the 'cool' of high school in the 'fifties'" echoes a widespread sense that the general culture was in some way harking back to that emotionally, as well as politically, less venturesome decade. A poem like Greg Kuzma's "Summer" suggests how neatly many of the characteristic feelings of the silent surrealist—the "dead wind" of anomie, the paranoia and unfocused yearning, the distrust of his own tools—could fit inside the feelings of the "silent majority":

> I am one of the citizens
> of this city I have my

small patch of grass my
sidewalk to protect my
mailbox stuck like an ear
to the front porch
my back yard where I lay
down my pointless tools
to run to the mailbox
to see what it has found
out and my new pale
refrigerator inside which
the igloo of beer cans stands
firm in a dead wind.

One cannot be quite sure whether Kuzma is mocking "the citizens," mocking himself, or exercising a genuine but rather terrible populist humility; and this ambiguity is characteristic of the poetry of the 1970s.[11] It is a relief, then, to find a clearer tone of political anger in certain books written in the period style, but slightly later, such as Denis Johnson's *The Incognito Lounge*, quoted at the beginning of the chapter. Johnson's self-hatred—which comes through much more clearly than the same emotion in Shelton or Kuzma—is intimately connected to his hatred for the prefabricated and paranoiac qualities in our communal experience. The face that, so characteristically, tries to study itself in a shop window finds itself "mired in alarm tape"; while elsewhere—in the valueless proliferation of images that helps make valuable identity so difficult—there are "eleven television / sets in a storefront broadcasting a murderer's face." There is something here of the grim and trenchant realism of 1960s poems— Lowell's image of "Hiroshima boiling / over a Mosler Safe, the 'Rock of Ages' / that survived the blast." And one feels Johnson recovering the sense of having a self, even if a loathsome one, as he finds he has strong responses, even of loathing, to his immediate world.

This brings us to a third limitation in the new surrealist poetry. The exclusion of the specific flavor of the poet's personality—or of any human being's, for that matter—from the poem is often carried farther than in any poet of the middle generation except Merwin. One senses a kind of territorial war with the personal or confessional poets. Greg Kuzma has even written a poem called "Advice on Reading the Confessional Poet," in which confessional disclosure is reduced to a perverse enjoyment of self-degradation. To the notion here that it is healthier and really more honest to keep one's secrets secret, other poets have added the notion that it is more artistic—thus, ironically, coming full circle to that very doctrine of Impersonality, of the necessary distance between poet and poem, for which the New Critics are still reproached. Mark Strand contends in an interview that the personal poets have "lost . . . in the fervor of this inner debate, the idea of poetry." He goes on:

> *Strand:* . . . If you're going to write about yourself and you sit down and begin a poem, you would be some kind of funky journalist if you said, "I am Mark Strand, and I'm five foot two and eyes are blue."
>
> *Interviewer:* But poets have done that, several recent ones have, you know, tried to speak to themselves directly in the poem, with the name and address, as it were, and so forth.
>
> *Strand:* Well, that . . . you know, that's boring.
>
> *Interviewer:* Yes, it is. I think it is.
>
> *Strand:* . . . I don't consider myself confessional, only because the "self" is an imagined "self" . . . I mean most confessional poetry is very specific; there is no attempt to mythify the self. And I think that, perhaps, that's what I'm doing: creating a mythology of self.[12]

But I think the personal poets are right to be suspicious of such a compartmentalization of the "boring" specific self and the interesting imagined one. The psychological danger is that the desire to "mythify" is really a defensive desire to dignify. The literary danger is that once the mystery, the exploratory stimulus, of the particular is removed, what remains will not be myth but, once again, allegory. Strand's " 'The Dreadful Has Already Happened' " is a case in point. Strand says in the interview that the poem "comes out of reading R. D. Laing's *The Politics of Experience*. It's about how we quickly learn how to participate in our own demise; how we pick up cues from our parents, and the world in general, that ultimately stifle us and destroy our imaginations and our individuality."[13] My difficulty with the poem is precisely that it is such a word-for-word translation of Laing:

The sky darkens. There is thunder.
"Break his legs," says one of my aunts,
"Now give him a kiss." I do what I'm told.
The trees bend in the bleak tropical wind.

> The baby did not scream, but I remember that sigh
> when I reached inside for his tiny lungs and shook them
> out in the air for the flies. The relatives cheered.
> It was about that time I gave up.

Nothing in the poem individuates these relatives; no detail convinces one (if one is disposed to doubt) that such scenes of torture are an adequate metaphor for their characters and motives. The one genuinely mysterious and dream-like element, the tropical setting, is too mysterious; Strand could have used the personal poets' richer diction, and their willingness to adumbrate the private history of an image. At the end the poem improves; the idea—that the maimed self becomes a kind of ideal beloved, glimmering and intruding between one and the world—is more Strand's and less Laing's, and the imagery seems more integral:

> Now, when I answer the phone, his lips
> are in the receiver; when I sleep, his hair is gathered
> around a familiar face on the pillow; wherever I search
> I find his feet. He is what is left of my life.

Still, that last sentence is easy and shrill; Strand's abstraction lets him in for a degree of self-pity which Lowell and Plath, at least, among the personal poets, would have known how to avoid.

This is not to imply that only confessional details can authenticate the personal feeling in a poem. But there is too much else in this poem that smoothes away individuality and facilitates an untested allegorical vision of life: the banality of the diction; its failure to characterize a speaker; the textbook source of the plot; and the very underlying premise, that one has long since been prevented by malevolent others from having unconfused or authentic reactions. And indeed, the three limitations I have discussed in the new surrealism have this common theme: a withholding of interest from the emergent or adult personality—the self that sees those visions it can see, takes definite, even if unhopeful, political stands, weights its words differently from even the most intimate group, and traces much of its pain to a particular life history. The results of this withdrawal remind me of a paradigm from the earlier Laing: that of the inevitable thinning out of the self which denies full reality to the active and visible portion of itself.

Such an anti-individualist stance is indeed recommended—or at least held to be characteristic of contemporary poetry generally—in one of the most influential books of criticism from the beginning of the decade in question, Richard Howard's *Alone with America.* Howard finds a central metaphor for contemporary poetry in the story of King Midas, who, horrified by the consequences of the golden touch, bathed in the river Pactolus to rid himself of it. Contemporary poets, Howard feels, are giving up the traditional goals of uniqueness of voice and artistic immortality—the "craving that whatever passes through one's hands shall be immutable, immutably one's own"—with a revulsion comparable to that of Midas, a "longing to *lose* the gift of order, despoiling the self of all that had been, merely, *propriety*": "From Ammons to Wright, the course of the river Pactolus may be traced here, and in its gold sand, moreover, we shall see what has been given over, gainsaid in order to gain a universe not yet *manhandled.*"[14]

True, Howard admits that the "sand" remains "gold"; and his words can be taken merely as an overstatement of something that has often been said about, for instance, the influx of disorderly personal content in confessional poetry. But the vehement anti-humanism of his closing pun reminds me of the more dramatic avant-gardism in painting, music, and fiction, which also repudiates the expression of the individual personality—or, in the case of fiction, an interest in character—and then calls on chance, arbitrary rules, various modalities of an all-too-logical "conceptual" formalism, to avoid "manhandling" the universe, essentially, by saying nothing about it. In one of his last lectures, delivered at the University of Virginia in 1975, the late Lionel Trilling maintained that the attraction of such avant-gardes lay in regression: a preference for the infinite unexercised potential of infancy over the lonely and limited freedom available to adult enterprises.[15] Though I do not altogether subscribe to the absoluteness of Trilling's either-or, his argument seems all too relevant to much of the new poetry. That poems like " 'The Dreadful Has Already Happened,' " or Merwin's "Habits," or Mezey's "New Year's Eve in Solitude" gesture not toward achieved Enlightenment so much as toward a pure potentiality, to which nothing has happened, seems obvious. That the use of a language as bland as Strand's in " 'The Dreadful Has Already Happened,' " like Warhol's practice of copying photographs, serves to avoid—without ever failing—the traditional tests of high art is less provable but, I think, true. Allegory itself—though seemingly the opposite of an avant-garde technique—can serve the same function, minimizing the need for an artistic response to particulars.

A more direct analogue to anti-art movements can perhaps be seen in the blankly unselective, almost "found" poems of middle-period Creeley or of younger members of the New York School such as Ted Berrigan. Here, chance and randomness are literally included in the act of composition, to offset the "manhandling" tendencies of the author. But I do not think it is an accident that these poetic enterprises arose at almost exactly the same time as the new surrealism; both have the same jaded, exhausted tone to them, and both presume the same sense of a passive or empty "I." And both offer a kind of invitation to literary mediocrity, insofar as they assume that no moment of experience is more significant, more worthy of detailed examination, than any other—indeed, that the very sense of significance is to be mistrusted, as one of the maneuvers by which the predatory ego misappropriates "the universe" to itself. There is perhaps no arguing with this philosophy as a philosophy; but carried to its extreme it can lead—as it has, at times, in the visual arts—to a climate in which a new individual richness of technique, or a genuine (and therefore selective) interest in the outside world, will be greeted with suspicion rather than celebration. (This is not to deny that great work has been produced, especially in the visual arts, out of an anti-epiphanic vision. And I have deliberately omitted from this discussion the one living poet, John Ashbery, who seems comparable to the Abstract Expressionists in drastic originality of technique. But Ashbery—like the best of the Abstract Expressionists—seems to me at once an epiphanic and an anti-epiphanic artist; and I shall discuss him, and his complex relation to the idea of the avant-garde, in the following chapter.)

II

But by now the reader may be more than ready to argue with me. After all, aren't boredom, indefiniteness, permanent uncertainty, the painful narrownesses of personality, part of our psychic life just as much as excitement, insight, coherence? Perhaps—my reader may concede—mediocre talents are disproportionately attracted to the period style, because it is in fashion, and sets little premium on effort; but aren't there *some* poets for whom these subjects do not weaken feeling or precision of expression, and in fact lead to a kind of patient wisdom?

And so I would like to conclude with a few examples of poems in which the anti-epiphanic emphasis, rather than destroying the complexity of introspective poetry, gives it a new dimension. "The Story of Our Lives," the title poem of Mark Strand's fourth and best book, is such a poem. Like many of Strand's poems, it is a fable, and a variation on the theme of the double—a theme Strand characteristically uses to represent alienating self-consciousness as well as (its more traditional application) the projection of the repressed. In "The Story of Our Lives," the issue is the shared self-consciousness of a married couple, who are represented as having to read their life from a book as they live it. Their efforts to do something the book does not predict, and to become so much at one with what it does predict that they forget its existence, are equally unavailing. But the fable suggests so many aspects of marriage at its bad moments—overfamiliarity, habit so entrenched it feels like determinism, identity blurred by a constant spectatorial presence and at the same time impoverished by loneliness—that it becomes symbolism and not allegory. The reading of the book offers a wealth of metaphors for awareness, the refusal of awareness, and the gestures that reveal them:

> You have the impulse to close the book
> which describes my resistance:
> how when I lean back I imagine
> my life without you, imagine moving
> into another life, another book.
> It describes your dependence on desire,
> how the momentary disclosures
> of purpose make you afraid.
> The book describes much more than it should.
> It wants to divide us.

I cannot see in the earlier Strand's flat overstatements the "gnomic wisdom" which Harold Bloom's blurb claims to find there, but I would apply that phrase gladly to much of the sharply aphoristic writing here:

> *They would patch up their lives in secret:*
> *each defeat forgiven because it could not be tested,*
> *each pain rewarded because it was unreal.*

These lines describe brilliantly the kinds of bargains people strike—demanding too much, or the wrong, merely compensatory, kind of "reward," and at the same time "forgiving" too much, out of guilt—

when they cannot get to the bottom of what is really at issue between them. It is an insight that belongs in the middle of a Kafkaesque fiction, because the processes it brings to focus impart a profoundly fictive, "as if" quality to life itself.

Two other poems in *The Story of Our Lives* also convince us, magnificently, that the opacity they describe is an irreducible psychological one, not an unearned premise about what life is like. "Elegy for My Father"—though marred by its more windily grandiose Lorcaesque passages—uses the surrealist litany to immensely powerful effect, in two sections, to render the obsessive urgency and frustration of the son whose father's dying seems merely a continuation of the emotional withdrawal and elusiveness he practiced in life. "The Untelling," a poem about memory and childhood, avoids the conventional Wordsworthian tonalities of such poems by concentrating on the mixture of boredom and fascination with which children regard the opacity of adult lives. The apparent purpose of the poem is to dispel this sense of suspension by later understanding. But the harder the poet tries, the more he finds not only that the opacity is the core of the childhood experience, but that his own effort to explain is the mysterious interruption that has put it forever out of reach. At this point, all ages become equal in their bafflement, and the poet experiences a communion of what Stevens would call "mere being"—the most elaborated, and powerful, of those negative or purgative ecstasies that recur intermittently through Strand's work.

A very similar emotion dominates in what seems to me the most philosophically sophisticated book to come out of the anti-epiphanic ethos (if one excludes Ashbery, who, again, seems a very special case), Jon Anderson's *In Sepia*. Anderson's poetry has one central fable—a fable quickly sketched out in "The Parachutist" from his earlier book, *Death & Friends*, then elaborated throughout *In Sepia*. The fable might be summed up as follows. We begin, in youth, with the mesmerizing fear of death as the pure opposite to selfhood. But in "the middle years"—as vivid points stand out less from the general flow of time, as we no longer expect our lives to form patterns or stories leading to conclusive revelations, and yet longing remains, diffused into our sense of indefiniteness—our experience of life becomes curiously like our fantasy of death, "The same measure, or passing of time, / Where we dissolve." Thus, the poem I have been quoting from, "Stories," begins with "a story declining, as landscape / Into its elements"—the decline of landscape being represented by a twilight drive through the Midwest, in which the individual trees and houses become

> Some processions you can remember awhile
>   Between which the land
> Goes on, gliding without force toward
>   Night & sleep.

Yet in this dissolution, even in this loss of force, there is a paradoxical release, or joy:

> How can I say this, only beginning to see
>   Such understanding as
> Can make you whole. These stories end, as

> Always, in our gradual belief. They are
>   The lands we live in,
> The women we finally meet as friends,

> The friends we overcome. We overcome
>   Ourselves.

Permanent indefiniteness places us indissolubly in our context, in greater "belief"; it frees us, among other things, from the need to give other people meaning solely in terms of their effect on us, our emotions, our story. It is true that in a darker poem like "The Inner Gate," this accepted alienness can modulate into the paralytic self-consciousness often found in Strand. Then, instead of the ritualistic, peaceful "processions . . . Between which the land / Goes on," we get: "These are the raptures of falling in space forever." But in a third poem, "In Sepia," Anderson's very preoccupation with death returns to save him. Each moment of consciousness—he seems to say—keeps its mysterious uniqueness, because we could not be sure we would survive it; and, by the same token, it leaves the subsequent moments free.

> By Death, you meant
>   *A change of character*: He is
> A step ahead, interlocutor, by whose whisper
>   The future parts like water. . . .

    Death was process then, a release of nostalgia
      Leaving you free to change.

Anderson's work is warmer and richer for the fact that it is almost as constantly concerned with the awareness of others, in friendship, as with self-awareness. (The title of his second book, *Death & Friends*, is not a parody of Sylvia Plath's "Death & Co." but a simple list of the only themes Anderson cares to write about.) How easily his mind moves between the two contexts can be seen from the last lines of "The Parachutist," in which the inevitable errors one makes in trying to imagine what it is like to die are compared to the errors of "those / who imagine the silence of a guest / to be mysterious, or wrong." And, indeed, the two contexts, life and death, friendship and solitude, present Anderson with the same problem of ambiguous boundaries. He fears loneliness, but fears still more the rituals that make connection seem greater than it is:

    And if, this morning
    I should turn & touch your face
    Or caress your throat lightly,
    As if in love . . .

    This is not love, but care.
    Yours is the world
    I dream in when I fail to dream.

                           ("The Inner Gate")

But he also struggles with extreme experiences of connectedness, both consoling and frightening: the sense of inter-identity ("friends . . . so enclosed within my reasoning / I am occasionally them") and the sense of others' personalities as pure essences, numinous forces. These sensations can never quite be explained away, because they reflect ambiguities in self-perception. Trying to correct the suspicion that people become pure spirits once out of sight—a departing guest rising "like a ghoul / Into the moon's face, laughing"—he reasons,

    No, she is just walking to her car,
    As you are walking to sleep,
    That alabaster sea whose tides the moon controls.

                              ("Other Lives")

But he immediately realizes that he too vanishes, into a translucent but not transparent medium. If the Richard Wilbur echo seems ill-advised, the other, half-given echo (of Saint John's description of paradise) is extremely effective.

And yet the less tactful echo, and the stilted rhythms of the last line, suggest an uneasiness with visionary modes, which other poems confirm, and which may be due to Anderson's quite strong commitment to low-key conversational norms. It is not that one would expect him to sound like Blake or Nerval; his more appropriate master might be Stevens, in whose poems visionary moments "occur as they occur," but epistemological honesty keeps them on the move. It is, however, precisely the authority with which Stevens raises and lowers his poetic voice that is, as yet, lacking in Anderson. "Please John Clare, there was time"—with its incongruous resemblance to Frank O'Hara's plea to Lana Turner—simply is not enough to involve the reader in the talismanic value which Clare's feelings (not his poems) have for Anderson. But there are moments when Anderson's "one-of-the-guys" tone serves him very well. In the line "Each house got personal" (from "In Sepia"), the ordinary guy's mixed feelings at a violation of "cool" correspond precisely to the philosopher's ambivalence about imaginative mergings.

My other reservation about In Sepia is perhaps graver, though it applies to fewer passages. Perhaps because Anderson has, by his own admission, "seldom mentioned . . . Those events or names by which / I was compelled to write," I grow uneasy when he takes an elevated moral tone—even in self-deprecation—about his unspecified personal life. The worst, and the only aggressive, instance occurs in "Rosebud," where Anderson asserts that his wife, in directing "an ironic comment" at him, has "hurt the land." There has to be a grain of priggish self-importance here, however many layers of sincere animist feeling have accreted around it. Anderson's justness of tone—perfect for the metaphysical ramifications of relationship—is less reliable on the terrain of strictly emotional autobiography. An exception is the fine (but dramatically situated) poem "A Commitment."

Finally, I would like to turn to one remarkable, and as far as I know unique, application of the current surrealist style to what would usually be considered confessional subject matter—in the sense of extreme, shattering, traumatic. It is by Gregory Orr, a poet who, until he came to this subject matter, had distinguished himself

from run-of-the-mill new surrealists only minutely, by a greater visual and epigrammatic crispness. "Gathering the Bones Together"—
the title poem of Orr's second volume—is a harrowing account of
living with the memory of having accidentally killed a brother at the
age of twelve. The story is told mainly through a series of recurrent
dreams, one of which, however, comes eerily before the fact. The
precise visualization of surrealistic scenes—a merit even of
Orr's more generic work—becomes stunningly effective here. The
speaker's changed sense of his body after the accident—its terrible
new importance, and, at the same time, the decreation of its simple
natural presence—is all rendered in one image and four mostly
monosyllabic lines:

> I crouch in the corner of my room,
> staring into the glass well
> of my hands; far down
> I see him drowning in air.

It seems almost impertinent to say in the face of such urgency, but
one feels that Orr has given the benumbed surrealist style its perfect
subject: not transcendence but traumatic repetition; not change but
living with something that changes everything and cannot itself be
changed. The static quality and the self-undermining of language
and vision that irritate one in a poetry purporting to explore, to seek
revelations, become under such circumstances legitimate demands
of the subject matter:

> But tonight the bones in my feet
> begin to burn. I stand up
> and start walking, and the slab
> appears under my feet with each step,
> a white road only as long as your body.

It is true that the poem lacks certain dimensions that a confessional
poet might find indispensable to honesty: a concrete exploration of
the family relationships, of the possible presence of unconscious intention in the killing, and thus in the guilt. But in its rendering of
traumatic obsession—an experience whose essential quality is its refusal to be untied by reasons—the poem could hardly be improved.
The very last section sounds inconclusive, and therefore weak, but

what it offers may indeed be the only conclusion possible: an anticipation of the speaker's own future death which is penitenitally excessive, and yet saving, because it returns both the speaker and his
brother to normal human fate.

There is generally a common reason why I admire, or fail to admire, works with a considerable element of reductive abstraction in
their handling of experience. Stated as a principle, it would go somewhat as follows. A good empty work of art allows one to extrapolate
something—the method, at least—of a full work that is missing,
while at the same time impressing on one an emotional or imaginative quality which could not exist without the emptiness. I can extrapolate a way of seeing landscape from Jackson Pollock's last
manner; I cannot begin to imagine how Andy Warhol would go
about painting anything unphotographically. Among the poems considered here, Jon Anderson's "Stories" begins with a sensation that
one might well experience at the end of a very long chronicle novel
about life in the Midwest. Mark Strand's "The Story of Our Lives"
could live inside a marriage poem by Robert Lowell or Adrienne
Rich, as a final quality of consciousness in the struggling protagonists; whereas Strand's poorer earlier allegories, like " 'The Dreadful
Has Already Happened,' " suggest no outer world, only the world of
ideas in vogue from which they take their structure. Orr's "Gathering the Bones Together" would illustrate the second half of my
principle: its self-limitation to dreams at once rests on and drama-
tizes the fact that, for the traumatized psyche, nothing really happens
except its own relivings of the trauma.

It is encouraging, at a time when anti-epiphanic ideas seem in
other quarters to have led to a uniform dullness and lethargy, to see
this kind of full/empty poem developing in the work of writers like
Strand, Anderson, and Orr. It suggests the possibility of a commerce
between the school of metaphysical alienations and the school of literal autobiography, a commerce which is also being opened from the
other side (see the discussions of Glück, Tillinghast, and Bidart, two
chapters hence), and which is much to be desired. It is evident that a
truly personal poetry needs to take account of the flickerings of self-
consciousness, the degrees and qualities of interior distance, that
dissolve into too easy transparency in the more factual confessional
styles. On the other hand, it is peculiarly self-defeating for poetry to
ignore the particular causes of things, if transcendental or archetypal
causes are posited, from the start, through a negative theology that
renders them unapproachable. When Gregory Orr wrote "Gathering

the Bones Together," he unmade, retracted, an earlier conventionally surrealist poem to give the new poem this epigraph:

> When all the rooms of the house
> fill with smoke, it's not enough
> to say an angel is sleeping on the chimney.

6

THE DIFFRACTING DIAMOND

Ashbery, Romanticism, and Anti-Art

But the point in contemporary American poetry where the epiphanic and the anti-epiphanic are truly married, to produce something rich, strange, and not quite like either, is in the work of John Ashbery. For all his new-found celebrity, Ashbery remains *sui generis*, a poet whom each of his admirers is likely to have a strong desire to rescue from some of the others, and even from aspects of himself. I, for one, cannot abide mention of that mythical chimera Ashbery-and-Koch; that is, I cannot see (or, at least, value) Ashbery's disjunctions and underminings of his own moods as ends in themselves, as the all-inclusive irony of Dada and anti-art. On the other hand, there are moments when I want to rescue Ashbery from his best philosophical critic, Harold Bloom, who tends, in his influence theory, to expect that with increasing "belatedness" poetry will not only be but sound like literary criticism, and so overrates Ashbery's speculative manner, however prolix, at the expense of what Bloom terms his "elliptical" manner.[1]

The—no doubt equally fragmentary—Ashbery I would rescue is, like Bloom's, a perpetuator of that long meditation on consciousness, on imagination and perception, subjectivity and objectivity, that runs through English and American Romanticism from Blake to Stevens. But he is also an inheritor of French traditions, not only Surrealist but Symbolist. At a moment when ideas about the nature and coherence of consciousness have become infinitely complicated, Ashbery takes up (for the first time in our poetry since Hart Crane) Rimbaud's *alchimie du verbe*: the aspiration to find verbal equivalents, rather than analytic descriptions, of states of consciousness, to write down silences, nights, vertigos. For me, this is the most exciting aspect of Ashbery's poetry, along with his perhaps related rediscovery of the Symbolist and Romantic theme of longing, the interior search for the lost paradise—a theme elsewhere muted, in contemporary poetry, by psychological knowingness and by Manichaean metaphysics.

Ashbery is, as almost everyone agrees, a poet of the mind very far off inside itself, dependent on the quality and intensity of its own responses for its final sense of reality, and therefore—a conclusion from which Ashbery does not flinch—ultimately isolated. The inner ground of reality is, to a degree, the common theme of the Romantic tradition. But Ashbery is an extreme not only in his denial of objectivity but in his equal, and peculiarly contemporary, diffidence about locating or reifying the imagination, the essential self. The differences can be seen in a passage from "Fragment" in which Ashbery is consciously replying to Wallace Stevens:

> Slowly as from the center of some diamond
> You begin to take in the world as it moves
> In toward you, part of its own burden of thought, rather
> Idle musing, afternoons listing toward some sullen
> Unexpected end. Seen from inside all is
> Abruptness. As though to get out your eye
> Sharpens and sharpens these particulars; no
> Longer visible, they breathe in multicolored
> Parentheses, the way love in short periods
> Puts everything out of focus, coming and going.

Where Stevens maintained in "Esthétique du Mal" that "We are not / At the center of a diamond," because of our bodily vulnerability, Ashbery responds that we cannot help being inside the diamond, since we cannot be aware of anything without also being aware of ourselves perceiving it. We attempt to escape from ourselves by sharpening our awareness of the outside, of "particulars"; but in the process we sharpen, make more salient, our own imaginative powers, until—as in the physical process of diffraction—the acuteness of focus disperses the image. The external world, if it comes alive for us, "breathes," will be "no / Longer visible." It is Ashbery's uniqueness that he identifies the state of imaginative ecstasy with the point at which the object goes out of focus, multiplies, dissolves. It is this that makes Ashbery, of necessity, the poet of disjunctions and uncompleted stories, the first abstract painter in our poetry, and the forever problematic special case for those who would see in him the continuation either of Romantic faith in the imagination or of Symbolist *alchimie du verbe*.

To complicate matters further, the passage from "Fragment" also hints at an opposite, anti-subjective metaphysics: the idea of the world as a thinking center, less "sharp" than our own, but nonetheless capable of regarding us as its peripheral and semifocused objects. Seen from this angle, our vagueness and disjointedness may simply reflect our (or its) inability to bring its purposes regarding us beyond the level of "idle musing." To leave the matter on a rational level, we might simply say that the content of the self is the world, as the content of the world is the self; therefore neither can be defined.

> Thus your only world is an inside one
> Ironically fashioned out of external phenomena
> Having no rhyme or reason, and yet neither
> An existence independent of foreboding and sly grief.

We should, however, acknowledge that the idea of a thinking cosmos resists being left on a rational level; and that its recurrences partly account for the tone of paranoia, of "foreboding," that often accompanies epistemological speculation in Ashbery. Sometimes, in his reflexive use of the second person, Ashbery seems to speak to himself as such a world might speak to him: as an older teacher, perhaps even a lover, and yet menacing in its withheld wisdom—like Robert Frost's guide, "who only has at heart your getting lost." Does Ashbery's assumption of such a persona imply a continuum—however inscrutable—between the self and the cosmos? Or simply that in our self-consciousness we are always watching ourselves "the way God watches a sinner on the path to redemption" ("The Bungalows")—that is, with an impersonality at once real, in the distance it creates, and factitious in its teleological presuppositions? In the ambiguities of Ashbery's concept of selfhood, both answers remain possible.

Given these concerns, Ashbery's relation to the devaluation of personality and self-expression in anti-art movements—on which, as an art critic, he has of necessity lavished considerable patience—is extremely complex. One might say that such ideas are at once necessary and poisonous to his ambitions. In the first place, he understands that what is in question is not really a rejection of personality but a desperate attempt to salvage personality, or at least the personal will, from what is conceived—particularly in the visual arts— as the commercially standardized character of traditional expression. In "Definition of Blue," Ashbery writes

> In our own time, mass practices have sought to submerge the
>   personality
> By ignoring it, which has caused it instead to branch out in all
>   directions
> Far from the permanent tug that used to be its notion of
>   "home."

Ashbery understands and resists the trap of the perpetual avant-garde: "But today there is no point in looking to imaginative new methods / Since all of them are in constant use." Still, there is, for him, no backtracking: "There is no remedy for this 'packaging' which has supplanted the old sensations." Indeed, the sense of "packaging," the extreme self-consciousness about style, which inhibits a spontaneous expression of sensibility has at least one real virtue. It makes us realize that the "old sensations," if they did not falsify, at least limited: like "architectural screens" in a landscaped garden, they created an illusion of harmony by judiciously breaking off the chains of connection which, in the mind or in life, are in fact endless. Hence the peculiarly Ashberian justification (and, at the same time, transcendence) of the avant-garde. Endless self-consciousness makes every gesture the possible occasion for endless self-knowledge. If the air is no longer air, at least it becomes a mirror:

> erosion produces a kind of dust or exaggerated pumice
> Which fills space and transforms it, becoming a medium
> In which it is possible to recognize oneself.

Here, as elsewhere, we see Ashbery's remarkable refusal to relinquish either surface or depth: either the avant-garde's insistence on randomness, on the destruction of hierarchies of the aesthetic—a world without "rhyme or reason"—or the Romantic-Symbolist-Freudian assertion that perception symbolizes and reveals the depths of the self. To quote again from "Fragment," "Like the blood orange we have a single / Vocabulary all heart and all skin."

Ashbery's skepticism about "imaginative new methods" is gently refuted by the remarkable innovations in his second volume, *The Tennis Court Oath.* To my mind, this obscure and often undecipherable book constitutes a "period" in the sense in which painters are said to go through them but writers are not: a stage at which all particular content is subordinated to the inventing and mastering of techniques indispensable to the expression of what one might call the artist's content beyond content. I am puzzled that Harold Bloom rejects this book from the acceptable canon so unequivocally, and in particular that he dismisses "the notion that this was a necessary phase in the poet's development."[2] It is not that I derive much more enjoyment from "Leaving the Atocha Station" than Bloom does; but that in these poems Ashbery finds the means of rendering blurred, in-between states of consciousness without which many of his later, clearer poems would be little more than dry philosophizing.

The techniques I have in mind are somewhat more structured than the pure free association, in the tradition of André Breton, that dominates a number of poems. The first is the use of an interrupted narrative or speech as an element in a collage, along with other narrative fragments, images, and free-associative chains of words. The technique differs from collage in Eliot and Pound mainly in that the narratives are rarely intended to become less mysterious through study, or through outside information. A better analogue is the mode of modern painting, from the Cubists to De Kooning, in which representational areas are interrupted or even interpenetrated by purely abstract areas. The unsettling power of Ashbery's technique lies largely in the psychological logic of the interruptions. An extraordinary number of his narrative fragments have mysterious erotic or violent undertones; and in these cases the break almost invariably occurs just as a crisis of revelation approaches. This suggests that the dissociating effect of the collage represents, in part, the dissociation of projection or fantasy, and that the break corresponds to a psychic censorship. In "The Suspended Life," for instance, a rather bland narrative suddenly acquires a decadent coloration—

> She started
> On her round-the-world cruise
> Aboard the *Zephyr*. The boy sport
> A dress. The girl,
> Slacks. Each carried a magazine—

and then, just as these interesting characters seem about to en-counter each other, the narrative dissolves in a dense associative jumble—

> A package of sea the observatory
> Introduced me to canned you

—in which one may, if so minded, detect both genital and oral sexu-ality, and even cannibalism. The crisis past, the bland narrative voice resumes, but there is now an unsettling discrepancy between tone and content:

> Only a few cases of plague
> Announced in Oporto, the schools
> Reopen in the fresh September breeze.

The issue these lines suggest—the uneasy boundary between inno-cence and experience, between perception and the refusal to per-ceive—is really the central issue throughout. It is an issue that obsesses Ashbery, and not Ashbery alone. How many movies have we all seen on the subject of runaway children who cross paths with a murderer—a subject whose appeal, surely, is to our own anxiety about the relation between normal venturesomeness and the com-pletely out of bounds?

> And hiding from darkness in barns
> They can be grownups now
> And the murderer's ash tray is more easily—
> The lake a lilac cube.
>
>   (" 'They Dream Only of America' ")

When the children "can be grownups," the evidence of evil is at once "more easily"—and I think the missing word has to be either "found" or "recognized." So that again it is precisely the recognition scene that is averted—averted by stopping time, freezing the journey of escape in an eternal present of pastoral beauty. And one notices how the same detail that makes the last line suggest an abstract painting also betrays the effort of psychic containment: the lake water held to the dimensions of a cube.

" 'They Dream Only of America' " is one of the most clearly structured poems in *The Tennis Court Oath*, possessing essentially a traditional double plot. The story of the children and the murderer reflects the shadowy story of the narrator's friend, whose journey to lose himself in America, driving "hundreds of miles / At night through dandelions," becomes more and more terrible, as he takes everything that happens for "a sign" (presumably of impending evil, the broken leg mentioned in the last stanza). He ends, like the children earlier, paralyzed between alternatives of ecstasy and destructiveness; "There is nothing to do / For our liberation, except wait in the horror of it."

I do not mean to maintain that all interrupted stories in Ashbery can be ascribed to psychic censorship. Often, the uncertainties of paranoia, the elusiveness of essentially nostalgic desires, provide more relevant explanations. My point is that it is the imitation of psychological tension—approach and avoidance, affirmation and denial—that gives Ashbery's disjunctiveness a force far exceeding mere aesthetic novelty.

A second disjunctive technique seems meant particularly to illustrate the notion that the mind and the world put each other out of focus. It is what I call the half-focused image: a kind of borderline structure between the mind and the world, possessing distinct sensuous qualities without ever quite becoming a visualizable object or scene. The effect is hard to describe, but fairly easy to illustrate. Consider the opening stanzas of "Our Youth":

> Of bricks . . . Who built it? Like some crazy balloon
> When love leans on us
> Its nights . . . The velvety pavement sticks to our feet.
> The dead puppies turn us back on love.
>
> Where we are. Sometimes
> The brick arches led to a room like a bubble, that broke when
>   you entered it
> And sometimes to a fallen leaf.
> We got crazy with emotion, showing how much we knew.

"Youth" becomes a building of unknown origin, all of whose attributes are paradoxes. It is made of bricks, yet resembles a balloon; its arches either lead to bubbles that burst, or else simply condense, into the minute fragility of the fallen leaf. In short, it is at once an extreme of heaviness and of lightness, evanescence, like the Rilkean leaning *Weltraum* of the nights of love. What Ashbery is really describing is the vertiginous quality of adolescent consciousness, in which the external world is alternately suffocatingly present ("The velvety pavement sticks to our feet") and almost dissolved in the "crazy" accesses of emotion. Such a state has much to do with the new importance the world beyond the self has acquired, through "love"; with the uncertainty about where love is to be found, what is expected of one; with the acute awareness of one's own presence as observer and observed—all of which Ashbery manages to suggest in a wonderful stanza of provocative, paranoid questioning.

> Do you know it? Hasn't she
> Observed you too? Haven't you been observed to her?
> My, haven't the flowers been? Is the evil
> In't? What window? What did you say there?

Out of this self-awareness grows that adolescent sentimentality which is so different from the sentimentalities of other ages, with none of their staleness, and which consists in the insistence that everything be special in the sense of precious, included, so that nothing will be special in the sense of incommensurate, cast out— the "dead puppies" turning us "back on love." For an extended narrative treatment of such states of mind, one would look to *The Catcher in the Rye* or to Randall Jarrell's fine and neglected poem "The Night Before the Night Before Christmas." But it is extraordinary how completely the condition is conveyed in Ashbery's unfocusable image—a Rimbaldian triumph at writing down a vertigo.

A later example of this technique (for it remains basic to Ashbery's epistemological enterprise, whereas the interrupted story becomes an occasional ornament) is the opening of "Fragment":

> The last block is closed in April. You
> See the intrusions clouding over her face
> As in the memory given you of older
> Permissiveness which dies in the
> Falling back toward recondite ends

The first sentence is quite oracular. We can give "block" the sense of "city block"—in which case the line suggests an abandonment, or a demolition project, of eerie proportions—or the sense of an element in a composition, a building block, or a block of color in an abstract painting. In the second sentence, the blocks become specifically "intrusions," the guardednesses, the new interests, which make the woman's face mysterious to her former lover. But in the continuation, both possibilities in the first line are taken up again: the allusive-elusive quality of abstract composition to convey the woman's slightly teasing attitude ("point of other / Space not given, and yet not withdrawn"), the urban destructiveness ("saw-toothed flames") to suggest the painful erotic possibilities of her other life.

It is impossible to gauge how much of the effectiveness of Ashbery's half-finished stories and pictures depends on his celebrated musicianship, and its power to induce an irrational sense of completion or suspension. How the completion is accomplished can be seen in the "murderer's ash tray" passage from " 'They Dream Only of America' "—the unexpectedly long penultimate line giving place to the tight concluding one, whose consonants (if one excludes the first and last) close as neatly as a rhyme-scheme: l-k-l-l-c-c. The congruent power to create troubling suspensions can be seen in the dangling feminine endings in the stanza just quoted from "Fragment" ("older," "in the," "point of other"), or, still more strikingly, in the following two-line vignette from "Civilization and Its Discontents": "The child's psalm, slightly sung / In the hall rushing into the small room." After the cramped first line, almost all strong accents, the second seems a "rushing," a release; and yet its only strong syllables are bunched in two spondees, the more noticeable because their first syllables rhyme and their second alliterate. Here one could almost regard the elements of poignancy in the plot—the childish hesitation, the curtailed "rush"—as an elaboration of what is already implicit in the metrical awkwardness. Thus, Ashbery's poetry approximates the qualities he has said he admires in music: "its ability of being convincing, of carrying an argument through successfully to the finish, though the terms of this argument remain unknown quantities."[3]

Having developed these techniques in *The Tennis Court Oath*, Ashbery proceeds to consolidate them with a poetry much clearer in its emotional and thematic directions, a poetry capable of discursive comment on itself, in *Rivers and Mountains*—his third book, and to my taste still the richest, the most energized balance of his various gifts. The philosophy is as yet more embodied than discussed; but the characteristic attitudes toward experience, the emotional key-signatures of the work, are now clearly articulated, with the freshness of early maturity. There is the strange combination of Baudelairean synesthetic blurring, *ténébreuse et profonde unité*, and a slight foreknowing irony, with which romance is greeted: "The miracle took you in beside him. / Leaves rushed the window, there was clear water and the sound of a lock." There is the eerily similar mixture of feelings (a resigned appreciativeness?) which attends the anticipation of death, or of some apocalyptic alienness equated with death:

> There is no longer any use in harping on
> The incredible principle of daylong silence, the dark sunlight
> As only the grass is beginning to know it,
> The wreath of the north pole,
> Festoons for the late return, the shy pensioners
> Agasp on the lamplit air.

There is the ability to relive, with equal vividness, the incommunicable intensities of adolescence and the monochrome fascinations—the collections, the chemistry sets—of the latency period. (Many writers can be classified according to whether their emotional touchstone is childhood or adolescence—but not so Ashbery.) There is, finally, the concern with "Civilization and Its Discontents," with the relation between the meaningless complex orderliness of daily behavior and the meaningful elusiveness of satisfied desire. For Ashbery is—as I hope to show a little later on—very much a poet of his historical situation, and his guardedly ironic assumption of the Freudian inheritance is, in its own way, as genuine as Snyder's or Lowell's.

All of these concerns are most lavishly illustrated in "The Skaters." It is, except perhaps for "Self-Portrait in a Convex Mirror," my favorite among his longer works, for rather old-fashioned reasons: the importance, and the variety, of its subjects, the suppleness with which its language responds. Since the poem is, really, an immense *assemblage* of half-told stories, long and short, it is a little hard to give an adequate sense of this variety and suppleness, while keeping one's eye on architectonics and thematic development.[4] I hope, by quotation, to make up for some of the deficiencies of commentary.

In the initial episode, the poet is watching skaters on an outdoor rink. The emotional atmosphere is that of "Our Youth"—a fearful but exciting adolescent vertigo before life:

> We children are ashamed of our bodies
> But we laugh and, demanded, talk of sex again
> And all is well.

Watching the scene, the poet seems to see an abstract visual design—"masses of inertia," "an incredible mess of dark colors"—alternate with heartbreakingly sudden assertions of individuality, of the particular:

>   hips
> Prod out of the violet-seeming into a new kind
> Of demand that stumps the absolute because not new
> In the sense of the next one in an infinite series
> But, as it were, pre-existing or pre-seeming in
> Such a way as to contrast funnily with the unexpectedness
> And somehow push us all into perdition.

"Perdition" is involved not only because these assertions have such a bewitching rightness, but because they fade: the sharpened profile cannot be remembered, the skaters merely "elaborate their distances" to return, inevitably, "to the mass." Only the alternating pattern remains in the mind; but this is not, initially, much consolation.

>   The human mind
> Cannot retain anything except perhaps the dismal two-note
>   theme
> Of some sodden "dump" or lament.

As Ashbery, in his new discursiveness, is quick to point out to us, the first symbolic function of the skating scene is to epitomize the method of the poem itself. Wisely, Ashbery chooses as the occasion for his digression one of the finest of his narrative fragments: the ecstasy of the Jersey City painter Helga, suspended in Crane-like inner spaces of latinate diction,

>   drawing death
> Again in blossoms against the reactionary fire . . . pulsing

> And knowing nothing to superb lambent distances that inter-
>   calate
> This city.

Immediately afterward, Ashbery intrudes *in propria persona* to justify
the technique, first by a rather defensive attack on naturalistic inclu-
siveness ("the floor sags, as under the weight of a piano, or a piano-
legged girl"), then by virtue of its inherent poignancy, "a bitter impression of absence, which as we know involves presence, but
still"—an impression, as it happens, peculiarly appropriate to the
self-annihiliating intensity of Helga's vision. Ashbery then goes on
to set forth his larger aesthetic premises in using the technique, in
terms that clearly parallel the alternation of fragile particularity and
blurred mass in the skating scene:

> This, thus is a portion of the subject of this poem
> Which is in the form of falling snow:
> That is, the individual flakes are not essential to the importance
>   of the whole's becoming so much of a truism
> That their importance is again called in question, to be denied
>   further out, and again and again like this.
> Hence, neither the importance of the individual flake,
> Nor the importance of the whole impression of the storm, if it
>   has any, is what it is,
> But the rhythm of the series of repeated jumps, from abstract
>   into positive and back to a slightly less diluted abstract.

Since the "rhythm" has already been given its reductive equivalent
("the dismal two-note theme / Of some sodden 'dump' or lament"),
it is not particularly surprising that Ashbery now says, with characteristic self-deprecation, "Mild effects are the result."

But the theme, more broadly considered, is not at all mild. It is a
considerable portion of human fate: the effort of the individual to escape from "inertia," and from the "mass," through energy, and to
attain some kind of specialness, "finer expression"—by beauty,
moral force, achievement, what you will. It is a tragic theme, for inertia always reasserts itself: the energy is used up in the attainment
of fineness, the profile slips from the mind, and, "somehow," "perdition" is always waiting. "But so little energy they have! And up the
swollen sands / Staggers the darkness fiend, with the storm fiend
close behind him!" (The fact that, at this point, "they" no longer lit-

erally refers to the skaters, but to childhood collections, underlines Ashbery's tragic doubt of the cohesive force of individuality.)

So that the poem proceeds logically from the skaters to a vast array of enterprises beginning to succumb to inertia: the poet's own life, as he enters middle age ("to go from 'not interesting' to 'old and uninteresting' "); his declining love affair ("I have a dim intuition that I am that other 'I' with which we began"); and finally history itself, its crusades and migrations ("Dim banners in the distance, to die"). To put it a little differently, the skaters' arcs—like the related symbol of the perspective lines—become a subsuming image for expansive motions that suggest, but do not attain, the absolute. And so it is appropriate that they blend at last ("Taking the exquisite theme far, into farness, to Land's End, to the ends of the earth!") into the Baudelairean theme of oceanic yearning: the poem of the voyage, which occupies most of Part II.

It is a pity that Harold Bloom is reluctant to carry his theory of influence and misprision across language barriers, and so mentions only Whitman and Stevens in connection with Part II of "The Skaters." For it seems to me that this passage cannot be grasped in its full import without locating Ashbery in relation to Baudelaire, as major precursor, and secondarily to Rimbaud, Eliot, and Crane: in short, to the great exponents and underminers of the vision of the voyage, *le vert paradis des amours enfantines* to be recovered in the tropics, in an art city like Venice, on the other side of an ocean. It is true that there are only a few direct echoes of this tradition. I suspect that the section is written in unrhymed quatrains (in pointed contrast to the uneven verse-paragraphs elsewhere) in partial homage to the form of "Un Voyage à Cythère," "Le Voyage," and "Le Bateau Ivre." The lines "Into the secretive, vaporous night with all of us! / Into the unknown, the unknown that loves us, the great unknown!" echo the desperate abandon of the end of "Le Voyage" ("Au fond de l'Inconnu pour trouver du *nouveau!*"). There is a line—"It is all passing! It is past! No, I am here"—that momentarily recalls Rimbaud at his extreme of subjectivist anarchism ("la terre fond. / *Ce n'est rien: j'y suis; j'y suis toujours'*"); and there is one significant echo of Eliot. But as Bloom says, the most important part of influence is not the relation of phrases but of total poetic stance; in this case, Ashbery's relation to the opposite attitudes held by Baudelaire at the beginning and end of his poetic career.

The vision of the voyage, in its initial form, is as mystical as anything the later Baudelaire may have found in Christianity. It is the notion that, through a kind of aesthetic and erotic saturation and co-ordination, the world becomes a language; it makes the self clear to itself by satisfying every desire.

> Les riches plafonds,
> Les miroirs profonds,
> La splendeur orientale,
> Tout y parlerait
> A l'âme en secret
> Sa douce langue natale.

("L'Invitation au Voyage")

The image of the mirror is rarely absent from Baudelaire's descriptions of this world, for there the distinction between subject and object almost vanishes. I say "almost" because Baudelaire still finds a correlation between the mystery of motive in the beloved's "treacherous eyes" and the mystery of any material presence. And in a sense, it is this "almost" that opens the wedge of Baudelaire's disillusionment: the discovery that no particular incarnation of the country at the end of the voyage satisfies as well as an imagined one, as one traced out by chance in the clouds. On the contrary, real voyages bring a continuously more reductive external view of the universal human impulses—sex, cruelty, religion—and of their common goal, an illusory freedom from destiny and time; which is, of course, the goal of the voyage itself, whose ideal country, "being nowhere, may be anywhere." It was the late Baudelaire's critical insight that T. S. Eliot codified, making "poetry of departure" a term of condescension in a line of anti-Romantic writers down to Philip Larkin.

Ashbery's misprision of Baudelaire—in Bloom's terminology—is to insist that both visions can be maintained at once; that since distance is an aspect of the sublime, the failure of the ideal country to maintain one fixed, graspable incarnation does not necessarily destroy its value as an imaginative intuition. In his mock-heroic address to the heavens, Ashbery alludes to the theory of the expanding universe, and—by an astonishing rhetorical introjection—makes this frightening enlargement of the twentieth-century sense of space feel like a rebirth of Romantic aspiration:[5]

> For I am condemned to drum my fingers
> On the closed lid of this piano, this tedious planet, earth

As it winks to you through the aspiring, growing distances,
A last spark before the night.

Is Ashbery in fact drumming his fingers, as opposed to playing? A little later, he echoes Baudelaire's discovery that the place one actually goes is always the wrong one—

"Why do you want to go *there*," they all say. "It is better in the other direction."
And so it is. There people are free, at any rate. But where you are going no one is.

—and yet there is no curtailment of mystery; the mystery, indeed, is that freedom reinvents itself, through sheer receptiveness, under "l'ennemi vigilant et funeste, Le Temps," as under other tyrannies:

Still, there are parks and libraries to be visited, "la Bibliothèque Municipale,"
Hotel reservations and all that rot. Old American films dubbed into the foreign language,
Coffee and whisky and cigar stubs. Nobody minds. And rain on the bristly wool of your topcoat.

"Mild effects," one can hear in the background. And yet the tone, though ironic enough, never quite manages to be mild, either in its startling but delightfully recognizable flickers of fear—

You have probably made travel arrangements, and know the feeling.
Suddenly, one morning, the little train arrives in the station, but oh, so big.

—or in its generosity, its will to create moments of absolute richness:

These sails are life itself to me.

I heard a girl say this once, and cried, and brought her fresh fruit and fishes,
Olives and golden baked loaves.

When, in his final assessment, Ashbery returns to Baudelaire's (and Hart Crane's) symbolism of the voyage as any and all love affairs—

> I think not to have loved you   but the music
> Petting the enameled   slow-imagined stars

—the enameled, smoothing recapitulation of sounds gives a timeless finish to the very sensations whose utter contingency is being asserted. Thus, in the end, despite the stops and starts of the literal story line, despite the continuous archness of the voice, one cannot shake the impression of having revisited that country of plenitude, where the presence of the phenomenal world in no way restricts the imagination, that first offered itself to Baudelaire.

The rest of the poem consists of essentially similar parables of situations of radical isolation in which satisfaction is found through imaginative surrender, "in remaining close to the limitations imposed." There is the child bent over his chemistry set; the castaway on his desert island; and, finally, one of those classical Chinese poets and civil servants who were always getting themselves exiled to remote posts in Szechuan. Even the ultimate limitation, "the problem of death and survival," is said to "age slightly"—though surely that choice of verb is grim and self-undermining—in the light of accidental continuities, "rhythm substituting for 'meaning.' " In the little astronomical joke with which the poem ends, the skaters', and the poet's, own disjointed rhythm—expectation outleaping possibility and then falling back—is accepted as if it were cosmic design.

> The constellations are rising
> In perfect order: Taurus, Leo, Gemini.

In turning from *Rivers and Mountains* to *The Double Dream of Spring*, I feel a complex mixture of gain and loss. Philosophizing has definitely come to the fore; there are, moreover, certain subtle changes in thematic emphasis which have farreaching effects on style. Ashbery's peculiar sense of distance modulates into an explicit concern with alienating self-consciousness: with the inability of the entire self to become absorbed in visionary moments, or to feel fundamentally changed by new insights. At the same time—and this is what separates Ashbery from the professional mourners of self-consciousness, Merwin and Strand—his introspective instruments are fine enough to detect that the self-observing part of the self has its own fluctuations of tone, among them a clear calmness amounting almost to ecstasy, in response to that from which it stands apart.

> The words sung in the next room are unavoidable
> But their passionate intelligence will be studied in you.
>
> ("Fragment")

Ashbery's classic study of a visionary moment that does not happen, yet—after this manner—happens, is "Evening in the Country."

The other new preoccupation, beginning with "Clepsydra" in *Rivers and Mountains,* is the sensation of passing time. Few writers give us such an unsettling sense of the trackless wilderness of everyday time, so even and monotonous in its demand to be filled up, yet never quite even enough to exclude fear. Ashbery says in an interview, "The difficulty of my poetry . . . is meant to reflect the difficulty of living, the everchanging, minute adjustments that go on around us and which we respond to from moment to moment—the difficulty of living in passing time, which is both difficult and automatic, since we all somehow manage it."[6] The treble to this bass (for Ashbery, like most time-obsessed writers, is a temporal dualist) is directed or distinguished time: change or nuance, a New Spirit, "the secret sweetness before it turns to life." In Ashbery, the greater part of the sweetness invariably dies when it turns to life. Yet it constantly, stubbornly resurrects itself; hence the seesaw of hope and disillusionment, the promise and dissolution of clarity, in so many of the later poems.

The stylistic effect of all this is the decreased frequency—and the indirect treatment—of epiphanic moments and, indeed, of sensuous images generally. The poetry is still very difficult; but now it is the time-haunted difficulty of shifting references and overqualifications, not the timeless difficulty of condensations and fragments. The vagueness of commonplace expressions and the jargon of the inexact sciences (economics, statistics, sociology, literary criticism) bulk ever larger in Ashbery's poetic vocabulary, presumably as a way of dramatizing cognitive difficulties. Similarly, the frequent reference to emblems, allegories, monuments, newspaper accounts, official versions tends to place a priori quotation marks of self-consciousness around all aesthetic apprehensions. Finally—especially in the longer poems, and especially where love is at issue—Ashbery arrives at a notation of nervous states, of half-fulfilled visions and expectancies, so exhaustive and yet so vague in its external references that by comparison *The Golden Bowl* is as extroverted a romance as *Pride and Prejudice.* The poetic effects of this enterprise are problematic. If I may, again, let the most ambitious poem in the book stand for all, consider the following passage from "Fragment":

Although beyond more reacting
To this cut-and-dried symposium way of seeing things
To outflank next mediocre condition
Of storms. The hollow thus produced
A kind of cave of the winds; distribution center
Of subordinate notions to which the stag
Returns to die: the suppressed lovers.

It is not hard to grasp, in a general way, what this and a number of similar passages are describing: the intensified rationalizing and internalizing activity by which the mind manages to weather the crises of an unstable relationship. But does the rendering of this condition really grow more vivid through such academic speech, circuitous grammar, and rather silly mixed metaphors (symposia outflanking storms, stags dying in the cave of the winds) as it seems to require, here and elsewhere in the poem? To my taste, the stretched but still integrated immediacy of the half-focused image gives Ashbery a more powerful means of conveying both the mediocrity and the vertigo of ongoing awareness:

Nothing is stationary
Nor yet uncertain; a rhythm of standing still
Keeps us in continual equilibrium, like an arch
That frames swiftly receding clouds, never
Getting deeper. The shouts of children
Penetrate this motion toward, as a drop of water
Slides under a lens. Soon all is shining, mined,
Tears dissolving laughter, the isolated clouds spent.

Ashbery uses this technique to particular effect in those isolated meditations on epistemological ambiguities which are the real triumph of the poem. For instance, in the discussion of privileged moments ("A time of spotted lakes and the whippoorwill / Sounding over everything") as a psychological artifice—

To speak the plaits of argument,
Loosened? Vast shadows are pushed down toward
The hour. It is ideation, incrimination
Proceeding from necessity to find it at
A time of day, beside the creek, uncounted stars and buttons.

—both a specific scene and a traditional imagery of erotic correspondences between macrocosm and microcosm (shadows and hair, stars and buttons) are so embedded in the argument that dismisses them that even the words "ideation, incrimination" lose their sense in their sound, and an extraordinary suspension of judgment results. Since "The Skaters," Ashbery's skepticism has become so ingrained, so sophisticated, that there is no longer any need to sound flippant in order not to sound credulous. Rather, there is an elegiac sense of arriving at the limits of possible understanding which is peculiarly suited to the dolmen-like rectangular dignity of the form.

The philosophical set pieces in "Fragment" are often—and, I think rightly—put forward as the best American poetry of their kind since Stevens. Harold Bloom, in his eloquent commentary, quotes all of the best of them: the diamond stanzas; the inquiry into privileged moments; the painful stanza on sex as an expressive medium, beginning "The volcanic entrance to an antechamber"; and the stanzas near the end dealing with ancestry, death, and survival. Indeed, if "Fragment" were to survive some future cataclysm—as Greek lyric poets survived the Dark Ages—only in Bloom's commentary, posterity might well believe that it was "the best longer poem by an American poet of my own generation, and unmatched . . . by anything in the generation of Lowell."[7] The difficulty is that the commentary amounts to an edition; it restricts the exhaustive treatment of the nervous states of "the suppressed lovers" to a paraphrase, and keeps anything sounding like "Although beyond more reacting . . ." carefully out of sight. Such passages make up more than half of the poem; and although many are much better written than the one I have quoted, the wasteful redundancy of their essential content becomes in the end exasperating, especially given the needless obscurity that is cast on what happens, to whom, in what order. (It is not even easy to agree about how many characters there are in the poem; Bloom appears, at one point, to think that "she" and "you" are identical, whereas it seems fairly clear to me that "she," "you," and "I" are a triangle.) Thus "Fragment," for me, is only a potential masterpiece—superior, in parts, to both "The Skaters" and "Self-Portrait in a Convex Mirror," but inferior to both in economy and the instinct for the center.

Perhaps prose is a more natural medium than poetry for the late-Jamesian explorations that concern Ashbery in this phase. The obscurity that lies between emotional states and their occasions grows denser still in the *Three Poems*; and yet the style seems consistently more welcoming, more sure-footed, less rococo than the "Although beyond more reacting . . ." manner in *The Double Dream of Spring*. It would require more close reading than space permits to show exactly where this new authority comes from; but I can at least indicate some of the contributing elements. The allusive reach of the prose is uniformly high and ambitious: to the Bible; to Shakespeare; to the most famous Romantic poems; at worst, to the overripe eloquence of nineteenth-century idealistic philosophy. On the other hand, the vagueness of everyday speech, though everywhere in evidence, is laid on lightly and delicately, so that the effect is less the deflation of cynicism than the attenuation of time, eating away at the overconfidence of philosophy but bringing out its darker ambiguities. The imagery, when it is not (as it often is) allusive, tends to be of a very particular kind: those half-present, fibrous bodies of light, air, and motion most likely to be familiar to us from Shelley or from Virginia Woolf. Like those writers, Ashbery finds such imagery extraordinarily useful for making visible gradations in the sense of identity:

> Do these things between people partake of themselves, or are they a subtler kind of translucent matter carrying each to a compromise distance painfully outside the rings of authority? For we never knew, never knew what joined us together. Perhaps only a congealing of closeness, deserving of no special notice. But then the eyes directing out, living into their material and in that way somehow making more substance than before, and yet the outward languid motion, like girls hanging out of windows . . . ("The New Spirit," p. 10)

Finally (and this effect is peculiarly difficult to illustrate briefly, but the last sentence I have just quoted gives a hint of it) Ashbery is brilliant at making arguments shift or reverse their emotional direction without changing their terms—a sine qua non for the study of thought at this level of rarefaction.

"The New Spirit" is in a way the most difficult of the *Three Poems*, because, despite elaborate indications of progression, it is essentially reiterative. From its opening pages it expounds a single doctrine, a fundamental one for all of Ashbery's later work: the doctrine of a Whole, mystically implicit in each of the parts, provided one does not interfere with their relations by choice, evaluation, or even clear distinction. This curious anti-Platonic Platonism contains a strong ethical imperative and promise: that if the arbitrary limits of one's life history are accepted absolutely, without regrets or even imagined alternatives, the value and interest of that life history will come to seem almost infinite.

"The System" is a more dramatic poem, because in it the passivity of totalism is challenged by an active pantheism, the uncalculated—even unwanted—by-product of violent love. Early on, Ashbery lets us know that he intends to avoid the "too well rehearsed" history of love itself, and concentrate instead on the "other tradition" of accompanying ontological sensations, which demand to be treated not from "an arcane historian's" point of view but from "the painter's"—that is to say, treated without reference to anything beyond themselves (p. 56). What follows, however, is less a painting than a Platonic dialogue: an exhaustive inquiry into the ways in which extended meaning or beauty can be conferred on an everyday life that remains substantially the same. The notion of the shape of a great career, and "the 'life-as-ritual' concept," are taken up, but—predictably—dismissed as an alienation of experience. Two kinds of happiness are then posited. The first—"frontal" or spontaneous happiness—Ashbery approaches almost with reverence, and dismisses, if at all, only as being largely a matter of chance, independent of the individual will.[8] The second variety—"latent or dormant" happiness—is one of Ashbery's most interesting and original psychological concepts. It is the sophistical conviction that one as good as lives an intuitive apprehension of perfect happiness by adopting an attitude of perpetually contemplating or awaiting it. Though the handiest examples of latent happiness are the religious ("their ears are closed to the cries of their fellow passengers; they can think only of themselves when all the time they believe that they are thinking of nothing but God"—p. 74), one rightly suspects a wider application. Indeed, the critique applies to Ashbery's own notion of the redeeming value of totalistic passivity:

> aren't we in danger of accepting these [the "first few steps" of love] only for what they are, of being thankful for them and letting our gratitude take the place of further inquiry into what they were like, of letting it stand both for our attitude as eternity will view it and also for the fulfillment of which this was just the promise? . . . So that in our way we are worse off or at least in worse danger than those others who imagine themselves already delivered from the chain of rebirth. *They* have their illusions to sustain them. . . . ("The System," pp. 75–76)

It is true that Ashbery draws back from this insight. Indeed, he salvages latent happiness by making it a kind of *felix culpa*, "a fleshed-out, realized version" of ideal happiness, "more to be prized because its now ripe contours enfold both the promise and the shame of our human state" (p. 81)—a more than slightly sophistical resolution, which, however, grows in authority through the fine passage in which true contact with the beloved is restored (pp. 94–98).

Notwithstanding this resolution—which grows more emphatic in the third poem, "The Recital"—it seems to me that Ashbery has broached a larger problem than he knows how to solve poetically. A rigorously applied totalism is not compatible with the explored inscape, the "painful freshness of each thing being exactly itself" ("Voyage in the Blue"), that it is supposed to facilitate. After *Three Poems*—and before "Self-Portrait in a Convex Mirror"—Ashbery sometimes seems only capable of writing one endless Ashbery Poem, a Hymn to the Indefinite into which new challenges to his negative capability (for instance, the Persian landscapes of "Scheherazade") break intermittently, like voices on a staticky radio.

If Ashbery's philosophy, in his recent books, can be a poetic liability, his work has another aspect far too little praised or even noticed: its social and historical intelligence.[9] I am not referring to the rare passages on specific social issues; these seem, like certain references to "the poor" in Stevens, sincere yet almost embarrassed at being so peripheral to the author's real vision. Rather, I am thinking of Ashbery's sense for collective nervous states, for the ontological "other tradition" which reflects off of a culture's moods as surely as off of a lover's. Ashbery is immensely sensitive to the undermeanings of the changing national aesthetic. "Forties Flick," as it moves from the decor of the film ("the silence that night alone can't explain. / Silence of the library, of the telephone with its pad") to a typical scene—

> In bra and panties she sidles to the window:
> Zip! Up with the blind. A fragile street scene offers itself,
> With wafer-thin pedestrians who know where they are going.
> The blind comes down slowly, the slats are slowly tilted up.

—evokes the absurd yet poignant ethos in which overtones of Existentialist *Angst* superimposed themselves on the heightened social anxieties of the conforming postwar years. Ashbery is just as acute in his portrayal of a radical period in our history. I can think of few chronicles that say more about what the spiritual *élan* of the New Left felt like, or why the more simple-minded versions of it were the more durable, than a passage from "The System" whose primary meaning may not even be political—though phrases like "these enterprising but deluded young people" and "the logical last step of history" make the topical bearing clear enough. The passage is so fine that it deserves to be quoted at length:

> Who has seen the wind? Yet it was precisely this that these enterprising but deluded young people were asking themselves. They were correct in assuming that the whole question of behavior in life has to be rethought each second; that not a breath can be drawn nor a footstep taken without our being forced in some way to reassess the age-old problem of what we are to do here and how did we get here, taking into account our relations with those about us and with ourselves. . . . To be always conscious of these multiple facets is to incarnate a dimensionless organism like the wind's, a living concern that can know no rest, by definition: it *is* restlessness. But this condition of eternal vigilance had been accepted with the understanding that somehow it would also mirror the peace that all awaited so impatiently: it could not proceed unless the generalized shape of this nirvana-like state could impose its form on the continually active atoms of the moving forward which was the price it exacted: hence a dilemma for any but the unrepentant hedonists or on the contrary those who chose to remain all day on the dung-heap, rending their hair and clothing. . . . So that those who assumed that they had reached the end of an elaborate but basically simple progression, the logical last step of history, came more and more to be the dominant party: a motley group but with many level heads among them, whose voices chanting the wise maxims of regular power gradually approached the point of submerging the other cacophony of tinkling cymbals and wailing and individual voices raised in solemn but unreal debate. ("The System," pp. 61–62)

By temperament, Ashbery understands civilization less as a matter of power or economic needs than as a precariously balanced collective nervous equilibrium. In his earliest and best philosophical poem about society, "These Lacustrine Cities," Ashbery seems to share Freud's view that historical progress is a matter of sublimation, of becoming "forgetful" of the bodily origins of our motives. It is, furthermore, a matter of continuous mutual adjustments between Thanatos and Eros—between hatred, whether directed at ourselves or at others, and the opposing pansexual energies that make possible the social bond.

These lacustrine cities grew out of loathing
Into something forgetful, although angry with history.
They are the product of an idea: that man is horrible, for in-
    stance,
Though this is only one example.

They emerged until a tower
Controlled the sky, and with artifice dipped back
Into the past for swans and tapering branches,
Burning, until all that hate was transformed into useless love.

In such a situation of artificial metamorphoses of feeling, people grow remote from, and uneasy with, each other; there is a "feeling of . . . emptiness" which "must be charged to the embarrassment of others / Who fly by you like beacons." But if the opportunities for projection tear the social bond apart, they also hold it together, providing a safety valve by which disturbing elements in the individual can be assigned to the general context. As Ashbery wittily puts it in "Spring Day," "night returns bringing doubts," but these "are fended off with clubs and knives" of outward violence.

But if we look again at "These Lacustrine Cities," we notice another balance, which is not Freud's but quintessentially Ashbery's: that of the future, associated with control and freedom, against the past, associated with beauty and familiarity. The sense of the need for such a balance grows out of Ashbery's conception of time in individual life. The past in Ashbery is often—as in Stevens' "The Auroras of Autumn"—a house. It encloses and protects unchallengeably; once part of it, our selves and our loves become objects, graspable and immortal. But if we lived in it entirely, we would be dead. We need to separate ourselves from it in order to live, as surely as we need to hold onto it for the ongoing sense of shape without which "the razor's-edge present which is really a no-time" ("The System," p. 102) would be unendurable. The ambivalence is so extreme that its expression requires a double and triple backtracking unusual even for Ashbery:

And the purpose of the many stops and starts will be made
    clear:
Backing into the old affair of not wanting to grow
Into the night, which becomes a house, a parting of the ways
Taking us far into sleep. A dumb love.

                                                        ("Song")

The same ambivalence afflicts the history of art, and the history of civilization. Out of the need to escape the past while keeping it available—as well as out of the need to transmute loathing into love—civilization progresses, accumulating its "pyramiding memories," knowledge, competences, its "mountain of statistics" which, in "The New Spirit" as in "These Lacustrine Cities," is finally the Tower of Babel. In a sense—and here Ashbery's own ambivalence becomes acute—this Tower of infinite consciousness is the philosophically desirable totalism. But the price it exacts is terrible, in terms of the attenuation of the individual into the thin film of his multiplied but conditioned perceptions. Against the animated, flying, but disembodied world of "others" in "These Lacustrine Cities" stands not a sensation but "an *idea* of yourself" (italics added).

It may be that this immensely extended but thinned-out mode of selfhood, half-detached from the body, is the real subject of Ashbery's more tenuous later poems.

> You have been living now for a long time and there is nothing
>   you do not know.
> Perhaps something you read in the newspaper influenced you
>   and that was very frequently. . . .
>
> ("Sortes Vergilianae")

Even the exhilaration of spring must be expressed as an act of signification, implying, though overleaping, a permanent gap between perception and the inner grammar of consciousness:

> All things seem mention of themselves
> And the names which stem from them branch out to other re-
>   ferents.
> Hugely, spring exists again.
>
> ("Grand Galop")

Seen from this angle, Ashbery's fondness for statistical jargon and empty everyday expressions seems a good deal more purposeful than before. It is now not simply a matter of metaphors for intellectual uncertainty, but of a literal mass of introjected language, preconceived ways of seeing and ordering, that interposes itself between the mind and reality. That such is Ashbery's intention can be seen from those very odd passages in which a fragment of public language—generally political—suddenly takes over a private argument conducted, elsewhere, in appropriately private terms. Thus, in "Fragment," we encounter the lines "We cannot keep the peace / At home, and at the same time be winning wars abroad," which in context refer to what Freud would have called ego- and object-cathexes, but which otherwise, given the date of the poem, would clearly belong to the debate about American involvement in Vietnam. Later in the same poem, in the phrase "Out of this intolerant swarm of freedom as it / Is called in your press," the implied voice of a foreigner criticizing the hypocrisy of phrases like "the Free World" momentarily takes over Ashbery's own meditation on the trickiness of similar terms in philosophy. The poem "Decoy" at once illustrates the practice and clarifies the analogy between public and private life that lies behind it. Beginning "We hold these truths to be self-evident," the poem proceeds to an exceedingly obscure account of why it is impossible to measure the honesty and success of a modern business through traditional economic analysis, or—and here the entire argument is instantaneously internalized—of a modern life through memory. The analogy—and the relativistic uncertainty—clearly extend to the arts as well; and we can see now that Ashbery's reluctant acceptance of an avant-gardism that treats all representational styles and all sensibilities as "packaged" data is not a purely aesthetic decision, but reflects a need to live with the mass consciousness at its most derealized and overburdened.

All of these themes—philosophical, public, aesthetic—come together in the long poem "Self-Portrait in a Convex Mirror." The "Self-Portrait" is one of those "last poems"—works that carry art a step forward by the act of defining final limits to art—of which we are sometimes told modernism largely consists. To Ashbery's own slightly peevish insistence that, while an "essayistic thrust" makes the poem seem accessible, "if one sat down and analyzed it closely it would seem as disjunct and fragmented as 'Europe,' " the critic must answer yes and no.[10] The poem has some of the meandering, overqualifying prosiness of other later Ashbery (though David Kalstone has argued very well for the purposefulness of the principal meanders); but it also has a rarely cogent and comprehensive symbolic structure, which vindicates the impression that many readers have apparently formed of a central, synthesizing work.[11]

On the first and clearest level, the Parmigianino self-portrait which is the ostensible subject illustrates the difficulties of defining the self as Ashbery has confronted them, at least since "Fragment." The painting's rounded, approaching-retreating surface suggests the inability of the self to move either very far into or away from the surface of life. It demonstrates "That the soul is a captive, treated humanely, kept / In suspension"; or, still more drastically,

> that the soul is not a soul,
> Has no secret, is small, and it fits
> Its hollow perfectly: its room, our moment of attention.
> That is the tune but there are no words.
> The words are only speculation
> (From the Latin *speculum*, mirror)

because, as the etymology already implies,

> We see only postures of the dream,
> Riders of the motion that swings the face
> Into view under evening skies. . . .

In the world of the painting, the surface is all there is, "a visible core," and yet—by virtue of the very elimination of comparison, of layered depths—there are "No words to say what it really is." It is the post-Einsteinian universe curved on itself of which we hear later in the poem, "Refusing to surround us and still the only / Thing we can see." (In keeping with this, the curved surface of the painting also represents the mysterious motion of time, "always cresting into [the] present.") Beneath these general rubrics, the poem subsumes many instances in which the self "crests" by a swerve into otherness—the "light or dark speech" of friends; the "nostalgia of a collective past" that pre-shapes, pre-interprets our experience of beauty; the independent life of an artistic medium.

None of this thematic material is altogether new. What is new is the tone of undisguised sadness with which Ashbery regards it in the light of inevitable death, *sub specie aeternitatis,* and the stately, almost old-fashioned, eloquence that results—a difference Ashbery seems to acknowledge indirectly when he writes that the painting, unlike Parmigianino's usual Mannerist work, retains "The consonance of the High Renaissance" because "The surprise, the tension are in the concept / Rather than its realization."

"In the concept," the painting is well suited to stand in for Ashbery's own art; indeed, it stands as progenitor to the whole tradition of the avant-garde with which Ashbery identifies himself. Like Ashbery's work, it is a psychological realism (Parmigianino "set himself

/ With great art to copy all that he saw in the glass") became "a *bi-zarria*" against its will, in the attempt to see the self reflected off of the largest possible surface of its relations; reflected, indeed, off of "the globe." It embraces randomness in the interests of absolute order, "to perfect and rule out the extraneous / Forever," and so overcome the limitations of sensibility, "The enchantment of self with self." These are, of course, common aspirations of painting since the Surrealists; and the self-portrait has two other qualities which contemporary art criticism is peculiarly prone to identify with artistic honesty, though they often lead to *bizarria*. It completely fuses or identifies surface and depth; and it includes the process of its own creation—the painter's hand—in the finished product. Thus, the self-portrait would appear to be a ne plus ultra of modern, self-conscious objectivity; and yet its actual effect, as Ashbery notes several times, is that of a "silver blur," a "neutral band," a "magma of interiors." The acknowledgment amounts to a self-imposed critique of the effect of Ashbery's own style—his even tones, his all-dissolving totalism. But at the same time, it suggests that the painting still exists—perhaps exists only—as a perpetuation of the autism of dreams, albeit in a negative form, "Like a wave breaking on a rock, giving up / Its shape in a gesture which expresses that shape." (In this connection, one should note that the ethereally beautiful figure in the painting, "rather angel than man," at times seems to represent the ideal self, and ideal beloved, whom Ashbery no longer expects to see emerge in experience. Perhaps that is why the figure's gesture, "neither embrace nor warning," almost duplicates the gesture which, in Rilke's Seventh Elegy, prevents the angel from appearing in the human world.)

Thus, Parmigianino's painting is itself a "last" work; by swerving from the extreme of objectivity back to the extreme of narcissism, it shows the limits of what art can accomplish. It thereby poses the perennial problem of avant-gardism, the problem of artistic exhaustion. For this reason—as well as because of what it reveals about the self—it is a "Life-obstructing task." In an amusing passage, Ashbery threatens the painting with being outmoded by "a new preciosity," only to conclude that the painting may itself imply all possible preciosities; "that it, / Not we, are the change; that we are in fact it."

We are, in fact, it, in a sense that extends far beyond our aesthetic premises. For as the mirror-portrait is to previous art, so modern civilization is to previous civilizations: "New York . . . is a logarithm / Of other cities." It is a logarithm because the exponent has become more important than the number; its literal, life-sustaining functions curve away from themselves in the collective attention to presentation, image. Single activities lose their privacy and a good deal of their solidity; the "mapped space" of the artist's studio turns, as in Parmigianino, to "enactments" (which I take to be a latinizing of "happenings"). "Business is carried on by look, gesture, / Hearsay" in "a society specifically / Organized as a demonstration of itself." (I remember noticing, on returning to America after two years abroad, how many public places, particularly restaurants, had redecorated themselves on a principle of *stating* what they had once simply, atmospherically, been: a Greek restaurant replacing its small sepia photos of the Acropolis with a life-size relief of nymphs and satyrs; a hamburger joint splashing murals of the movies, 1930s vintage, across its high, once smoke-streaked walls. Here I think Ashbery cuts to the core of what is disturbing about American popular culture in the 1970s and 1980s, and suggests one reason why the younger poets discussed in Chapter 5 find it so hard to believe they will learn anything real about themselves from their responses to the outside world.)

Yet Ashbery insists, as always, that "There is no other way," and in the last, most startling metamorphosis of the central image, the mass-mind of New York itself becomes the convex mirror:

> We have seen the city; it is the gibbous
> Mirrored eye of an insect. All things happen
> On its balcony and are resumed within,
> But the action is the cold, syrupy flow
> Of a pageant.

If, in the second sentence, we emphasize "*All* things happen," we have the fabled dangers of life in New York, and the fabled blaséness of its inhabitants; if we emphasize "happen / On its balcony," we have the sense of lack of privacy, of the spectatorial presence looming larger than any conceivable occurrence. In either case, the effect is of saturation leading to derealization, to the illusion that all events are aesthetically intended: "the action is the cold, syrupy flow / Of a pageant." The underlying horror-movie image in these lines hardly needs to be pointed out. But what it suggests of the destructive potential of our childish, benumbed, inexhaustible curiosity is borne out by the earlier description of Parmigianino's hand finishing the portrait, "big enough / To wreck the sphere" (and perhaps even inclined to do so, since within the sphere it is condemned to "weave delicate meshes / That only argue its further detention"). In such passages, "Self-Portrait" comes near to being not only an elegy for the self and for art, but—like "Waking Early Sunday Morning," *Gravity's Rainbow*, "For Now"—one of those putative elegies for the entire human race which make up a disturbing but inevitable part of our more ambitious writing. Yet the poem ends on a note of very muted, minor-key affirmation of the self that obscurely feels it has known a "whole," even if only, like the wave earlier, in a sort of negative space, "cold pockets / Of remembrance, whispers out of time."

Ashbery's more recent work seems to me to have come out onto a wide, high plateau. There is no advance beyond the thematic finalities of "Self-Portrait"; but for the first time, all the stylistic resources of his earlier career seem simultaneously available to the poet. The essayistic tone is much in evidence, and is handled with less, or gentler, self-irony than before:

> *It's sad the way they feel about it—*
> *Poetry—*
> *As though it could synchronize our lives*
> *With our feelings about ourselves,*
> *And form a bridge between them and "life"*
> *As we come to think about it.*

At the other extreme, there are condensed, surrealist eruptions of the ecstatic and the forbidden, of a kind rarely seen since *The Tennis Court Oath*: "flesh / Of ice cream and sting," "A shelf of breasts and underwear packaging / Rumored in the dark ages." Occasionally the essayistic and the eruptive interpenetrate, in a new kind of half-focused image:

> *Nothing here is like the*
> *Wet, hot vigil*
> *That loneliness erected:*
> *There is nothing here that can be seen*
> *The way that city could be seen,*
> *Most precisely at night, perhaps*
> *When thousands of tongues inspect it*
> *And the outline of its state of mind*
> *Tapers off hard and clear*
> *Until the next time.*
> *The noises in the bedroom dissolve slowly*

Almost everything here can be read as sexual innuendo, and, concurrently, as a meditation on those metaphorically phallic monuments of desire and "loneliness," the "city" and the poetic "state of mind." The dexterity with which this interpenetration is carried out could not have been managed by the earlier Ashbery, at least not without a heavy accompanying machinery of totalistic rhetoric. And one feels that something important has been added to Ashbery's vision of the seamless unity of the mind—the sexuality of abstract thought, the metaphysical complexity of sexuality. But beyond that, the implicit themes and the thematic tone of the passage are altogether familiar ones: skepticism, unfulfillable desire, mass consciousness, the pluralism that resists any pull toward singleness of vision. How, one wonders, could such themes ever change?

And so Ashbery's recent work leaves one with a curiously mixed impression of growth and stagnation. As often before, much of the best of it is concentrated in a long poem; and all of my quotations have been taken from "Litany." The peculiar premise of the poem, which has so worried and exasperated reviewers—two "simultaneous but independent monologues" set in parallel columns on the page—has two breathtakingly simple virtues where Ashbery's style is concerned. It keeps the lines short, and so exerts a pressure toward simplicity; and it spares either voice the burden of containing all of the poet's ambivalence. The lyric feeling can become stronger on its own before—actually while—it clashes with an opposing feeling. Thus, at the end of Part I, the second voice is allowed to drift off into a lush, very folksy, very American nostalgia for the old days:

> *Sometimes*
> *We would all sing together*
> *And at night people would take leave of each other*
> *And go into their houses, singing.*
> *It was a time of rain and Hawaii*
> *And tears big as crystals. A time*
> *Of reading and listening to the wireless.*

The other voice, meanwhile, has been asking grimly, "But what difference did any of it make / Woven on death's loom [?]" With the approach of death comes the now familiar realization (ironically reinforced by the very fact of the opposing voice's recovery) that there will be no dramatic resolution, no conclusive knowledge:

>   You knew
>   You were coming to the end by the way the other
>   Would be beginning again, so that nobody
>   Was ever lonesome, and the story never
>   Came to its dramatic conclusion, but
>   Merely leveled out like linen close up
>   In the mirror.

At the end, this voice turns away, in utter weariness, from the possibilities of companionship, perception, and even thought—

>   And no one longed for the great generalities
>   These seemed to preclude. Each thought only
>   Of his private silence, and hungered
>   For the promised moment of rest.

—just as the second voice, in a stunning dissonance, reaches its climax of heartfelt illusion: *"We never should have parted, you and me."* (The *"you and me,"* one can't help feeling, are the two voices themselves, emotion and reflection, the pleasure principle and the reality principle, as much as they are any actual pair of lovers.) One wishes that the aesthetic purpose of *Litany*'s "simultaneous but independent monologues" were always as clear as this; but when it is, the two voices together become as haunting, sad, and authoritative as the single voice of "Self-Portrait."

I have always enjoyed Randall Jarrell's habit of ending his essays—especially when his judgment was mixed—with a private anthology. I hope the reader will not mind my aping this practice. The underlying judgment would be more or less as follows. Ashbery is an uneven poet, whose repetitiveness and tendency to disperse energy, even more than his difficulty, place a heavy burden on his readers. He is fascinating—if not indeed indispensable—as a tragic epistemologist, in whose work the demystifying intelligence of the twentieth-century avant-gardes enters into a dialectic with the highest claims, emotional and aesthetic, of Romanticism and Symbolism. But he touches greatness by his extraordinary command of montage, rhythmic progression, and the half-focused image, through which he renders visible in-between spaces, uncertainty principles, in consciousness. The greatness, I think, is to be found chiefly in "Self-Portrait in a Convex Mirror" and in the best passages of "The Skaters," "Fragment," and "Litany"; and then, perhaps, in "A Last World" (especially the fourth stanza), "Our Youth," "These Lacustrine Cities," "Civilization and Its Discontents," "Summer," "Evening in the Country," and "As One Put Drunk into the Packet Boat." A little lower and to one side, as it were, one might place certain unusually clear, or unusually elegant, poems, which both refresh and (very slightly) disappoint one by the absence of the usual Ashbery desire to "put it all down": "Some Trees," " 'They Dream Only of America,' " "If the Birds Knew," "Song," "Definition of Blue," "Forties Flick," "Syringa." And as a balancing group, neither lower nor higher, certain versions of the Ashbery Poem that single themselves out by the eloquence with which they state their case, or by brilliant inset passages: " 'How Much Longer Will I Be Able to Inhabit the Divine Sepulchre,' " "Soonest Mended," "Parergon," much of "The New Spirit" and "The System," "Scheherazade," "Pyrography," "Daffy Duck in Hollywood," "Houseboat Days." The list could be much, much longer if one went simply by brilliant lines or an appealing quality of voice; but perhaps it defines a view of Ashbery more clearly if left brief.

7

THE FUTURE OF PERSONAL POETRY

It would be surprising if the sense of the impossibility of knowing the self, or of the elusiveness of what is "deep" and valuable in it, that preoccupies the range of poets from Ashbery to Strand to Wright had not affected the writing of explicitly autobiographical poetry in America. Moreover, the very success of "confessional" modes posed a threat to younger personal poets, since the idea of authenticity—as we saw in Chapter 2—virtually demanded a reinvention of the tactics of autobiography to correspond to what was unique in the self under examination. In the early 1970s, there was a sense of diminishing returns. As more and more young confessors began their sentences and stanzas in the same way, combining a blurting factual candor with an uneasy complacency at assuming the rhetorical mantle of Lowell, Plath, or Berryman, what had begun as a method of investigating sensibilities became, itself, a sensibility. And there was a revulsion of taste against the whole enterprise, ushering in not only the surrealist impersonality discussed in Chapter 5 but a counterbalancing formalist one.

Nevertheless, it seems to me that some of the most distinguished work being done by poets in their thirties and forties continues to be autobiographical. This chapter is devoted both to substantiating that claim and to exploring how current ways of handling personal material differ from those prevalent in the heyday of confessional poetry.

The typical confessional poem (if I may now be taxonomic, as I preferred not to be when discussing the detailed merits of such poems) is a kind of true dramatic monologue. It leads the speaker through a gamut of emotional responses to something in the world—a person, a situation, very often a specific moment—until the reflexive net of the self's possibilities of response is drawn tight; or, to put it more simply, a character is created. This paradigm fits both the *Life Studies* poems and the more experimental *Dolphin* sonnets; many, if not most, of the *Dream Songs;* and (if one allows the monologue somewhat fantastic premises) "Daddy" and "Lady Lazarus" as well as, more obviously, "The Night Dances" or "The Bee Meeting."

For later poets, I think it was easy to feel not only that this convention was artificial and confining (as all conventions eventually become), but that it assumed too easy a presentational mastery over the mysteries of the self. More recent poetry has tended to take a more petitionary attitude toward those mysteries, going deeper or else going shallower. Going deeper, one finds a poetry that has absorbed many of the ideals of the middle generation, emphasizing dream-like images, symbols of identity at once more central and more enigmatic than the flux of daily feeling. Going shallower, one finds a poetry that confines itself to the drama, the bafflement, the abstraction of a person explaining himself to others, risking the prosaic and even the banal in a new version of the perennial Wordsworthian return to actual speech. In this poetry one finds a reaction against the cult of the image, a defense of the "discursive" (as it is called in Robert Pinsky's *The Situation of Poetry,* in many ways the manifesto of this current of taste) which might have troubled even the poets of Lowell's generation, committed as they were to Eliot's ideal of unified sensibility, and with it to a fairly continuous presence of sense impressions in poetry.

But the most important distinction to be made is the relative humility of both modes toward the self, in comparison with the typical confessional mode. The first mode, by restricting itself to a kind of dream narration, concedes or pretends to concede that the inner language is not reducible to paraphrase past a certain point. At the other extreme, the plain style poet, by insisting on the need for paraphrase, for explanation, implicitly sides with the puzzlement of others—even admits that the conscious self shares in that puzzlement—thus abandoning the Rimbaldian project of finding an equivalent for the narcissistic taste, or atmosphere, of his own psyche.

The composite portraits I have just given are, of course, fictions, fitting no single poet perfectly and no two poets in exactly the same ways. Nevertheless, the poets treated in the opening and closing sections of this chapter have in common, at a minimum, a traditional lyric beauty which the confessional poets (except, occasionally, for Plath) neither achieved nor particularly desired; while the poets treated in between are all in one way or another explainers, exploring the borders—both in terms of subject matter and of style—between prose and poetry which remain controversial, even into the 1980s.

I

In Chapter 5 we saw how certain poets of the "deep image" group, notably Strand and Orr, have occasionally been able to use their method to write a very good and very original kind of personal poem. Louise Glück is perhaps the most splendid, certainly the best known, of the poets who have crossed the same divide from the other direction. Glück's first volume, *Firstborn*, though widely acclaimed, illustrates the good reasons a young confessional poet at the end of the 1960s might have had for feeling an acute "anxiety of influence." It is heavily dependent on Lowell: on his tense iambics and emphatic rhymes; his apostrophes and choked sentence fragments ("O innocence, your bathinet / Is clogged with gossip"); and on his imagery, sometimes with embarrassing closeness ("Their bed / Stood, spotless as a tub"—compare with "During Fever"). Beyond this, there is Lowell's clever, obtrusive use of proper nouns, with its frequent undersong of corrosive skepticism about all timely (and earthly) involvements:

> In every room, encircled by a name
> less Southern boy from Yale,
> There was my younger sister singing a Fellini theme. . . .

Other characteristics of *Firstborn* belong more generally to the group sensibility that confessional poetry was becoming: the numinous sterility of the landscapes; the use of foraging animals to symbolize human, and particularly sexual, needs; the inverse narcissism of bodily grossness. Even the typical New England seacoast setting, though beautifully done ("breakers . . . foam through bracelets / Of seabirds"; "the drained sun / Sinks through insects coalesced / To mist") comes to seem a convention. How often, and how memorably, all of the confessional poets have used it, even Berryman in *Homage to Mistress Bradstreet*—as if the contrast of long winters and fiery thin-leafed summers, the meagreness of tourist towns and scrub pine against the overpowering oceanic presence, said all that needed to be said about the peculiar confessional vision of love and death.

Glück does make valiant and sometimes successful efforts to individuate her style in *Firstborn*. By such experiments, for instance, as subjectless sentences, or a series of iambic lines systematically a foot or a syllable too short, then too long—as in the first quotation above—she creates a new tension, more brittle than Lowell's, more unreasonable than irrational, but by that very brittleness more her own. Still, one's dominant impression is of a very talented young poet swamped by a period style too congenial to her own—perfectly real, perfectly sincere—themes.

Turning from *Firstborn* to Glück's second and third books, *The House on Marshland* and *Descending Figure*, one is almost overpowered by how drastically either personal change or the need for literary independence has remade her style. The short-line free verse seems designed to exorcise anything reminiscent of Lowell's grim definitiveness, though one still feels, as in the following passage, the instinctively formal poet's tendency to make an architecture, a procession, of seeing:

> It is all here,
> luminous water, the imprinted sapling
> matched, branch by branch,
> to the lengthened
> tree in the lens. . . .

While an a priori pessimism still controls (sometimes overcontrols) many poems, a tone of brooding melancholy, occasionally almost Victorian ("root, rock, and all things perishing") has replaced the corrosive, accusatory tones—so full of contempt for the self and for others—that dominate in *Firstborn*. The poems now concern themselves with feelings almost to the exclusion of causes or attendant circumstances; and the Lowellian definition of family relations by realistic detail disappears in favor of fables or nature epiphanies.

The paradigmatic instance of the very suggestive and original kind of autobiographical poem that can result is the peculiar variation on "Sleeping Beauty" called "For My Mother." In it, the poet imagines herself as existing within her mother's body as a full-grown parthenogenetic embryo, until her father arrives when she is thirty.

> Screened
> through the green glass
> of your eye, moonlight
> filtered into my bones
> as we lay
> in the big bed, in the dark,
> waiting for my father.
> Thirty years. He closed
> your eyelids with
> two kisses.

The meaning of this parable is, and remains, elusive. The repeated specification of thirty as the age at which "spring" and birth occur, at which male otherness and sexuality become real to the poet, lead me to suspect that it is the age of her own motherhood. This reading goes outside of the poem, but it accords with a common psychological insight: that only parenthood makes one's own existence seem as real, as prior, as one's parents'. Other details, however, suggest that the real issue is the changing psychological identifications and understanding that come with age. The imagery of screens, filters, shades attached to the mother's consciousness acquires, as it accumulates, more and more of its normal and unfavorable connotations. There is a world of ambiguous sexual war and tenderness in the "two kisses," recalling as they do both "La Belle Dame Sans Merci"—as Helen Vendler has pointed out—and coins on the eyes of the dead.[1] And yet the most important function of this detail is to prepare for the idea that being born is a loss of vision, of "absolute knowledge," in which what was previously sufficing and central becomes accidental and extrinsic—the mother left outside on "the brick stoop," "shading" her eyes against a universe that has become mere neutral extension, mapped by "the small tin markers of the stars." Thus, on a third level, the poem seems to concern itself with pure epistemology: with poetic and anti-poetic worlds, with the in-fantile element in the desire for coherence, in the architectures of intense sensibility. Here, an immense suggestiveness, extending to many levels of psychic experience, is the poem's reward for not con-fining its sense of persons and relations to what can be realistically pinned down.

A great deal of Glück's recent work is purely lyrical, with no overt autobiographical element, so that some readers might question my grouping her among personal poets at all. I would argue, however, that a subtle tissue of implicit psychological preoccupations links the impersonal poems to the personal ones, and helps give the imper-sonal ones a delicate complexity of feeling we have missed in some of the ontological lyrics that try to leave the specific self too com-pletely behind. Reading the lovely poem "Messengers" alongside "For My Mother," one finds the same concern with birth, separation, and feminine identity informing the same kind of subtle meditation on the workings of the imagination. The poem uses the attributes of Artemis—moon and huntress—to define elements of extreme sepa-ration, chastity, and violence in the artistic mission. To receive the world as if it were a message implies a distance from it like no other. The very attributes that make Artemis' deer resemble poetic intui-tions (their delicacy of movement, the need for the observer to re-main absolutely still) suggest to this poet what Helen Vendler has called an "almost posthumous" quality.[2] They move "as though their bodies did not impede them"; they seem to wait for a liberation ("until their cages rust") which is at least winter, if not death. The "release" of art is at the same time a terrible injury, both to the artist and to the subject; and the imagery suggests a birth trauma, albeit in scientific disguise:

> that cry—*release, release*—like the moon
> wrenched out of earth and rising
> full in its circle of arrows
>
> until they come before you
> like dead things, saddled with flesh,
> and you above them, wounded and dominant.

(My students tell me that this account of the origin of the moon is no longer good science; but in Louise Glück's, and my, schooldays, it was.) The paradoxes of these lines are a key to the poem's deepest

tensions and vitality. The "fullness" of the moon inheres in its re-
pellence of everything, its "circle of arrows." The animals, while
they are alive, are domestic, "saddled," out of the hunter goddess's
realm. Yet the "wounds" are transferred from them to her—her very
need to stand "above" a radical testimony of incompleteness, of the
mutual injury of separation, and of yearning, inherent both in the
relations of mother and child, and of artist and subject.

Hart Crane called for an "absolute poetry" that would crystallize a
"state of consciousness" by the internal integration of its elements,
without recourse to paraphrasable "precepts" or—one might extrapolate—to explanatory narration.[3] In Chapter 5 I dwelt on what I
think is the error of believing that absolute poems are made by refusing the solicitations of the particular, by dwelling explicitly on the
idea that the "state of consciousness" is beyond embodiment and
beyond language. Although it is not a great poem, "Messengers"
does show how absolute poems—poems that interpret themselves
only by the internal coherence of the images—are sometimes made
successfully. In this case, it is by a delicate attention to the suggestive
undertones of words; a willingness to make intelligent use of the
past, literary or mythic; and, above all perhaps, a sensitivity to the
ramifications of a feeling in the psyche that differs more in form than
in substance from that encountered in confessional poetry—as the
intertwining themes of "Messengers" and "For My Mother" make
clear. Glück raises the odd possibility that personal poetry can in
some sense come to the rescue of absolute poetry.

A no less distinguished, though less well known, meeting point
between the "deep" or mythic image and autobiography is to be
found in the work of the Southern poet Richard Tillinghast, whose
first book, *Sleep Watch*, appeared in the Wesleyan Series in 1969.
"Southern" deserves signaling, because, though many influences
have supervened (Robert Lowell; W. S. Merwin; popular music of
the 1960s; the mystical and revolutionary West Coast Countercul-
ture), Tillinghast surely owes much of his unfashionable Romantic
wistfulness, as well as his carefulness, to early immersion in the Fugitive tradition. Indeed, what most sets him apart from contemporary "surrealism" is the yearned-for, exotic lavishness of the inner
world invoked—a Baudelairean *paradis artificiel* where sensuous and
aesthetic harmonies adumbrate, without quite encompassing, religious ones.

Yet Tillinghast does not simply plunge, luxuriating, into this paradise; there is a tension, an occasion for wit, and a distinct element of

danger in the passage between it and our common world, as the echo of the phrase "death watch" in Tillinghast's title makes plain. The peculiar quality of his mediations can be seen in a seemingly slight poem called "On the Night Ferry." The poem begins with a kind of throw-away wit, an almost New York School randomness, not un-characteristic of Tillinghast's this-worldly voice:

> too fidgety to include
> Jane Austen,
> too fatigued and changing
> to write these letters
> my handwriting veers around the upright.
> I put the cap back onto the pen
> the way a court reunites a
> mother and child.

But as we soon realize, this is randomness informed by the Freudian premise that the more truly random one becomes, the more quickly one will get to what is unpleasantly, even intolerably, central. The exclusion of Jane Austen, a writer entirely, if somewhat rationalisti-cally, preoccupied with tension-ridden relations between men and women; the pen which ceases its less than "upright" recording as a court ends the wars of divorce—one does not need the context suc-ceeding poems eloquently supply to see that the speaker is in deep unhappiness and indecision about his domestic life. His wish to limit his own awareness is given a very peculiar, very characteristic for-mulation two stanzas later:

> We are best
> seen in terms of our cars
> facing forward   the children in back
> limited by the glass, locked in by the doors.

Our lives are "best" and "best / seen" going forward automatically, without the exertion of our wills—as our parents' lives no doubt seemed to do when we were "the children in back." Yet it is this wry, poignantly tidy picture of the "cars . . . in the hold" that drops the poet into deep reverie, into a visionary image of a life at once pro-tected and immensely articulated, clarified:

> the springs and shock-absorbers
> shift in their clear grease

with intense precision.
Those well cared-for move in silence
in a still place under the heart of the ship
as she rolls in the arms of her winter lover.

That is to say, the surface regressive wish shadows forth the primordial image, or memory, of a prenatal paradise. We remember that,
from the start, the poet's imagination is drawn to the situation of
"mother and child" rather than to that of husband and wife; and the
final image delineates very delicately what he sees and fears in the
avoided role. To admit the full range of masculine feelings is become
unbounded, like the sea outside, and, what is more, a "winter
lover"—a figure like Hart Crane's "winter king," violent to himself
and to others in his self-division.

"On the Night Ferry" is not Tillinghast's most ambitious poem,
but it shows very clearly what distinguishes his marriage poems—
which make up a considerable portion of *Sleep Watch*—from those
earnestly but drably decent, "other-directed" ones so common in the
1960s. The difference lies mainly in Tillinghast's acknowledgment,
witty and sardonic ("Our life, all the grace of a record-changer") yet
stubbornly respectful ("All I wanted / was music that could care for
me"), of the near-solipsistic dimension of nostalgia that feeds and
yet undermines our specific relationships. Indeed, there is a whole
side of *Sleep Watch* that is not autobiographical at all, though Freudian enough (or Ferenczian: Tillinghast is an ultimately thalassic
poet, for whom the birth trauma and the Nirvana instinct sometimes
seem to be the only important psychic realities). Here, nostalgia—
and the states of desolation and fear that so often shadow it—are
dealt with not in terms of the situations that release them but as permanent and irreducible categories of inner experience. These categories emerge in their pure form in the "sleep watch" states (dozing,
insomnia, psychedelic hallucination, and—in an odd way—travel),
in which the external world remains available but is interpenetrated,
brought to life, by the world of the imagination and the unconscious.
Thus, "Passage" reworks some of the material of "On the Night
Ferry"—as Glück's "Messengers" reworks the themes of "For My
Mother"—in more dislocated, more purely archetypal, terms. The
poem begins by envisioning the quotidian world as a claustrophobic
limitation of inlets and outlets:

In the house with telephones,
no one can see beyond the windows

> where taxis cruise,
> their headlights mooning on our ceiling
> like aquarium lights.

But within this world, the poet senses a secret life (the automobile engine "cutting down" until it is "all vibration"), which one might descend into, as into an underground tunnel. This fantasy, however, proves less than adequate to the expected revelation, and for a moment the desire itself becomes frightening, a drowning in inexhaustible nostalgias:

> When our cat was gone,
> I heard her drowned voice everywhere
> crying down the gently sloshing paths of stone.

But at that very moment, the terms of consciousness go through a kind of Blakean vortex; downward becomes upward, the tunnel becomes the sea.

> Miles above is the real
> sea   and a happiness we never know—
> the happiness of ants on white paper,
> the mind pliant
> like blank film lying in solution.

The mind realizes its own secret life—as in Buddhist meditation—when it can entertain the shapes of all objects, without being constrained by, identified with, any. Even as it is being excluded, this oceanic happiness seems to arrive, in a reverie of an Aegean cruise—"a brightness coming off the air."

Tillinghast's vision and his poetic technique are remarkably congruent. The sharpness of detail is counterweighted by a drifting syntax—detached phrases, floating line-breaks—learned from Dickey and Merwin; so that the images become epiphanic moments, vivid but dreamlike, irretrievable. One of the special graces of Tillinghast's poems is their way of veering off at the end, as though into space, the velocity itself part of the meaning. "In the Country You Breathe Right" sinks for several stanzas into rural sensations, lovely, but increasingly still and thalassic—

> a calf drinking milk that sloshes through a sieve
> a cat running down a well
> ferns growing through a roof

—before a specific "I" appears and instantly vanishes, with the poem, saying eerily:

> My hands are so cold
> I hope you can read this.

It is not for nothing that Tillinghast's emblems are the cat and the wave.

There are times, though, when technique and temperamental wistfulness betray Tillinghast into a Shelleyan nebulousness, an Emmeline Grangerford melancholy, which must be positively poisonous for some readers:

> You are becoming all the women I ever love
> We hear the rain   float to the far edge of sleep
> The years come to my door
> and knock and walk away sighing

At such moments one realizes how much Tillinghast needed the stress on irony and particularity he found in one side of the Fugitive tradition, and in Lowell.

Still, in spite—and partly because—of the Romantic risks he takes, Tillinghast stands with Glück among the few younger poets who have given a new lease on life to the mode of self-sufficient, drifting visual imagery, by grounding it more richly in language, in the quirks of a particular sensibility, and not least in our experience of a real outside world. His work since *Sleep Watch* is also excellent. As I have said elsewhere, it seems to me the best—if not the only— poetry to give a distanced but still sympathetic account of the experience of being radicalized in the 1960s, and then not so much disillusioned as worn down, exhausted.[4] But the very public character of this work makes it less relevant to our concerns; for that reason I shall not discuss it here.

II

Before turning from the poetry of inner imagery to the poetry of explanation, I should like to pause over a poet who has, at different periods, fitted both categories, but whose particular distinction is inventiveness of structure, a new variation on what I have called the reflexive mode. Diane Wakoski has been one of the sadder casualties of the shift in taste in the last decade; she is so fixed in many

readers' minds as an artless instance of heart-on-the-sleeve confes-
sionalism that a serious, discriminating discussion of her work from
the formal point of view is almost impossible to find. Wakoski has
partly invited this reputation, by overproduction, self-repetition, and
a peculiarly unfortunate habit of arguing with her critics in her own
poems. Still, I don't think the reputation will survive even a cursory
reading of her early poems, or a careful reading of the best of her
later ones.

All of Wakoski's best poems do essentially the same thing: they
use a governing image or group of images to look at the same situation from a number of perspectives, rather as a cubist painting (to
use one of Wakoski's favorite points of comparison) might look at a
chair from three sides at once. The images tend, especially in the
early poems, to be splendid, scary, even over-romantic (gold scor-
pions, green horses, a girl joining hands with the wind). One feels
that the legacy of Spanish surrealism came almost too ready to hand
to a lonely young woman already inclined to prefer fantasy to reality. And yet the design of the poems works to correct this, from the
very beginning. The cumulative effect of the repetition of images is
claustrophobia, not escape. "There are so many ways / of telling the
story," a very inventive poem concludes: but the feeling—in context—is clearly one of gloom and entrapment. The poems insistently
speak of emotions as static things, "structures": "The structure of
anger / is repetition"; "the structure of dream, / like a har-
ness / lowered over my head." The macabre ending of the early
poem "Tour"—

> I hope you will not be alarmed to learn
> that you may not leave this place again;
> because you have seen the black fox
> mate the white,
> and to satisfy your curiosity
> let me say,
> both animals are now
> dead

—is paradigmatic both in its dry crispness, and in its sense of what it
means to close a symbolic circuit, to purify and mate the mind's internal opposites. And one remembers that Wakoski's other early
love, besides Lorca, was Stevens—the Stevens of *Harmonium*, whose
rather chilly factorings of aesthetic impressions (think of "Domina-
tion of Black") convey the same sense of the mind's inability to

escape from itself, in epistemological terms, that Wakoski's poems do in emotional terms.[5]

Given these preoccupations, Wakoski would be a born writer of rather tight formal poems, and one can't help being ambivalent about the early identification with the idea of the avant-garde that steered her in other directions. A sestina, for instance, seems the perfect vehicle for her sense of proliferation and sameness, the mind trapped by its images; and when she in fact writes one, "Sestina from the Home Gardener," it is at once one of her best poems and a strong contender for the best contemporary example of the form.

The choice of end-words tends to be the *pons asinorum* of sestina-writers. If the words are too emotionally laden, too wide in their applications, the poem gets easy and dull. If they are too narrow, it becomes gimmicky. Wakoski chooses with discrimination. Three of her words, "sections," "precise," and "pointed," are narrow enough to be a challenge, yet resonant: they can suggest the pleasant crispness of work with tools; they can also turn into images of self-division, dismemberment, aggression. ("Pointed" also carries a phallic suggestion, and a suggestion of direction or distance.) The other words run an ascending scale from the ambiguously mechanical to the unequivocally emotional: "removed," "unfamiliar," "losses."

The title suggests the poem's rather wistful, charming premise: a woman turns to fixing up house and garden (or a woman artist to art) to fill the empty time, and the emotional emptiness, after a marriage ends. But the tasks quickly become a language for her emotions and bodily sensations. There is a touch, here, of Plath's sense of being victimized to the point of being turned into a thing by one's relations to others; but with a difference:

> These dried-out paint brushes which fell from my lips have
>   been removed
> with your departure; they are such minute losses
> compared with the light bulb gone from my brain, the sections
> of chicken wire from my liver, the precise
> silver hammers in my ankles which delicately banged and
>   pointed
> magnetically to you. Love has become unfamiliar

We feel at once how much more various in tone, and gently witty, Wakoski's images are than Plath's: from the gritty feel of the inner scratchiness, raggedness of lust (associated with the liver in Elizabethan physiology), to the wonderful image for a delicate, sexually self-aware woman walking. Wakoski's poems from this early period are full of similarly arresting, original uses of mechanistic imagery to convey the helpless indwelling force of erotic feeling: "Blue of the heaps of beads poured into her breasts," or the "delicate / displacement of / love" that "has / pulled all my muscles / diagonal." These images surely enhance, at least as much as they diminish, the humanity and femininity of the speaker. Yet they have disturbing implications, which grow stronger as the sestina advances: that emotions, like tools, have an existence separate from the will and consciousness; that, like objects, they can be "removed"; that the poem's sense of the self is a fragmented one, allowing the possibility of integration through love, but not of self-integration.

The poem proves this, in a sense, by exploring all the avenues of autonomous integration. For a while, art seems stronger, more powerful, in the absence of the lover ("each day my paint brushes get softer and cleaner—better tools, and losses / cease to mean loss"). Yet there is an uneasy awareness that parts of the self are becoming "unfamiliar," and so given over to nightmare or paranoiac projection: "the unfamiliar / corridors of my heart with strangers running in them, shouting"; the "sections / of my brain growing teeth" while "unfamiliar / hands tie strings through my eyes." The mind sinks, wittily and honestly, from art to money as a source both of power and of connection:

> and I explain autobiographically that George Washington is
>   sympathetic to my losses;
> His face or name is everywhere. No one is unfamiliar
> with the American dollar, and since you've been removed
> from my life I can think of nothing else. A precise
>
> replacement for love can't be found. But art and money are
>   precise
> ly for distraction. The stars popping out of my blood are
>   pointed
> nowhere.

Not the least graceful aspect of the poem is the way in which this rather outrageously relaxed conversational voice—which points up the speaker's search for autonomy, and not incidentally breaks up the potentially drab unity of the form—plays off against the entrapping returns of surrealistic imagery. At last the speaker bursts out:

> But there are losses

> Of the spirit like vanished bicycle tires and losses
> of the body, like the whole bike, every precise
> bearing, spoke, gear, even the unfamiliar
> handbrakes vanished.

Only through the body does the self cease to be fragmented; and "the real body has been removed."

> Removed by the ice tongs. If a puddle remains what losses
> can those sections of glacier be? Perhaps a precise
> count of drops will substitute the pointed mountain, far
>   away, unfamiliar?

The concluding metaphor drives home the terrible central insight: how the emotional equipment of the self in isolation is precisely the same as, yet utterly different from, that of the self integrated in the body, through love; and how nothing can be done about it. But the "precise count of drops" is also, of course, the sestina form itself—its exhaustive monotony, the sum of parts that will never be a whole.

This poem is a perfect instance of the reflexive mode, in its tightly drawn net of images, its unity-in-diversity, and above all in the way in which the self is driven, fighting all the way, to a recognition of the limits of its mastery over itself. Other poems may use the method with a more "cubist" clash of contradictory perspectives; they may also lead it toward a happy ending, but with the same sense of the mind's confusions and misdirections. Consider, for instance, the lighter and happier "Rescue Poem." It is another poem about tools: "the tools to chop down an invisible telephone booth." The telephone booth is, fairly clearly, the solipsistic sensibility, the "shadow foot between the real foot and the ground." The "tools" are the body made vivid to itself, in the metaphorical extensions of sexuality ("diamond breasts and a silver penis"), in an almost frightening imagery of perception as incorporation ("an apple inside the ear"), and in a vision of passive desires become active faculties ("teeth chipped out of the navel," a "saw made of all the soft parts of / a cheek"). But if the images can proliferate endlessly, the event is single, simple, and unexpected: "Need I say the obvious? / That you found the door?" And yet, the sealed consciousness is not, finally, left behind; rather, it becomes one with the resurrected body—in what is at once a sexual image and an image of the brain's electrical intricacy—as the poet says

Join me
on the silver
wirey
inside.

It is a charming, rather Zen-like strategy: two incompatible endings which are in reality the same ending. And again it enforces a
sense of the mind's limitations, its tendency to look in the wrong or
the half-right place, its need of the body, and of others, for its fulfillment.

Some readers, I suspect, will recognize the merit of these early
poems but still feel that the discursive turn Wakoski has taken in the
last ten years has been an unmitigated disaster, given her lack of critical distance on feelings of self-pity and defensive anger—so obviously unpromising in a poet of wisdom. Four-fifths of the time,
perhaps, these readers would be right. Yet Wakoski continues to insist that she is just as much interested in questions of form in these
later poems as in her early ones. And every once in a while a poem
comes along that is so ingenious in its structural play with its bare
and prosaic terms, that it triumphantly vindicates her.

One such poem is "The Story of Richard Maxfield" in *Virtuoso Literature for Two and Four Hands.* The poem deals with the suicide of a
homosexual electronic composer, who once made a composition out
of tapes of people coughing at concerts, called "Cough Music." More
centrally, the poem is a meditation on the mystery of psychic
strength: why it is available to some people and not to others of
equal intelligence and talent. From the beginning, Maxfield's death is
at once an enigma and a banality:

He jumped out of a window.
Or did he shoot himself?
Was there a gun,
or was it pills?
Did anyone see blood?

Banality continues to be the poem's chosen method. It drives home
our ignorance concerning psychic strength by its merciless, deliberate overuse of two conventional question-begging expressions: a
person who has such strength is "well organized"; one who loses it
"falls apart."

He was brilliant and well organized.
And then he fell apart.
He was homosexual and took drugs.
He was brilliant and well organized.
I loved "Cough Music" and could not see how such a fine
composer could fall apart as Richard fell apart.

But as the words are rubbed clean of what little explanatory value
they ever had, the concepts are subtly, unexplicitly given new metaphorical bodies: music for organization—

a piano piece by
Debussy, delicate and sparse,
like a dress you can see through

—and the sensation of coughing for falling apart. And so Maxfield's
own subject becomes a way of refiguring and elucidating his fate.
The question, why do people cough more during a piece like the
Debussy, suggests rich if unexhaustive answers to the question, why
do people fall apart? Is it a wish to draw attention to oneself; a wish,
on the contrary, "just to join the whole crowd"; or a kind of panic in
the face of the sexual and existential nakedness of the clarified life?
And the poet, restraining herself from coughing during the Debussy
though she feels the mysterious temptation to do so, arrives at a
small illustration and assurance of why "I would never fall apart."
There is a kind of structural genius in this poem, deliberately choos-
ing the most unpromising materials in order to redeem from within
our commonplace, confused ways of "telling our troubles." Most of
Wakoski's more controlled later poems aim at something like this,
though only a few succeed so completely ("Searching for the Canto
Fermo" is one that comes to mind). But at this level of accomplishment in extending the range of poetry, a few are enough; they de-
serve the envy of many writers who have gotten into the habit of
dismissing Wakoski without reading her.

III

It is no great leap from "The Story of Richard Maxfield" to a kind
of poetry of explanation that (while it would be placed far from
Wakoski in most maps of literary movements or fashions) is
equally challenging to conventional notions about prose and po-

etry. I am thinking of Frank Bidart, James McMichael, and Robert Pinsky—poets who, different as they are, have in common a distrust of merely decorative imagery and description, and an essayistic latitude of voice, which reaches to the scholarly and argumentative as well as to the matter-of-fact and quotidian. All of them are inclined to feel that explicit intellectual inquiry is an undervalued resource of poetry; that the pendulum has swung so far in the direction of rendering, or at least of imagery, that the strengths of speech and prose—what Pinsky, in his book *The Situation of Poetry*, calls "the discursive aspects of poetry"—are now more likely to convey the real freshness and urgency of a life.

Frank Bidart is the most extreme of these poets—the cruelest test for those raised on traditional notions of literary beauty. He is a stylistic ascetic, who manages whenever possible to avoid the senses, description, and even metaphor. He also, as Pinsky has remarked, shocks us because he uses the speech truly natural to himself and his typical audience—fellow intellectuals—rather than an earthier "common speech" which, whatever its virtues, must have for this audience a pastoral and escapist element:[6]

> I've been reading Jung, and he says that we can
> never get to the bottom
> of what is, or was . . .
>
> But *why* things were as they were
> obsesses; I know that you
> the necessity to contend with you
> your *helplessness*
> before yourself,
>   —has been at the center
> of how I think my life . . .

The poetry of speech here goes beyond matters of vocabulary, of course. There are the subtly registered tempi: the hurtling rush into utterance in the long first line, followed by a slowing-down for emphasis, for pondering. The way the speaker neglects to say "obsesses *me*"; lets grammar go—but not the poetic grammar of parallelism— as he becomes entangled in the contradictions of his situation (he is addressing his dead father); then draws breath, with a mid-line break and a superfluous dash, to reassert a kind of mastery in the unidiomatic "think my life"—all these details catch and intensify what is most expressive, most existentially engaged, if you will, about explanatory speech. Elsewhere in his work, Bidart's ways of underscoring this expressiveness become positively baroque: profuse punctuation, multiple margins, hieroglyphic stanza-shapes. But he also makes good use of more traditional tactics such as buried rhyme: witness the repeated *s* in the middle lines quoted above; witness also the passage in "Another Life" about "older wisdom" (Charles De Gaulle's, amazingly enough)—

<blockquote>
without
illusions, without force, the austere source
of nihilism, corrupted only by its dream of Glory
</blockquote>

—where the dying fall of "Glory" does, in fact, "corrupt" a solidity the rhyme has given "force" and "source" in spite of their subverted meaning. Bidart's skill in dramatizing the immediacy of the speaking voice sometimes reminds one of the great masters of the conversational mode, Frost and Jarrell; but his poems, unlike theirs, must often carry on voice alone—on voice, and on the naked importance of what is said.

Bidart's first book, *Golden State*, begins with a harrowing tour de force—the confession of "Herbert White," a child-murderer and necrophiliac. But what is most harrowing about Herbert White, as Richard Howard suggests in his introductory note, is his similarity to the Frank Bidart we come to know in the book.[7] Beyond the common anger at parental neglect and sexual cheapness, there is the desire "to *feel* things make sense," to complete a pattern, to make the world "somehow, come alive," that White experiences, horribly but convincingly, in his crimes. "When I hit her on the head, it was good," White's voice opens the book; five pages later, Bidart asks in a "Self-Portrait," "What *reaches* him except disaster?" Another of White's traits that will haunt Bidart in his technique of fragmenting himself, to protect his essence from his actions: "somebody else did it . . ." The terrible effects of the inability to confront oneself whole dominate the central autobiographical sequence, incarnate in a culture and a man. The culture is Southern California, no Golden State for Bidart, but an endless, overstylized Hollywood set, an imaginary frontier with real corpses in it. The man is Bidart's father, a millionaire, violent, supermasculine, yet helplessly self-destructive, whether through the disappointment of his "trivial desires" for self-escape—"Why can't I look like a cowboy?"—or through some underlying, obscure self-hatred. The story of the father and son's struggle and ultimate failure to accept each other is—despite an ado-

lescent scornfulness in the earliest of the poems, "Book of Life"—
one of the most painfully moving of its kind in contemporary literature. Bidart succeeds in his intention of becoming "not merely . . .
the 'eye,' but a character," as he charts his rebellious shaping of the
Eastern intellectual identity which, for him, must always mean both
weakness and sanity. He comes to dream in medieval allegory, of
faceless figures on a stage labeled "Insight." Yet there is always
something in him that fears the stasis of wisdom—"the austere
source / of nihilism"—and pulls back toward unformed energy, the
Hollywood Freeway at midnight, the bisexual abandon of Catullus,
the protoplasmic "glitter of mere life" in his father's photographs.
There is even the fear that Insight, at the moment when it becomes
the live exhilaration of art, may, as with the great prototypes, Proust
and Oedipus, exact the completion of a pattern of self-destruction.

Bidart's stylistic bareness works, I think, because it is a part of the
drama, the visible sign of a spiritual poverty. It is like the moment in
the strange, beautiful dream-poem "Another Life" when a character
splits apart from himself into a photographic double image, in order
to avoid the literally cannibalistic preying on himself that returns
with unity. To approach the matter from another angle, we might
invoke Hemingway's dictum that the artist can always afford to leave
out what he knows—only what he does not know is a danger to him.
Here the magnetic power of emotional indulgence, of decadence and
the apocalyptic, is so completely known in the story itself that it
would be a kind of insult to work such feelings up in the reader
through a more sensuous, alluring style.

Richard Howard, in his original introductory note, is inclined to
romanticize a "Satanic" element in Bidart's unconditional acceptance—both thematically and stylistically—of his impoverished and
tormented self. But at ten years' distance, one is struck by how well
the book captures—even while refusing—the optimism, the sense of
weightlessness, which the very idea of "change," of the malleability
of the self, could engender in people of Bidart's (and my) generation,
the first generation, probably, in which even student-age writers
would, as likely as not, have had some experience of psychotherapy.
The real heart-knowledge that things are not so simple belongs not
to *Golden State* but to Bidart's second volume, *The Book of the Body*. A
motto for that book might be found in the quiet sick joke elaborated
in the poem about the one-armed man: that "one," if it means "unified," "whole," means, where arms and legs are concerned, "two." In
one way or another, every poem in the book asks whether we are
more or less "one" when we attempt to double the gravely limited

self our history has given us with our ideal. The speaker of "California Plush" wished "to change"; the speaker of "Elegy" decides to, resolving his sexual ambivalence by falling in love with a woman friend and begetting a child. But he soon finds himself in a false position rather than a resolution, because his motives turn out to have more to do with an old and bitter quarrel with his mother than with the woman friend herself; and in the end he falls back on homosexuality and isolation, not necessarily as desirable, but as his own truest inclinations. Around this crisis, at the center of the book, one senses an expanding preoccupation with the limits rather than the potentialities of selfhood.

But Bidart's strongest work, in *The Book of the Body* and since, is found not in the autobiographical poetry but in the series of narrative poems and dramatic monologues extending from "The Arc" and "Ellen West" to "The Sacrifice" and "The War of Vaslav Nijinsky."[8] These poems, like "Herbert White" in *Golden State*, deal with violent extremes of human experience—suicide, anorexia, mutilation, madness—and their pitch is heightened by Bidart's increasing tendency to use italics, capitals, italicized capitals to differentiate levels of intensity in an already intense voice. It is Bidart's seriousness and triumph to make the reader feel that these extremes are not curiosities but instances of universal moral and ontological problems—indeed, clarifications of the ways in which these problems may be beyond solution. (This is, of course, an extension of the methods of *Golden State*, where "Herbert White" and "Another Life" illuminate the predicaments of the marginally "normal" autobiographical speaker.)

The two contrapuntal monologues in *The Book of the Body* both deal with the question of the body's adequacy to express what Bidart and his speakers persist in calling "spirit" or "soul." The speaker of "The Arc" cannot recover from the accidental loss of an arm because this central intrusion of "chance" into his biography signifies, to him, the loss of a personal essence. Ellen West's anorexia seems to her "NOT trivial" because the desire to be thin,

    all profile

    and effortless gestures, the sort of blond
    elegant girl whose
                    body is the image of her soul

reveals, by its implication of the removal of all fixity, all impediment to expression, a deeper desire *"not* to have a body" at all. The poem does not ignore the unmetaphysical meanings that eating has for Ellen (having to do with pollution and sexual penetration,. with the acknowledgment of emotional dependence on others); indeed, it makes them clear enough that one is somewhat puzzled as to why the psychiatrist concludes that therapy is of no use, and that Ellen must be left to her fate. At the same time, Bidart succeeds—largely through the brilliant poem-essay on Maria Callas and *"the History of Styles"* that he puts into Ellen's mouth—in making the problem Ellen poses, the incompatibility of pure expression and material presence, seem in its own terms unresolvable.

One can already observe in *Golden State* Bidart's fascination with the cyclic unities attained by divided selves. In this book, both narrative poems end with elaborate balancing acts, although one leads toward death and the other back toward life. Ellen West indulges her appetite—and sees that appetite return to normal, satiable proportions—in the knowledge that she will kill herself, by poison, the following night. In her last letter, which, since she knows it will arrive after the news of her death, is already half *d'outre tombe*, she is able for the first time to apply her name to her whole self, and then offer it to someone else: "Your *Ellen.*" The speaker of "The Arc" also realizes that he must encompass both what might have been—the ideal—and what is, just as he must go on feeling the cramps in his "phantom hand." But he is finally consoled by the belief that every "resonant" identity is similarly double, containing what has been destroyed in it as much as what it has preserved, as "Paris is still the city of Louis XVI and / Robespierre." Elsewhere in the book, in the most fascinating speculative passage in Bidart's writing, the notion of acts that at once affirm and deny physical reality is grafted onto the libido theory itself: sex is "the type of all action" because the orgasm is both "reconciliation with the body" and "annihilation of the body."

Bidart's major long poem since *The Book of the Body*, "The War of Vaslav Nijinsky," seems to me an even more substantial achievement, partly because of the greater intelligence and complexity of the speaker, partly because the sense of the universality of the extreme is carried over for the first time into the realm of politics and history, as it was so often and so fertilely carried over in the work of Bidart's teacher and friend (but only barely visible influence), Robert Lowell. "HISTORY IS HUMAN NATURE," Nijinsky proclaims at the crisis of the poem; and the dancer's preoccupation with World War I and his descent into madness are understood throughout in the light of his inability to transcend the mutually exacerbating interplay of aggression and guilt in his own life. The facts that we take for granted about Nijinsky—that his precocious talent helped drive a jealous older brother insane; that he entered, partly opportunistically, into a homosexual relationship with Diaghilev; that he then "betrayed" Diaghilev by marrying, but, though he loved his wife, could not forgive her her contented worldliness—these facts, as Bidart brings them to focus, *are* the madness, insofar as they are the cumulative proof of Nijinsky's conviction that *"All life exists / at the expense of other life'"* and that "GOODNESS and BEING / are incompatible." Nijinsky's last public action, his one-man ballet of the War, is another of those almost sacramental acts in which Bidart's characters unite the irreconcilable opposites in themselves: aggressor and victim, horrified accuser and sacrificial scapegoat. But it is a failed sacrament, because it wins approval, and so remains a form of aggression: a spectator compliments Nijinsky for being "able / 'to smell a good subject.' "

Bidart's work, I have found, can provoke sharp disagreement among intelligent readers whose ideas of poetry are otherwise reasonably compatible. One reason for this (aside from the shock of his kind of colloquialism) may be that the philosophical and psychological subtlety of his design tends to be under, not on, the surface. Again, the comparison with Hemingway seems odd but apt. The bareness and explicitness of both styles eliminate many of the opportunities a richer, more oblique style affords of making clear just where, and how, the author's understanding goes beyond the speaker's. Let me give one instance of the kind of subtlety I have in mind. Near the midpoint of "The War of Vaslav Nijinsky," the dancer has a dream—one which does not appear, as far as I know, in any of the records of the historical Nijinsky. In it, he is "slowly climbing / a long flight of steps." His wife and Diaghilev appear, "arm in arm," behind him; he hurries, "so that / they would not see me"; but the distance narrows.

> Soon, they were a few feet behind me,—
> I could hear them laughing,
>
> gossiping, discussing CONTRACTS
> and LAWSUITS . . .
>
> They understood each other perfectly.

I stopped.

But they

DIDN'T STOP . . .

They climbed right past me,—
laughing, chatting,

NOT SEEING ME AT ALL . . .

—I should have been happy;

yet . . .
        wasn't.

The conflict between Nijinsky's loneliness and his contempt for
others is clear enough. But to appreciate the central, prophetic character of this dream we must look elsewhere: back to those preemi-
nent instances of height, Nijinsky's famous leap and the dance of the
chosen virgin in *Le Sacre du Printemps;* forward to the chosen virgin's
death, and to Nijinsky's final posture in the asylum, unable or un-
willing to rise above his hands and knees. We might also look to the
significance of images of height and depth in the psychology of Ludwig Binswanger—the source for "Ellen West" and, I think, the great
hidden influence for all of Bidart's poetry since *Golden State.* Such
images, for Binswanger, relate to the idea of the "ground"—a complex concept involving the body, ancestral sources, the material context of life, but also the pragmatic and self-preserving body of our
worldly relations ("CONTRACTS / and LAWSUITS"). Images of
flight and soaring imply an unrealizable desire to transcend, be free
of, repudiate all that this implies (Nijinsky tells his chosen virgin to
leap *"BECAUSE SHE HATES THE GROUND"*). Images of sinking,
entombment, imply the reverse—the sense that one is not really
alive, that life is a machine, a tomb, that arises when no sense of significant freedom attaches to our actions at or above the surface. Nijinsky, like Ellen West, is a figure who cannot exist at ground level;
he must rise, or he will sink. We understand now his unexpected depression in the dream when Romola and Diaghilev—the people who
accept the "ground," and who have been his "ground"—rise above
him without seeing him, as he has wished. And when in the suc-

ceeding section (which *is* based on a real incident) Nijinsky shoves his wife and daughter down a flight of stairs because their noise has kept him from working, we are prepared to understand it not as simple brutality but as a desperate literalizing of the symbol, an attempt to regain the transcendence, the perspective-from-above, which alone enables him to "work" and live with others. The incident, of course, also underlines the paradoxical connection, throughout the poem, between Nijinsky's Christian, vegetarian, otherworldly transcendence and his anger or aggression—the connection that binds Nietzsche to him as a kind of demon-brother, and that finally reduces him to hopelessness. In the end, Nijinsky must unlearn not only dancing but walking—not only self-expression but the whole development of the self beginning in infancy—to escape from the aggression inherent in "BEING."

If Bidart's designs are often spread out unexplicitly over the whole length of a poem, as here, there are moments, nonetheless, when his sense of tragic pattern blazes out in a kind of epiphany likely to impress almost any reader. It is often at these moments that the imagistic is finally allowed a place in Bidart's poetry—as in our last view of the poet's mother in "Elegy" from *The Book of the Body:*

> her obsessive, baffled voice
>
> says that when she allowed herself to love
>
> she let something into her head which will
> never be got out—;
> > which could only betray her
> or *be* betrayed, but never appeased—;
> whose voice
>
> > death and memory have made
> into a razor-blade without a handle . . .
>
> "Don't forget;
> I want to be buried in a mausoleum at eye-level."

It is an ideogram of tragic necessity: first the chilling metaphor for the inability to compromise, not with the beloved, but with one's own internalization of the beloved; and then the inevitable retributive conversion, driven home by the rhyme of "handle" with "level"—the wish to be immortal by slipping into other minds in the same manner.

This sense of tragic cohesion, so rare in contemporary poetry generally—and made possible in Bidart, one feels, not only by the subtlety of his philosophical and psychoanalytic thinking, but by that love of subsuming actions which, as the speculative passage on sex in "The Book of the Body" makes clear, verges on the mystical—gives Bidart his real if problematic claim to be becoming one of our most moving and important poets. It certainly explains, when taken together with his tireless respect for at least one material aspect of poetry, the pitch and tempo of speech, why his poems, abstract as they are, never seem dematerialized or merely schematic, as Merwin's and Strand's sometimes do. His thought has become as Manichaean as theirs—as pained by the shortcomings of the self and, indeed, of material presence—but his poetry continues to speak from a central and adequate involvement with the whole reality of a life, his own or his characters'.

Another recent poet who achieves wholeness (indeed, a kind of wholeness in some ways new to poetry) by sticking with prose and explanation is James McMichael. After two good but not startlingly original earlier books, McMichael in 1980 published a long, astonishingly compendious verse autobiography called *Four Good Things*. A profoundly anti-Romantic poet, McMichael sees the world not as shape, or color, or as an equivalent for his feelings, but as a manifestation of will, an aggregate of mostly hidden purposes. *Four Good Things* astonishes not, as with Bidart, by an abstention from description but by a sheer, encyclopedic appetite for fact: how an organ is put together; how the Industrial Revolution began; what sections of McMichael's native city, Pasadena, were settled first:

> Below
> Millard and Poppyfields and Chaney Trail, there had been
> orchards mostly with an interspersed few streets of
> modest bungalows for the retired Mid-Western
> patrons of the cafeterias downtown. By private
> rights-of-way and by electric motive power,
> they'd take the Red Car from the cemetery to the
> sheds below St. Andrews. . . .

Such a way of writing an autobiography is almost bound to seem dry, lacking in plangencies of sensibility, to readers nourished on

Wordsworth or even on Lowell and Plath. Yet it allows McMichael to see, and find significance in, aspects of personal behavior which an emphasis on mood might screen out. These, again, have to do mainly with will, with our uneasy, half-conscious managing of reality: how we feel about travel, its maps and schedules; how we pace a conversation with a friend, or react to being accosted by a stranger. Or take this wonderful passage about how an insomniac self-consciously tries to outwit his own self-consciousness, to achieve the bemused moment that opens the door to sleep:

> And even the
> giving up is trying, a counterfeit that takes me into
> harmless things, a seagull, my socks, into the drowse of
> someone giving up who meets that first improbable
> ellipsis, slips beyond it to a second and a third and,
> losing count, goes off between the scatter, sleeps,
> is someone who's asleep, not me at all, who's only
> almost there and pleased to be this close, too pleased,
> now coming to my hold again with all the shifts
> intact and unrelieved. I've lost my chance.

There is a peculiar congruence between the novelty of McMichael's interests as a poet and the ingeniously original metric he has hit upon. Blank verse, the traditional meter for long ruminative poems in English, reasserts itself in a pure form (as in the last line of the passage quoted above) just often enough to establish a clear norm. Yet certain characteristic irregularities—six- and even seven-stress lines; a predominance of falling rhythm; an obsessive tendency to end on peculiarly weak words, prepositions, articles—seem constantly to be stretching the line beyond itself, not toward a new boldness of assertion but toward flaccidity, entropy. (One remembers Alexander Pope's description of the "needless alexandrine . . . Which, like a wounded snake, drags its slow length along.") There is thus a kind of yielding to the entropy of fact operating within a cumulative principle of formal (as of intellectual) shapeliness. The same could be said of the structure of the book as a whole, which has a peculiar seamlessness, a reluctance to place topics in a hierarchy of importance. Everything, as one reads and rereads, is relevant to everything else; yet there never seems a clear reason for any single section to be exactly where it is, and transitions are glides, feats of sleight-of-hand, rather than dramatic builds.

With McMichael, as with Bidart, the limitations and the acute-
nesses of the style come to seem an objectification of the psychic
predicament at the center of the poem. A sense of displacement and
fear of life have been at the core of the poet's experience from the
very beginning:

> With my conception, I was virtually
> coincident with cancer in my mother's body.
> To exist is to be *placed outside,* where there are
> things to fear. My body. Me. The visible
> pulse at my right ankle, thick blue vein, the skin. . . .

When to this primary trauma are added the concealment of the
mother's illness ("My mother was dying. I didn't know that"), the father's withdrawal into work, and his subsequent, unannounced remarriage, the poet's obsession with mapping, explanation and
prediction, with knowing the facts behind the facts, becomes all too
understandable. And the accompanying dryness comes to seem not
lack of concern with a richer dimension of feeling, but despair of
finding it. This is particularly evident in a vignette near the beginning of the book, in which the boy is taken along by the father—as a
rare special treat—to visit a family whose house the father is, in fact,
in the process of condemning for a public works project. Stirred by
the token kindness—but probably, unconsciously, identifying the
family's plight with his own—the boy bursts into uncontrollable
tears when an older daughter of the household is friendly and somewhat maternal toward him. By his outburst, he feels he has spoiled
his chance to remember the occasion "some good way," and wishes
"I'd / kept myself from watching her." Now, instead, he fantasizes
the demolition of the house—partly as revenge, partly, one feels, as a
way of possessing it and its inhabitants unconditionally. The sense
here that the exercise of intellectual or imaginative control is at once
a substitute for and a destructive exclusion of intimate contact with
others will be acknowledged, explored, combatted throughout the
book. "My worrying and fear," the poet admits, are congenial to him
because they are "as free of people as a / garden is, or as a plan."

The same insight informs and dominates the remarkable public
side of the book. McMichael is, with Bidart, one of the very few
poets since Lowell's generation—or since the Vietnam War years—
to find fresh ways of drawing the psychological-political analogy,
seeing "HISTORY" as "HUMAN NATURE" writ large. The

ground-theme is, as in the autobiographical sections, the compulsion to know and control all possible sources of contingency and threat. The Industrial Revolution (as McMichael argues in an astonishing nine-page tour de force verse lecture) was an effort not only to produce goods faster and more cheaply but to secure an organization, a surplus of capital, an inexhaustible supply of powerless, interchangeable laborers, sufficient to withstand any vicissitudes of the market. As luck would have it, this aspect of capitalism—or industrialism—reached its pure form in the place where McMichael himself had his beginnings; "Pasadena," as he puts it in his rather laconic jacket statement, "looked the way it did because there had already been a Manchester." That is to say, Pasadena was, economically, the place where it became profitable simply to organize information and predict from it, without carrying out any of the practical applications; just as, residentially, it was a community that existed because it was planned for and advertised, not because people spontaneously settled around existing resources and jobs. For all his empathy with the human insecurity underlying it, McMichael is keenly alive to the dangers of information technocracy (one particularly blameless citizen of Pasadena, he informs us, "helped to plan the arsenals" of *all* the nations that fought in World War II), just as he is alive to the potential emptiness of a packaged private life. There is a particularly poignant passage about the sadness of the retired Midwesterners in the cafeterias—beyond consolation precisely because they know they are in Paradise:

> Their sense of
> where they lived depended strangely on their
> fitness to change, as if they couldn't know
> without those changes where they were or what they
> wanted in their lives. Living here was too much what they'd
> thought it would be. The sequences of perfect days were
> unavoidably what they'd come for.

Pasadena is, in real history, what it is in the poet's emotional history: a place all but drained of presence by the intrusions of the anxious consciousness and its ubiquitous planning.

When the consequences of fear are so omnipresent, what is feared can come to seem almost a redeemer. Perhaps the most moving passage in the book comes when the poet, having reduced Pasadena to an end-point of conscious social planning, suddenly restores an absolute lyrical value to its sights and hours by invoking "pain"—by seeing them through his dying mother's eyes. It is, in a way, the emotional breakthrough that makes the rest of the book endurable; yet it is done without compromising the book's relentless cleaving to the surface of fact:

> She was reading about North Borneo, about a
> concentration camp, the Japanese, their curious
> honor and the cruelty that came from it. She hadn't
> seen that in them, doubted it. She wondered what the
> spareness of the things they'd lived with meant to
> sailors on the carriers.

But now fact is what people share, not what displaces or distances them. A kind of transfiguring existential companionship—whose object may be the self, as well as any or all possible beloved others—springs from the double awareness that one is now present in the world of facts, and that one will not always be. The mother is consoled by the seamlessness of her connection with that world, in a way that oddly but, I think, intentionally prefigures and justifies the seamlessness of her son's poem:

> From the promenade, on each crossing, late,
> later than this, she'd watched the clouds curve up in
> tumbles that brought no wind. Alone, it had been like
> seeing a place for someone else whom one might never
> tell about it, filled, as one was, with the colored
> presence of what was there, with how it all spread
> back and away and rounded, shone, went dim.
> It filled one with the ease of trusting that the
> other person too was in a place.

And so, entirely within its own terms, McMichael's anti-Romanticism leads to a deeply Romantic affirmation of location and connection, the imagination at home in the world.

James McMichael and Robert Pinsky were both students of Yvor Winters, and both seem heirs—in the spirit if not in the letter—of Winters' insistence that the poetic intelligence must resist its own impulse to merge emotionally with the world in any kind of Emersonian monism. Pinsky's originality as a personal poet (the one side of his many-faceted endeavor as a man of letters that concerns us here) rests, like McMichael's, on a complex and critical sense of how our feelings attach themselves to the factuality of the world. Or rather, perhaps, a sense of mystery and fragility about the very possibility of such attachment—a lurking Stevensian fear of the world as it really is, the "cold wide river of things." (Curiously, some of Pinsky's acutest negative insights as a critic concern the motives and the implications of the New Surrealists' tendency to reduce the world to "the blank, simple substances—snow, water, air."[9] Like many good critics, Pinsky seems at once far from and peculiarly close to what he attacks.)

Pinsky's own sense of fragility and blankness receives a fine opening statement in his best early poem, "Poem About People." Brief glimpses of people ("The jaunty crop-haired graying / Women in grocery stores," a workingman's "porky walk / Back to the truck, polite") can make us

> feel briefly like Jesus,
>
> A gust of diffuse tenderness
> Crossing the dark spaces
> To where the dry self burrows. . . .

But love becomes extremely problematic when confronted with the specific "dry self" in its burrow of ego and weakness,

> When anyone's difficult eyes come
>
> Into focus, terrible gaze of a unique
> Soul, its need unlovable: my friend
> In his divorced schoolteacher
> Apartment, his own unsuspected
>
> Paintings hung everywhere,
> Which his wife kept in a closet—
> Not, he says, that she wasn't
> Perfectly right. . . .

The gap between the emotion and its possible particulars is resolved, or at least made more endurable, in one of the strangest and most effective touches I know of in recent poetry, by a landscape description:

> The weather
> Changes in the black of night,
> And the dream-wind, bowling across
>
> The sopping open spaces
> Of roads, golf-courses, parking lots,
> Flails a commotion
> In the dripping treetops,
>
> Tries a half-rotten shingle
> Or a down-hung branch, and we
> All dream it, the dark wind crossing
> The wide spaces between us.

The poem has beautifully prepared the reader to work out the underlying metaphor, in the best New Critical manner, and arrive at a subtle, immensely suggestive epiphany. The "wind" (the "gust" of feelings) "tries"—and, implicitly, finds wanting—all the "dry," "half-rotten," "down-hung" shortcomings of the specific self. Yet it also unites us, on the preconscious level, because we have all felt this impulse and this testing—just as a sound in the night might enter many people's dreams, in many different disguises. But symbolic structure isn't quite adequate to explain what I think many readers will find most startling and memorable here: the amount of space and loving attention given to the night landscape. This very plain, very plainly seen America—the blank world of phenomena, the accretion of the sad tidiness of our efforts to do something with life— with its weight of pathos, gives the poem an unexpected surplus of visionary truth. It is an "objective correlative," in the best sense of that too easily invoked phrase.

When a poet with this kind of vision turns to autobiography, as Pinsky has done in a remarkable group of poems that have been appearing in magazines over the past two years, one may expect something out of the ordinary. The *moment privilégié* can hardly be privileged in a Proustian or Wordsworthian sense, in the face of so sweeping an intuition of the neutrality of life and the poverty of individual character. Indeed, to content oneself with describing and savoring the moment's uniqueness—so like the uniqueness of all other such moments—might be a self-defeating endeavor, preventing one from asking the more general questions that might finally account for the poignancy and specialness. It is such questions that give shape and originality to Pinsky's long poem "History of My

Heart."[10] The poem begins with a moment that is privileged for the poet even though it occurred before he was born—his mother's memory of Fats Waller improvising for a Christmas shopping crowd in Macy's, where she worked as a high school girl. That this unexperienced moment can be special speaks not only for the intimate connection between the sense of specialness and familial love, but for some more abstruse criterion that it will take the poem its whole length to define. At the beginning, the memory is simply a "scene from the romance of Joy,"

> Co-authored by her and the movies, like her others—
> My father making the winning basket at the buzzer
>
> And punching the enraged gambler who came onto the court—
> The brilliant black and white of the movies, texture
> Of wet snowy fur, the taxi's windshield, piano keys. . . .

"The brilliant black and white of the movies" is itself a brilliant image, not only for the conventionality of "Joy," but for the way it at once heightens and reduces the reality it transforms. That is the common element linking this image to the succeeding one, the magic of falling snow, which in turn provides the link to a wonderfully fresh episode of adolescent sexual awakening:

>   what I felt
> Dancing close one afternoon with a thin blonde girl
>
> Was my amazing good luck, the pleased erection
> Stretching and stretching at the idea *She likes me,*
> *She likes it,* the thought of legs under a woolen skirt,
>
> To see eyes "melting" so I could think *This is it,*
> *They're melting!* Mutual arousal of suddenly feeling
> Desired: *This is it: "desire"!* When we came out
>
> Into the street we saw it had begun, the firm flakes
> Sticking, coating the tops of cars. . . .

By the ambiguous pronoun "it," the qualities of the snowfall (monochrome, blanketing, "melting" like the eyes, but also poignantly "clinging" in "soft / Separate crystals") read back onto that other "*it,*" "*desire,*" the categorically anticipated great moment that at once glorifies and dismisses the individual particular. Pinsky deflates our expectations for such a scene in other ways as well—the bald and funny stress on the "pleased erection," the relative casualness about the object, "a thin blonde girl." Yet in deromanticizing the scene, he holds all the more strongly to what is really generous and charming about it—the amazement at being liked, the liking for oneself that comes with being able to make someone else happy. (Pinsky speaks later in the poem of Fats Waller's "giving them / A thrill as someone might give someone an erection, / For the thrill of it.")

The rest of the poem meditates at length on the mysteries of egotism and generosity; and of our ability, sometimes, to be pleased simply because others wish to give pleasure—the circularity of desire:

> the way feeling pretty or full of erotic revery
>
> Makes the one who feels seem beautiful to the beholder
> Witnessing the idea of the giving of desire. . . .

Perhaps this is possible because, at the happiest level of our infantile experience, all these things blur. The child's self-assertion is received as a gift by the parents, and, conversely, their gifts seem to enter into and change his innermost being. When "pain buzzed / Scaring me because it twisted right inside me," and the mother nurses him,

> It was as if she had put me back together again
> So sweetly I was glad the hurt had torn me.

The gifts that really touch us later in life, the poem suggests, restore us to this unquestioned mutuality. But the theme has its tragic side too, in the power that this symbiosis gives others over the self—as the poet has occasion to discover in his more difficult mature relations with his mother. Toward the end, the poem takes a particularly dark turn (reflecting back, inevitably, onto its generally celebratory, if bemused, treatment of imaginative transformation), when the mother's brush with madness turns the son away into the solitude of art—at first, as a jazz musician. But art, at least, gives him the terms with which to understand more clearly the "abstract" and arbitrary yet bodily, egoistic yet self-sacrificing, character of all of the heart's ventures:

My heart following after a capacious form,
Sexual and abstract, in the thunk, thrum,

Thrum, come-wallow and then a little screen
Of quicker notes goosing to a fifth higher, winging
To clang-whomp of a major seventh: listen to *me*

Listen to *me*, the heart says in reprise until sometimes
In the course of giving itself it flows out of itself
All the way across the air. . . .

My impulse is to go on and on quoting from this poem, to show how Pinsky's special angle of vision leads to near-perfect renderings of things—like the content of jazz—that haven't been seen, or seen in quite this way, before. Though he is finally a softer, more traditionally nostalgic poet than McMichael, Pinsky likewise shows the oddly liberating effect that an intellectual framework can have, in guiding recollection away from the conventions of recollection. (Rereading Proust, one is struck by how much energy he puts into elaborating his almost eighteenth-century "laws" of human nature, when one had remembered only the madeleine, the three church spires . . .) It is for this reason, I think, that Pinsky and McMichael have done so well with the compendious, various kind of autobiographical poem, where others in their generation have avoided it. (They have, of course, the added advantage that their obvious models and threats, Lowell and Berryman, rather feared abstract explanation, whereas their own teacher, Winters, positively encouraged it.) Bidart's case is somewhat different—the narrow centrality of the tragic; but with him, too, we feel the power of prose, of anguished inquiry, to deliver the shock of a human predicament, more strongly, perhaps, than imagistic rendering could at this point. While remaining essentially within the tradition of a psychological realism like Lowell's, these writers have brought new resources to bear on it, which our poetry, one hopes and expects, will be a long time in exhausting.

IV

But I would like to conclude—for the sake of our sense of possibility regarding the future of personal poetry—with a poet whose originality lies in reaching out to include, not the prosaic and the explanatory, but the loftiest and most traditional kind of grand style. Allen Grossman in fact had his beginnings as a pure, and too derivative, high-style poet; it was only in his forties, after years of failure to win recognition with his early style, that he came to the fractured and almost confessionally intimate mixed mode that is unmistakably his, in his recent volumes *The Woman on the Bridge over the Chicago River* (1979) and *Of the Great House* (1982).

In a curious way, Grossman's mature poetry remains a poetry of failure. It identifies itself with, even as it struggles to overcome, the state in which the words that come to one to tell one's story fail to ring true, to give one the sense of real presence in one's story (a state familiar, I'm sure, to many people who have never written a poem). Grossman's poems are psychologically preliminary—rather as Wallace Stevens' are epistemologically preliminary—to what would truly be poetry.

It is perhaps for this reason, paradoxically, that Grossman has finally been able to use so much more of the grand style successfully than any other contemporary poet can. He is freed from constraint because he in no way claims the grand style as his personal property, as appropriate to his experience. On the contrary, the grand style becomes the type, like Stevens' "central man," of that adequacy—emotional, sexual, expressive, cognitive—to experience which his own individual life fails to attain:

<blockquote>
the voice
That remembers
A man who has no horizon,

the hero
Whose language is a heart, the strong heart
Of a bridegroom, who runs in the sun's brightness—
Wide-eyed, thinking. . . .
</blockquote>

This image is—like the grand style in its original, epic sense—collective and not individual. Part of the wholeness that the poet yearns toward is the sense that his painful idiosyncratic experience can be seen as a version of shared, universal experience.

Thus, the poem that may stand as a paradigm of Grossman's grand-style confessional work, "Bow Spirit," begins with a quotation from Homer which in the original is merely ironic: "But tell me of your lineage, for you are not come from a famous oak tree, or stones." But for the speaker of the poem, there is no irony: "a famous oak tree" is all too apt a description of his mother's wild but autistic oracular intensity; "stones" of the businessman's impersonality, the "flickering / Minerals" of "Louis's small eyes, my father's." Grossman could say, as Robert Lowell said in a late poem to *his* mother, "you are as human as I am . . . / if I am."[11] The whole matter of "lineage"—and therefore of being part of a human continuum, not a special case of monstrous consciousness—is problematic, in a way unimaginable in the Homeric world.

"Lineage" is a word with many overtones of meaning; in the resonance between them lies the strange, difficult unity of "Bow Spirit." It is the "line-work" of a poem; the "lines" of a face; the "lines" of a ship's rigging, pulled taut to catch the wind and set forth. The meanings are all one meaning: to write a true poem is to give oneself a face, to set forth on an existential voyage into the world, hence to be born, hence at once to recognize and to become separate from one's ancestors. At the beginning of the poem, the poet despairs of all these things. His face is seen with almost unremitting self-loathing, as a deformity, an un-face: "the wen upon the brow" (later in the poem it is "my / Ghastly wen"), "the mouth never right— / never right" (later it is "the knotted" or—in context, quite unpleasantly— "this / Flowing mouth"). The mouth that is "never right" does not truly possess a voice, and for this the poet is inclined to blame his mother. She has been unable, he feels, really to recognize another person; he asks her, "Mother, have you ever seen a man's face?" and her reply—the one thing she says in the poem, and the one use of the poet's own name—is "Allen, I / Have never loved anyone." (There is a terrible contrast here with the most famous naming of a poet in his own poem, by another "Unteachable Beatrice," in *Purgatorio*, Canto 30.) She has therefore been unable to confer on him either the sense of selfhood or the power to communicate—which she did not herself possess. This is the force of the title: the mother is the "bowsprit" and beckoning "spirit" of the existential voyage; she must go before into all the territories of possibility her child can naturally inhabit. The writing of poetry—"This poem in the likeness of a countenance"—is, then, the effort to attain unnaturally, by a kind of second birth, the sense of real presence which is naturally lacking.

"Bow Spirit" is a poem about a poem that never quite gets written—and thus at once a painful account of creative blockage and a rather lovely meditation on those prior emotional resonances which are never fully made visible, even in the very best poems. The lines which, with great difficulty, "materialize" in Part I are conventionally Romantic ones, their elegiac tinge perhaps betraying the expectation of failure: "It is October, and the air is dry"—and then simply, "The wild blue aster." But for the poet, his "October" is already much more than conventional; it is "a deep, deep lake" in which he sees emerging first a picture and then, tremulously, a face. The picture, though identified in a note with Breughel's "October," is clearly one of those dream-pictures that throughout the volume *Of the Great House* "stand . . . in the / Place of what I know"—that is, both interpret and displace reality.[12]

> Hoi. On the mountain
>
>   the dark cattle
>
>   (on
> The blind breast of the mountain in the death-
> Winds of October)
>
>   are driven from the
> Upland pasture with blows. Hoi. Light.
>
>   —The boat
> Is upon the water, the harbor and the
> Harbor islands shine

From a depth-psychological point of view, we are dealing with two contrasting pictures of the separation experiences of early childhood. In one, the mother's inadequacy to recognize and nurture, her "blind breast," is death-dealing, and separation becomes compulsory and violent. In the other, separation is seen, more hopefully, as birth and as a recognition of invitingness in the outside world. (The lines following the image of "islands," returning, in the endless recirculation of images characteristic of Grossman, to the face, now emphasize what is chosen, created in it—a Christian addendum to the Jewish substrate, which, not accidentally, sets the poet at odds with his father: "The beard is for the resurrection. Louis / Hates it.")

I think "pictures" like this one constitute for Grossman a language for feeling, which, like nature for Wordsworth, is healing partly because it is grand and impersonal. If a mountain stands for the mother's breast, a harbor for the vagina, a journey by boat for birth or maturation, it is not through the accidents of any individual biography, but through a general and irreducible integration of mind with body, body with world. In any case, the creative displacement of the picture allows the poet, finally, to glimpse his face; and in the next section, after an access of "terror / For the children," his voice comes too. Wonderfully, what it says first is not poetry but something more real, and less uniquely individual—the protective command and invitation to the children which his own mother was incapable of offering:

> What would he say, if the trying and not
> Succeeding were to end
>
>   and his opened
>
> Mouth
>
>   (tears streaming down his face, as linnet-
> Like the lines weave
>
>   of sere flax the sheer
> Facial shroud)—?
>
>   Come in, children. Come in
> Now. It's going to rain.

In this climactic passage, all the central images begin to come together. The "lines" of the poem weave the face, which is also the cloth sail, the "shroud," raised to begin the existential voyage (and the "shroud" of the dead—since, in Grossman's poetry, to exist, to carry identity beyond the provisional, is always to begin to die).

But the recovery of the voice, far from providing the poem with a happy ending, leads directly into its darkest section. The "man who has begun" must confront the mother, with an intensified guilt, since she cannot at this point go through a parallel development, and so cannot experience the son's kind of knowledge except as a mortal wound. This realization is initially so embittering that it brings on both a renewed access of physical self-hatred and, for the only time in the poem, a complete repudiation of the mother: "I do not love you, mother. / Die where you will."

The next section, however, finds the poet exhorting the (now largely internalized) mother to "imagine" a different mode of existence, and to

> Let be,

> Mother—

> Let this light be

> that is.

The whole psychological movement forward is contained in the wordplay. By "letting be"—relinquishing her hitherto endless claims on the speaker—the mother allows the world to "be" for him, simply because, and as, it "is," beyond the self. This access to a world truly not the image of the self is the ideal, or vanishing point, of most of Grossman's poems, and is figured here by the "islands," bits of land detached from the mainland, "in the shine" of the harbor, with which the poem ends.

This reprise and transformation of the Breughel picture in the last two sections sheds a good deal of light on the function of Grossman's characteristic recirculation of images. The circularity of the method—and the culturally derived character of many of the images—makes it, in one sense, evidence of the poet's frustration, his inability to speak from the center ("Forty years unable to concentrate / My mind"). But in another sense, the method imitates processes of therapy or psychic growth—the obsessive subject seen, each time it returns, from a slightly different angle, and with a cumulative clarification. Thus, when the picture of mountain and harbor is revisited, it is in one way demystified. The brutal physicality of the birth image has now emerged from behind the pretty landscape (*"inter urinas et faeces* / The beautiful roads"). But in another way, far from being reduced, the significance of the image has expanded to include the equally soiled birth that takes a lifetime, the journey of self-creation:

> From the mountain down, by the mountain path

> (Forty years unable to concentrate
> My mind)

past the reeking gibbet, and the
Harrowed sidehill field, to the sullen valley
Stream

(Louis is alive still but mad)

and out
Into the dazzling estuary, and the air

The harbor now becomes the release of death, as well as the release
into life. After this epiphany of endings, the lines about the aster finally complete themselves, as a fragment that will never be a poem,
unless it is the poem "Bow Spirit." They form, appropriately, an ac-
knowledgement of "the Fall"—the dryness of the self, the irretrievable loss of youth—but also an almost ecstatic opening of the way to
continued wildness and blossoming:

O this blue aster is an autumn, a dry-
Wood flower,

a wild flower

of the Fall.

It is, I think, the real right ending for the poem (the last section being
a lovely but slightly programmatic effort at more total optimism). It
is also a good instance of Grossman's way of wringing grace out of
awkwardness and hesitation—the process of self-correction yielding, as if by accident, the powerful nominative force of "autumn"
and even of "dry-," the off-rhyming stepwise descent from "wood
flower" to "wild flower," the mimesis of "Fall."

Grossman's poetry studiously avoids the language of psychotherapy or of "confessional poetry"—giving only the scantiest anecdotal
evidence for his view of his parents' characters or his own predicament. Indeed, in "Bow Spirit," most of the evidence of this kind
comes in parentheses, forming (as in the last reprise of the mountain
passage) a delicate subtext or counterpoint to a meditation whose
terms in themselves remain lyric and impersonal. And yet Grossman's use of blockage and failure, his recirculation of images, his
pendulum-swings between darkness and light, the very peculiar distance of his relation to his own high style, place him profoundly

within the mode of difficult interior truthfulness which I call re-flexive. While avoiding psychotherapeutic language, Grossman oddly comes closer than almost any poet we have discussed to the experience of successful therapy: the deepening sense of authenticity, beyond words; the continuing dialogue with internalized parents or obsessive images, which is a different thing from insight about them; the sense of the widest bearing of images which sometimes arrives when their bodily meaning is no longer suppressed. Grossman's achievement is to make visible the process or quality of psychological growth, by all but eliminating its particular terms. (Those that he does not eliminate are profoundly telling, suggestive, painful; there is no question here of an evasive appeal to a "mythic self.") While perhaps aiming only at being a high lyrical poet, Grossman has discovered a new way of being an honest personal one.

I wished to conclude with a poet who is something of an anomaly precisely in order to avoid the predictive note on which books on contemporary writing often end. We tend to think of a high lyric grandeur like Grossman's—with its tendency toward the universalized, even the formulaic—as what had to be given up in order to achieve the personal, intimate kind of truth with which this book is concerned. Frank Bidart's Nijinsky sums up the ideals of the "traditional 'academic' dance"—"the illusion of *Effortlessness, / Ease, Smoothness, Equilibrium*"—and then concludes: "When I look into my life, / these are not the qualities / I find there." We have seen here many powerful renunciations of such traditional ideals, from the later Lowell to Ashbery to McMichael and Bidart himself. (Even the poets of the middle generation, despite their preoccupation with visual beauty, qualify by their willingness to minimize the auditory dimension of poetry.) So that, whatever we expect to come next in the development of our poetry, it is not likely to be another Yeats, Rilke, or Crane; we may even concur with Stanley Kunitz's slightly ungenerous prediction that we may now expect "great poems" but not "great poets."[13]

And yet . . . Such predictions, I think, always put too much weight on a quasi-Marxist logic of the next step, too little on the accident of particular writers appearing just when they do. Whitman, Eliot, Frost, even Ashbery, all now present themselves almost as stances, not poets—but what is stance in them could easily have been quite mediocre, without the peculiar chemistry of an individual temperament and its often contradictory affections and sourcings. No one could have anticipated Whitman's combination of opera and democracy, Eliot's mix of music hall, sexual nightmare, and nostalgia for the strictness of Metaphysical wit. Grossman is not a poet of this order, of course; but no one could have predicted the precise combination of virtues that makes his style successful. As soon as he is there, we realize that the grand and the lyrical are legitimately part of the intimate economy of the psyche—that it takes only the right point of view to make them compatible with, even enabling to, a new kind of reflexive verisimilitude. And we reflect that perhaps, after all, all roads are always open in literature; it is only a question of the writer who knows how to travel them.

NOTES

1. INTRODUCTION

1. Robert Lowell, *Writers at Work: The Paris Review Interviews, Second Series* (New York: Viking, 1965), p. 346.
2. Sigmund Freud, *The Interpretation of Dreams*, tr. James Strachey (New York: Avon, 1965), p. 613.
3. Arthur Rimbaud, *Oeuvres complètes* (Paris: Bibliothèque de la Pléiade, 1954), p. 233; p. 270 (my own translations).
4. For these latter, probably the least well-known to American readers, the classic source in English is Rollo May, Ernest Angel, and Henri F. Ellenberger, eds., *Existence* (New York: Basic, 1958).
5. Sigmund Freud, *Civilization and Its Discontents*, tr. James Strachey (New York: Norton, 1961), p. 12; idem, *The Interpretation of Dreams*, p. 585.
6. Paul Breslin, "What the Signs of Promise Are," *Ploughshares* 7, no. 2 (1981): 155; Charles Molesworth, *The Fierce Embrace* (Columbia: University of Missouri Press, 1979), esp. the chapters on "Confessional Poetry," Kinnell, and Bly. The happy exception to this recent deemphasis on the self is, of course, David Kalstone, *Five Temperaments* (New York: Oxford University Press, 1977).

2. "I AM THAT I AM"

1. Thus, for example, Irving Howe, "The Plath Celebration: A Partial Dissent," in *The Critical Point* (New York: Horizon, 1973); Howe acknowledges, and nonetheless suffers from, an inculcated prejudice that a truly first-person "I" is the exception and not the rule.

2. Robert Duncan, *Caesar's Gate* (San Francisco: Sand Dollar, 1972). All quotations are taken from pp. i–iii. For Rosenthal's discussion of the poem, see M. L. Rosenthal, *The New Poets* (New York: Oxford University Press, 1967), pp. 182–184.

3. It follows from this that the obscure "private" detail in personal poetry can only be judged—like initially unreadable signals in other modernist modes—in the totality of its formal relationships (as Duncan, in fact, implies). This is not to deny that factual exposition in lyric poetry poses special, though subordinate, problems of grace.

4. Adrienne Rich, "Caryatid," *American Poetry Review* 2 (September/October 1973): 42–43. It is true that the first remark was made of *History*, the second of the original *Notebook*; but I do not think it seriously distorts Rich's meaning to apply both to all of Lowell's work in the unrhymed sonnet form.

5. See Rollo May, Ernest Angel, and Henri F. Ellenberger, eds., *Existence* (New York: Basic, 1958), esp. the introductory essays, Minkowski's "Findings in a Case of Schizophrenic Depression," and Binswanger's "The Case of Ellen West."

3. REAL AND NUMINOUS SELVES

1. See Jon Rosenblatt, *Sylvia Plath: The Poetry of Initiation* (Chapel Hill: University of North Carolina Press, 1979), which at least attempts to bridge the gap, though psychoanalytic perspectives are resolutely ignored. Judith Kroll, *Chapters in a Mythology* (New York: Harper & Row, 1976), contains valuable research on the mythopoeic and religious side of Plath, but suffers from the apparent belief that this dimension will be annihilated if a pathological side is also explored. At the other extreme, David Holbrook, *Sylvia Plath: Poetry and Existence* (London: University of London, Athlone Press, 1976), a Freudian-Laingian study, seems indeed to intend such an annihilation. There is much learning and brilliance in Holbrook's book, but I found myself increasingly at odds with his rules of evidence and his notions of the moral purpose of art. Perhaps the best single discussion of Plath's imaginative vision is D. F. McKay, "Aspects of Energy in the Poetry of Dylan Thomas and Sylvia Plath," *Critical Quarterly* 16, no. 1 (1974): 53–67.

2. The reminiscent and biographical pieces by Lois Ames, Wendy Campbell, Ted Hughes, Aurelia Plath, and Nancy Hunter Steiner have all been most illuminating; also Edward Butscher, *Sylvia Plath: Method and Madness* (New York: Seabury, 1976). If they occasionally make one think of the story of the five blind men and the elephant, that too is usefully cautionary.

3. Sylvia Plath, *The Bell Jar* (London: Faber & Faber, 1966), p. 27. All subsequent citations refer to this edition.

4. Carl Jung, "Psychological Aspects of the Mother Archetype," in *The Basic Writings of C. G. Jung,* ed. Violet S. de Laszlo (New York: Modern Library, 1959), p. 336.

5. Nancy Hunter Steiner, *A Closer Look at Ariel* (New York: Harper's Magazine Press, 1973), p. 45.

6. If this interpretation seems true but not quite adequate to the intensity of the hatred, biography can cast a further grim light. I doubt that I am the only reader who has come away from a first reading of the poems with the vague impression (compounded perhaps out of a montage of "Suicide off Egg Rock" with "Full Fathom Five," the pond "Where the daft father went down" in "All the Dead Dears," and the "head in the freakish Atlantic" in "Daddy") that Plath's father was himself a suicide. In a sense, he was. Aurelia Plath's courageous memoir introducing *Letters Home* tells how Otto Plath, believing he had diagnosed his own illness—in fact, diabetes—as incurable cancer, refused to be treated by a doctor until it was too late to avoid the amputation which led to his death. Thus, his "autocracy," his need to be in control, did lead to one savage and murderous act; but it was an action against himself. Only this—combined with the long shadow which his illness and melancholic anticipation of dying must have cast over his daughter's childhood—quite explains how he could be conflated with the worst of tyrants and at the same time be so bitterly regretted and loved.

7. "My mother hadn't cried either. She had just smiled and said what a merciful thing it was for him he had died, because if he had lived he would have been crippled and an invalid for life, and he couldn't have stood that." *The Bell Jar,* p. 177; also pp. 40, 175.

8. Lois Ames, "Notes Toward a Biography," in Charles Newman, ed., *The Art of Sylvia Plath* (Bloomington: Indiana University Press, 1981), p. 166.

9. R. D. Laing, *The Divided Self* (New York: Pelican, 1965), p. 42.

10. "The Munich Mannequins" brings together the "blood flood" and De Chirico's "Disquieting Muse" in a horrific image of the purely erotic, unmaternal woman (probably, in this case, a refiguring of Plath's actual rival for her husband's affections).

11. It is not only in relation to men that the idea of a scapegoat—that is, the idea that intrapsychic contents can be embodied in another per-

son and then carried off to a suitably bad end—arises. Both Doreen and Joan are regarded in this light in *The Bell Jar.*

12. Holbrook, *Sylvia Plath,* p. 176.
13. Steiner, *A Closer Look,* p. 42; Butscher, *Sylvia Plath,* p. 104; Sylvia Plath, *Ariel* (New York: Harper & Row, 1966), p. ix.
14. Louis Ames, "Notes Toward a Biography," in Newman, ed., *The Art of Sylvia Plath,* p. 166.
15. *The Basic Writings of C. G. Jung,* p. 164.
16. The ambiguity of the imagery of birth here was first discussed in Harriet Rosenstein, "Reconsidering Sylvia Plath," *Ms* 1 (September 1972): 44–51, 96–99.
17. See Heinrich Zimmer, *Philosophies of India* (New York: Meridian, 1956), pp. 172–177, chapter entitled "The Palace of Wisdom."
18. *The Basic Writings of C. G. Jung,* p. 126. Judith Kroll has already pointed out (*Chapters in a Mythology,* pp. 232–233) how Plath's lines echo a related passage in "Archetypes of the Collective Unconscious" (*Basic Writings of C. G. Jung,* pp. 300–303), in which water is "a living symbol of the dark psyche," and the "treasure" or reflected light in its depths the archetypes—recognized as internal, thanks to the decay of religion. The vertigo of this recognition is itself dangerous; Jung warns, "More than one sorcerer's apprentice has been drowned in the waters called up by himself. . . . The prudent man avoids the danger lurking in these depths, but he also throws away the good which a bold but imprudent venture might bring." It makes a good epitaph for what remains stubbornly beautiful and suggestive—beyond the claustrophobia—in Plath's transfiguration of her experience.
19. Kroll, *Chapters in a Mythology,* pp. 183–184, also discusses this sound-pattern, and the significance of its last metamorphosis.
20. Holbrook finds it "strange" to call the dew "suicidal," but he forgets how Marvell used the same image to describe the soul "careless of its Mansion new"—the body—and yearning, instead, to "run / Into the Glories of th' Almighty Sun" ("On a Drop of Dew"). Holbrook, *Sylvia Plath,* p. 160.
21. Newman, ed., *The Art of Sylvia Plath,* p. 188.
22. John Frederick Nims, "The Poetry of Sylvia Plath: A Technical Analysis," *ibid.,* pp. 136–152, draws the distinctions between the two books very nicely, and does much more justice than I have done to the achievements of *The Colossus.*
23. For Alvarez's view, see Newman, ed., *The Art of Sylvia Plath,* pp. 56–68, esp. p. 66. See also Butscher, *Sylvia Plath,* esp. pp. 326, 341–342.
24. See Newman, ed., *The Art of Sylvia Plath,* pp. 77–88.
25. According to Butscher, Plath was obsessively preoccupied with the idea of having more children—and with her rival's supposed sterility. The lines "my sheets, the cold dead centre / where spilt lives congeal and stiffen to history" draw an emotionally clear—if not altogether

logical—connection between the failure to procreate and the negative vision of "history," of merely sequential time.

26. See Newman, ed., *The Art of Sylvia Plath*, pp. 66–68.

27. Gilbert Bettman, "Some Continuities in Sylvia Plath's Poetry" (honors thesis, Harvard University, 1970), describes the increasing staticness of the late poems very well, though from different initial premises.

28. *The Collected Poems of Sylvia Plath* (New York: Harper & Row, 1981), p. 295.

29. The idea of an evil mother is probably in play, unconsciously, earlier, since the "counterfeit snake" image closely echoes a savage description of the protagonist's mother in Robert Lowell's "Between the Porch and the Altar."

30. Robert Pinsky, *The Situation of Poetry* (Princeton: Princeton University Press, 1976), pp. 129–133.

31. Peter Orr, ed., *The Poet Speaks* (New York: Barnes & Noble, 1966), p. 172.

32. See Charles Mauron, *Introduction to the Psychoanalysis of Mallarmé*, tr. Archibald Henderson, Jr., and Will L. McLendon (Berkeley: University of California Press, 1963).

33. Irving Howe, "The Plath Celebration: A Partial Dissent," in Howe, *The Critical Point* (New York: Horizon, 1973).

34. Quoted in Newman, ed., *The Art of Sylvia Plath*, p. 32.

4. LANGUAGE AGAINST ITSELF

Note: The deaths, within a few years, of Robert Lowell, Elizabeth Bishop, and James Wright have given a sad irony to the title of this chapter. I retain it because I think that, for many readers, these poets remain in the "middle": still heavily defined by what they have reacted against; their own ultimate stature still hard to assess.

1. Cited in A. Poulin, *Contemporary American Poetry*, 2nd ed. (Boston: Houghton Mifflin, 1975), p. 435.

2. Gary Snyder, *Earth House Hold* (New York: New Directions, 1969), pp. 118, 122.

3. Robert Bly, "Looking for Dragon Smoke," in Stephen Berg and Robert Mezey, eds., *Naked Poetry* (Indianapolis: Bobbs Merrill, 1969), pp. 161–164.

4. Poulin, "Contemporary American Poetry: The Radical Tradition," in *Contemporary American Poetry*, p. 464.

5. Snyder, *Earth House Hold*, p. 111.

6. Ibid., pp. 92–93.

7. Gary Snyder, *Turtle Island* (New York: New Directions, 1974), p. 91.

8. See, in this context, Alan Williamson, "Music to Your Ears" (a review

of *This Tree Will Be Here for a Thousand Years*) *New York Times Book Review*, March 9, 1980, pp. 8–9, 14–15.
9. Robert Hass, "James Wright," *Ironwood* 10 (1977): 74–96.

5. "SURREALISM" AND THE ABSENT SELF

1. See Christopher Lasch, *The Culture of Narcissism* (New York: Norton, 1978).
2. André Breton, "The First Surrealist Manifesto," in Lucy R. Lippard, ed., *Surrealists on Art* (Englewood Cliffs, N.J.: Prentice-Hall, 1970), p. 20.
3. See Robert Pinsky, *The Situation of Poetry* (Princeton: Princeton University Press, 1976), esp. pp. 56ff, 81ff.
4. Richard Howard, *Alone with America* (New York: Atheneum, 1971), p. 39.
5. Ibid., p. 42.
6. Robert Pinsky, "Said, and Unsaid," *Poetry* 122 (June 1973): 168–173; idem, "Far from Prose," *Poetry* 123 (January 1974): 241–247.
7. For a fairer view of the range of Simic's work than is given here, see Alan Williamson, " 'Fool, Said My Muse to Me,' " *Poetry* 133 (November 1978): 100–107.
8. William Stafford, "Poetry in the Classroom (8): 'People of the South Wind,' " *American Poetry Review* 3, no. 1 (1974): 44–45.
9. Paul Breslin, "How to Read the New Contemporary Poem," *American Scholar* 47 (Summer 1978): 357–370.
10. Ibid., p. 366.
11. For a disturbing extreme of populist humility, in a poet considered radical at other stages of his career, see Robert Bly, "The Network and the Community," *American Poetry Review* 3, no. 1 (1974): 19–21: "The important thing is the community itself and its continuity, because it is a living forest of people, ecologically sound; that is important, not the flying fragment. The 'prophet' knows this; that is why in such a true community he allows himself to be killed without a lot of self-pity, and without writing 'An Enemy of the People' or 'Crucible.' "
12. "A Conversation with Mark Strand," in Robert B. Shaw, ed., *American Poetry since 1960* (Cheadle Hulme, England: Carcanet, 1973), pp. 206–207.
13. Ibid., p. 200.
14. Howard, *Alone with America*, p. xiii.
15. The lecture finally appeared under the title "Art, Will, and Necessity," in Lionel Trilling, *The Last Decade: Essays and Reviews, 1965–75* (New York: Harcourt, 1979).

6. THE DIFFRACTING DIAMOND

1. See Harold Bloom, "John Ashbery: The Charity of the Hard Moments," in Bloom, *Figures of Capable Imagination* (New York: Seabury, 1976), pp. 169–208. Since the sentence in my text was first penned, a good deal of noteworthy, if less philosophical, criticism on Ashbery has appeared. The very best pieces, in my judgment, are David Kalstone, *Five Temperaments* (New York: Oxford University Press, 1977), ch. on Ashbery, which deals mainly with "Self-Portrait in a Convex Mirror"; and Helen Vendler, "Understanding Ashbery," *New Yorker*, March 16, 1981, pp. 108–136, which deals with *Houseboat Days* and *As We Know*. Another intelligent, though more disenchanted, assessment of the later Ashbery is Paul Breslin, "Warpless and Woofless Subtleties," *Poetry* 137 (October 1980): 42–50. David Shapiro, *John Ashbery* (New York: Columbia University Press, 1979), is almost a textbook example of what I have called avant-gardism; its evaluations are therefore suspect, but it provides valuable information about Ashbery's avant-garde affinities, especially in the visual arts. There are many useful essays on Ashbery in David Lehman, ed., *Beyond Amazement* (Ithaca: Cornell University Press, 1980): John Koethe, "The Metaphysical Subject of John Ashbery's Poetry," in particular, offers an interesting alternative to my view of Ashbery's conception of self.
2. Bloom, *Figures of Capable Imagination*, p. 174.
3. Cited by Richard Howard as coming from a *"curriculum vitae."* Howard, *Alone with America* (New York: Atheneum, 1971), p. 29.
4. According to an interview with Richard Kostelanetz ("How To Be a Difficult Poet," *New York Times Magazine*, May 23, 1976, pp. 18–31), the stories were originally more clearly distinguished, by virtue of section titles; but Ashbery chose to imitate Joyce rather than Eliot, in the interest of being "more mysterious" (p. 31).
5. The echo of "Prufrock" in the preceding lines ("I call to you there, but I do not think that you will answer me") has a similar effect, suggesting that the lack of response need not rescind the Prince Hamlet in the poet.
6. Kostelanetz, "How To Be a Difficult Poet," p. 31.
7. Bloom, *Figures of Capable Imagination*, p. 174.
8. Bloom, I think, overstates the rejection of "frontal" happiness; but he is profoundly right in attributing Ashbery's diffidence in the face of it to "the anxiety of influence and more primordial Oedipal anxieties" (ibid., p. 206).
9. This statement, again, requires qualification in the light of recent criticism. The essays by Douglas Crase and Keith Cohen, in Lehman, ed.,

Beyond Amazement, examine the same phenomena I consider here, without drawing quite the same conclusions about them.

10. Kostelanetz, "How To Be a Difficult Poet," p. 31.

11. See Kalstone, *Five Temperaments,* pp. 170–199, for what will probably remain the definitive close reading of this poem.

7. THE FUTURE OF PERSONAL POETRY

1. Helen Vendler, "A Quarter of Poetry," *New York Times Book Review,* April 6, 1975, p. 38.

2. Helen Vendler, *Part of Nature, Part of Us* (Cambridge, Mass.: Harvard University Press, 1980), p. 308.

3. Hart Crane, "General Aims and Theories," in Crane, *The Complete Poems and Selected Letters and Prose* (New York: Anchor, 1966), pp. 220–221.

4. See Alan Williamson, "At Borders, Think" (a review of *The Knife and Other Poems*), *Parnassus* (Fall/Winter 1981): 247–254.

5. Wakoski's undergraduate thesis at Berkeley was on *Harmonium,* considered as the American equivalent of Surrealism.

6. See Robert Pinsky, *The Situation of Poetry* (Princeton: Princeton University Press, 1976), pp. 139–144.

7. Richard Howard, "A Note on Frank Bidart," in Bidart, *Golden State* (New York: Braziller, 1973), pp. vii–ix.

8. "The Sacrifice" and "The War of Vaslav Nijinsky" are included in Bidart's third book, *The Sacrifice* (New York: Random House, 1983).

9. Pinsky, *The Situation of Poetry,* p. 163.

10. *Poetry* 141 (February 1983): 251–258.

11. Robert Lowell, "To Mother," *Day by Day* (New York: Farrar, Straus and Giroux, 1977), p. 79.

12. Allen Grossman, *Of the Great House* (New York: New Directions, 1982), p. 9. For Grossman's own gloss on this line, see Mark Halliday, "A Conversation with Allen Grossman," *Ploughshares* 7, no. 2 (1981): 29–30.

13. Stanley Kunitz, *A Kind of Order, A Kind of Folly* (Boston: Little, Brown, 1975), p. 302.

CREDITS

Grateful acknowledgment is made to the following:

Atheneum Publishers, for permission to reprint excerpts from "Spring," by W. S. Merwin, from *The Moving Target*, copyright © 1963 by W. S. Merwin; excerpts from "Habits," by W. S. Merwin, from *Writings to an Unfinished Accompaniment*, copyright © 1973 by W. S. Merwin; and excerpts from "Breath" and "The Dreadful Has Already Happened," from *Darker*, copyright © 1970 by Mark Strand;

Georges Borschardt, Inc., for permission to reprint excerpts from *Rivers and Mountains, The Double Dream of Spring*, and *Three Poems*, by John Ashbery;

Carcanet Press Limited, for permission to reprint excerpts from "Self-Portrait" and "Forties Flick," from *Self-Portrait in a Convex Mirror*, by John Ashbery; and excerpts from "Litany," from *As We Know*, by John Ashbery;

Doubleday & Company, Inc., for permission to reprint excerpts from "Sestina from the Home Gardener," from *Inside the Blood Factory*, by Diane Wakoski, copyright © 1962, 1968 by Diane Wakoski;

The Ecco Press, for permission to reprint lines from "The Shad-blow Tree," "For My Mother," and "Messengers," copyright © 1975 by Louise

INDEX

N